I0798517

Reconceiving AI

What if everything we assume about artificial intelligence rests on a misconception of human intelligence? This book challenges that assumption. Human cognition cannot be reduced to data and processing power. Instead, the book proposes a "Blue Orange Mind" that emerges from collaboration between humans and machines.

Reconceiving AI: The World as an Apple or a Blue Orange draws its central insight from Paul Cézanne, a painter who spent thirty years learning to see an apple and discovered what neuroscience would take another century to confirm: seeing is not receiving but creating. The book pursues this discovery into the nature of intelligence. What does it mean to perceive? To understand language? To reason morally? To imagine what does not exist? Each question leads through artists and poets, philosophers and neuroscientists, novelists and filmmakers, toward a richer understanding of human consciousness and its relationship to artificial minds. The current AI paradigm, which builds machines as mirrors of narrow human rationality, fails to grasp this. Human intelligence thrives on paradox, contradiction, and uncertainty, emerging from embodied experience, symbolic thinking, and the irreducible diversity of minds. Beyond this "cracked mirror," the author proposes the Blue Orange Mind, a form of intelligence that neither humans nor machines can achieve alone, arising from the interplay between what we are and what we might create.

Written for AI researchers, developers, students, and anyone curious about the future of intelligence, this book offers an invitation to see intelligence anew, to understand why consciousness cannot be copied, and to imagine what becomes possible when we stop building machines in our image and start building them as genuine partners in the construction of meaning.

Reconceiving AI

The World as an Apple or a Blue Orange

M. R. Hasan

CRC Press
Taylor & Francis Group
Boca Raton London New York

CRC Press is an imprint of the
Taylor & Francis Group, an **informa** business

Designed cover image: © Shutterstock (Cover design by M. R. Hasan)

First edition published 2027
by CRC Press
2385 NW Executive Center Drive, Suite 320, Boca Raton FL 33431

and by CRC Press
4 Park Square, Milton Park, Abingdon, Oxon, OX14 4RN

CRC Press is an imprint of Taylor & Francis Group, LLC

ISBN: 978-1-041-03342-4 (hbk)
ISBN: 978-1-041-03341-7 (pbk)
ISBN: 978-1-003-62340-3 (ebk)

DOI: 10.1201/9781003623403

Typeset in Nimbus Roman font
by KnowledgeWorks Global Ltd.

To Maa and Suparna
My being and becoming

One gave me breath, the other offered song.

Contents

Part IV The Three Dimensions of Moral Intelligence

Part V Becoming the Blue Orange Mind

One evening, a neighbor found Nasruddin searching the ground beneath a streetlamp.

“What have you lost?”

“My key.”

“Where did you lose it?”

“Inside my house.”

“Then why search out here?”

“The light is better.”

— *A Nasruddin tale*

Prologue

I am driving to work.

I have a goal.
Reach the office.
On time.
Earlier.

A vehicle moves slowly in front of me. I want to overtake.
Another races past. I feel an urge to chase it.
These are decision-making moments.

They arise from my expectations about the world.
Is that a Mini Cooper? Who is driving?
I catch a glimpse at the person behind the wheel.
A man with broad shoulders, thick forearms.
Not what I expected!

I have a model of the world in my mind.
It is flexible.
I update it constantly.

Decision-making is a form of thinking.
It presupposes a plan, a goal, a chain of subgoals.
It needs a world model to make reasoning possible.
It is a process.
But the process is not linear.
It is often fragmented, uncertain, and fuzzy.

I close my eyes at the red light.
The world disappears.
Lincoln traffic, digital billboards, the woman in the red skirt. Gone.
I open my eyes. It all rushes back.
I sense a seamless flow of experience.
But I know the flow is an illusion.

At the light, my gaze finds the barely visible crack across the windshield.
I remember it happened in 2019.
I was driving back to Denver after visiting the Garden of the Gods.
Phebe was with me, along with her father and her sister.
Her family was visiting us from Bangladesh,
the first time since we had moved to the USA.

It was raining heavily.
Why do we say it is raining cats and dogs?
Why not horses and lions?
Or elephants and ants?
Or seagulls and zebras?
Language is so strangely arbitrary!
Suddenly, a stone kicked up from roadwork.
The crack appeared instantly across the glass.

The light changes. My foot hesitates on the brake.
For a moment, I am still in Colorado, not Lincoln.
This is how memories shape decisions,
how time folds within consciousness.

After the signal comes the quietest part of the road.
I glance at my phone.
I get distracted.
I know I should not be looking at the phone while driving.
But I do anyway.
Often unconsciously.
The conscious "I" wants to avoid harmful things.
But another "I" moves behind the curtain,
pulling strings, eluding reason.
I never quite know which "I" is the real one.

My mind drifts to the sound from the radio.
It has been playing since I started the car.
Why does it feel as if I haven't heard it until now?
The host says something. A new song plays.
I cannot recognize it. I have never heard it before.
It sounds familiar.
Is it similar to something I know? How do I even compare?
My mind does it automatically,
always measuring.

The melody stirs something in my mind.
Suddenly I remember my mother.
She is in Bangladesh.
I miss her.
I want to see her, be with her, hold her.
I miss my distant country.
Bangladesh, my home,
before the world became my home.
I feel that familiar ache whenever I think of the political turmoil there.
A three-minute song becomes a geography of loss and longing.

A car just cuts into my lane.
Too close, too fast.
Adrenaline floods my system.
For an instant, I am purely animal.
Reactive, alive, present.
The subtle touch of death.
I press the brake.
I feel alive because I am not dead.
The thoughts come back.

At the next stop signal, I see a girl crossing the road.
One more intersection, and I will reach my office.
I like seeing her.
She reminds me of someone I cannot quite remember.
There is something satisfying about not recognizing that person.
I love the mystery.
Sometimes not remembering brings joy.

Now the girl is gone.
I drive toward an industrial building.
It is shaped like an array of giant cylinders.
I see it every day, just after the stop signal.
Wide and tall.
Gray, or maybe white.
It fills my entire field of vision.
The structure stands on the far side of town.
Yet it feels impossibly close.
Too close for something so far.

I am getting nearer to my office.
I see a cafe on the corner.
I was here last year with a colleague
whose name I cannot recall.
Why this blank?

Some names fade so easily.
But I can remember the texture of my father's voice.
From twenty-four years away.
I can feel the familiar warmth of my long-blurred grandmother's presence.
The mystic aroma of her betel nut.

I reach my office parking lot.
Two minutes earlier than I expected.
I feel happy.
I text Phebe a nonsense joke with a made-up word.
She will laugh. Or roll her eyes.

I see a colleague getting out of his car.
I like him.
But I don't want to talk.
I walk quickly toward my office.
This is not rational.

I see scattered dandelions.
They line the sidewalk.
Bright yellow against the green grass.
People call them weeds.
Even those who love flowers mow them down.
Why?

If they survive the mower, the dandelions turn white.
Their yellow petals wither.
Then they disappear.
Everything disappears.
Everything morphs into something else.

I reach my office.
I take the first sip of coffee.
I love its taste. Its aroma.
Joy is sensuous. Joy is flesh.

My room feels quiet in the morning.
I open my journal and write,
reflecting on what I did in the past twenty-four hours.
I cannot remember everything.
I don't want to.
I remember the woman's red skirt, her hairstyle,
but not the color of her top.
I forget the colleague's name, the unfamiliar song,
but vividly remember the pain I felt for Bangladesh,
the ache of missing my mother.

My busy work day begins now.
Lots of duties.
"Promises to keep."

I am human.
I am intelligent.
At least, I believe I am.
But I have flaws and limitations.
I cannot stay focused on a single task for long.
I get distracted.
My thoughts are fluid, often disturbingly irrational.

My memory is far from perfect.
My sense of space and time is bent.
Distant objects appear near to me.
Time feels kaleidoscopic.
And I often do foolish things.

Am I intelligent despite these imperfections?
Or are these flaws part of my intelligence?
Can I think of a version of me without these flaws and yet still be me?
Would that make me more intelligent?
Can we create such intelligence?
Should we create an intelligence that is a smarter version of us,
one that has none of our flaws?

Perhaps this is the wrong question.
Maybe we should first consider:
How does the human mind
form understanding from paradox,
make decisions amid uncertainty,
create meaning from contradiction?
And what is the essence of human intelligence?

I think of something I read once.
A line that should not make sense but somehow does.
Paul Éluard wrote, "La terre est bleue comme une orange."
The Earth is blue like an orange.
But oranges are not blue.
And the Earth bears little resemblance to citrus fruit except its roundness.
Yet something happens when I read these words.
A spark of insight.
Reality subtly reorganized.
The ordinary suddenly luminous.

Perhaps the "blue orange" captures the essence of human intelligence.
Our ability to create understanding from impossible,
meaning from contradiction.
We are intelligent because maybe we are incomplete,
driven by longings we can never fully satisfy.

This book embarks on a journey to understand human intelligence.
Artificial intelligence will serve as our counterpoint.
We will explore what makes human intelligence unique.
And through that lens,
we will examine machine intelligence.

Our journey will progress through a tension between two versions of AI.
The AI that *is*.
And an AI that *could be*.

There is something deeply wrong about the way we have conceptualized AI.
And with everything that has followed from it.
The technology built to realize it.
The culture that sustains it.
The expectations and fears that spring from it.

"*Something is rotten in the state of Denmark.*"

Our dominant paradigm envisions AI as a mirror of ourselves.
Or rather, a reflection of only a narrow slice of who we are.
The so-called neurotypical, rational, "smart" human.
Our obsession with artificial general intelligence,
super intelligence,
super super .... intelligence,
all fixated on amplifying the reflected photon streams
of an incomplete and biased fraction
of the vast and diverse spectrum of human minds.

The book holds the view that this mirror paradigm is
jaundiced,
inherently flawed,
wasteful,
counterproductive,
doomed to fail,
or, even if it succeeds by its own standards,
it will do so at the cost of becoming self-destructive.

How do we move beyond the AI mirror paradigm?
This book is a search for that key.
We traverse two intertwined dimensions of human existence.
The enigmatic space of human creativity
and the dazzling diversity of human minds.

In our search, we will stand on the shoulders of
painters and poets,
sculptors and musicians,
novelists and filmmakers,
philosophers and scientists.
They will guide us toward deeper truths about consciousness.
We will try to decipher what intelligence truly is,
what it means to perceive,
to comprehend,

to create meaning
through our engagement with the world.

We are about to confront:
What happens when we build minds that think differently than we do?
What do we gain?
What do we lose?
And in enabling machines to become intelligent,
what might we finally learn about the future of intelligence?

This story is not just about human or machine intelligence.
It invites us to an interface,
a space where human and post-human intelligence
can meet and mingle meaningfully.

At this interface,
Human retains
what makes humans human.
Post-human intelligence offers
capabilities unconstrained by human limitations.

The post-human intelligence,
the *could be* AI, will no longer be a mirror version.
It will be designed from our growing understanding
of its categorical difference from us,
the realization that it need not be bound
by our existential truths,
or embodied constraints.

The story unfolds a trajectory that
neither started with humans,
nor will culminate in humans.

It inspires us to imagine
what otherwise seems unnatural,
yet is the most natural progression:
the emergence of an evolved intelligence
created from the productive contradiction between
human and post-human minds.

Like Éluard's "blue orange,"
which makes the apparently impossible possible,
we dream of a "Blue Orange Mind."
Not human.
Not machine.
But a new form of existence

sustaining itself on this "pale blue dot,"
and daring to venture beyond.

* * *

The journey begins in our world of vision.
Before entering the complexities of language, culture, and ethics,
we pause to understand a more fundamental feature of intelligence.
How do we see? What does it mean to perceive?

To seek the answer, we turn to a 19th-century painter.
A man who spent thirty years learning to perceive a single piece of fruit.
His name was Paul Cézanne.
And he discovered something about perception
that will crack the mirror of current AI.

About the author

M. R. Hasan is an AI researcher and professor at the University of Nebraska-Lincoln, where he directs the Human-First AI Lab (HAL 2.0), named in pointed contrast to Kubrick's rogue creation. This book began at a Cézanne retrospective in Chicago in 2022 with a question: What did a painter who spent thirty years on apples understand about perception that the most sophisticated AI still misses? That question became this book. Born in Bangladesh, Hasan writes from the productive contradictions of immigrant consciousness: between languages, between cultures, between the home he left and the home he is still making.

Part I

The Construction of Seeing

Our everyday reality feels solid, external, unyielding. We open our eyes, and the world simply *is*. The coffee cup on the table, the distant rumble of traffic, the dandelion pushing through a crack in the pavement, the weight of our body in the chair. We operate under the intuitive belief that we are passive recipients, impartial observers soaking up data from a world that exists independently, fully formed, and only waits to be seen.

This passive-recipient model of vision has deeply shaped how we have built artificial intelligence. For decades, we have designed machines to identify objects and recognize patterns from supposedly objective, external input.

But what if this effortless certainty is, in fact, a grand illusion? What if the act of seeing is an intense, collaborative act of creation, and reality is less a fixed terrain than a continuous, improvisational performance between our brains and the world?

This is the central question we pursue in Part I. We will peel back the layers of everyday visual perception through the eyes of Cézanne, who saw the world so differently, he changed it forever. Cézanne intuited the constructive nature of visual experience, an insight modern neuroscience is only now confirming and one that current AI systems, for all their advanced capabilities, still miss.

For Cézanne, seeing was never passive recording but active creation, a phenomenological process in which consciousness does not merely receive but collaborates with the world to generate meaning. His paintings look "wrong" to us because they reveal a hidden truth. Representation is always a form of distortion. The embodied vision can never be passively copied, only constructed through transformative engagement.

Cézanne developed many forms of distortion, strategic departures from optical correctness intended to capture deeper dimensions of sight, to visually construct different aspects of this active visual experience, each responding to specific perceptual challenges. While his large oeuvre presents a rich tapestry of these experiments, in Part I, we focus on three categories of distortion, each chosen to show how he grappled with the demands of interacting with objects, vast natural scenes, and, ultimately other conscious beings. By examining Cézanne's distortions, we uncover an artistic revolution and, with it, fundamental principles of embodied, temporal, and constructive vision that will prove central for understanding human intelligence and the challenges that artificial systems face in replicating it.

Part I opens with a deceptively simple question. *How does one paint the weight of an apple*?

1 The Weight of an Apple

In the autumn of 1899, in a cramped studio on the rue Boulegon in Aix-en-Provence, an old man sat before a wooden table. On it lay some apples, draped cloths, ceramic pots. Nothing more. Cézanne had been painting variations of this arrangement for nearly thirty years. And he was still not satisfied.

He would stare at these objects, sometimes dedicating a month to a single apple and claiming after thirty sessions that the work remained unfinished [72]. He would wait twenty minutes between two brushstrokes, his bloodshot eyes seeming to pop from his head with the strain of seeing. The fruit would rot and had to be replaced with artificial ones, which he abandoned because, as he would say, "they fade, the bitches" [113]. But the work never felt complete.

For decades, the French post-impressionist painter had obsessed over apples, painting them endlessly, alone, in bowls, on plates, nestled amongst oranges and pears. He painted them with such singular focus it seems absurd. What deeper truth could a simple apple, or a bowl of fruit, contain that so captivated him? Was he trying to create the most faithful visual representation possible?

If accuracy were the goal, the hyperrealistic techniques of classical masters such as Ingres or Meissonier, who rendered every surface texture and play of light with meticulous precision, had already reached the pinnacle of faithful representation. The camera of Cézanne's era could record even greater "objective" detail with mechanical consistency. The trompe-l'oeil painters of earlier centuries had long perfected the art of making painted objects appear so convincingly real they seemed to leap from the canvas.

Cézanne, however, turned away from optical trickery and photographic fidelity. He was after something far more elusive. **The sensation of the apple**. He wanted to convey its weight, its solidity, its presence in space, less how it looked to the eye than how it felt to exist in relation to it. He was not only observing it. He was experiencing it, and trying to translate that physical encounter onto canvas.

But how does one represent such embodied sensation beyond appearance? This challenge prompts a deeper question. What are we actually ***re*-presenting** when we represent the world?

The apple on Cézanne's table embodies this puzzle. Does it exist only for a single moment, the instant when light strikes it at 3:47 PM on a Tuesday afternoon in 1899? Does it exist only from one viewpoint, exactly where we happen to be standing? Does it exist in isolation, floating in empty space with no relation to the cloth beneath it or the bowl beside it?

Or is there something more? When we reach for an apple, we do not just see its surface. We feel its weight in our hand, anticipate its texture, sense how it rests in space among other objects. We experience the apple as something we can move around, examine from different sides, and interact with through time. We do not see

DOI: 10.1201/9781003623403-1

an isolated color-shape. We engage with a situated thing, embedded in relationships, heavy with presence, alive with possibilities.

Cézanne confronted the challenge of capturing how the apple exists in lived experience, in its phenomenological weight and the way it shows up to an embodied, sensing being in motion. He aimed to paint perception, the experience of seeing as it unfolds through time and space, where eye, hand, and world are joined in a single act of attention.

THE FIRST LABORATORY: INDOOR OBJECTS AND CONTROLLED PERCEPTION

Cézanne's obsession with still lifes was an investigation into how we construct the visual world through our sensory experiences. Over thirty years, he would develop three distinct approaches to representing visual experience, each responding to a different kind of perceptual challenge.

His first exploration focused on **objects in a controlled indoor environment**. These are objects smaller than us and within our close vicinity, such as apples, ceramic bowls, cloth arrangements within the room where we are located. The lighting condition is typically controlled and mostly unchanged, offering a sense of temporal permanency. As observers, we can look at these objects from various perspectives as we move around them, from sitting or standing, at different angles. This results in a dynamic perception, a continuous re-evaluation of the object over time.

The challenge, then, was how to translate this dynamic, embodied process of seeing onto a static canvas. Cézanne was not recording an apple's shape and color at a single moment, but conveying its weight, its spatial presence, and our lived experience of interacting with it through time. An apple is never only an apple. It is always a situated thing, enmeshed in a web of relationships and experienced through our moving, sensing bodies.

Cézanne's radical solution to this challenge was strategic **distortion** in representation. Since no flat canvas can capture the full spectrum of our visual experience, representation inevitably becomes a form of creative translation. To "see" is not just to record what lies before the eye but to participate in the act of experiencing it. Vision operates as a phenomenological process, rooted in the body's movements and perspectives, which makes our visual experience inherently embodied.

To convey this lived, constructive process in his still lifes, Cézanne turned distortion into a deliberate method. What might seem as flaws or liberties were in fact purposeful strategies for translating the experience of seeing into paint. Through them, we identify three interconnected challenges at the core of visual representation.

How do we convey the phenomenological weight and three-dimensional presence of objects? Traditional perspective assumes a single, fixed viewpoint, but human perception synthesizes multiple perspectives through movement and time. We do not merely see an apple's surface. We experience its solidity, its weight, and its occupancy of space.

How do we convey the relational fabric that gives objects meaning? Objects do not exist in isolation. They inhabit networks of spatial, temporal, and experiential relationships that shift with context and observer position. The apple exists in relationship to the cloth, the bowl, the table, the room, and most of all, to us as experiencing observers.

How do we convey that perception is active construction, not passive recording? The act of seeing involves creative interpretation and physical engagement. We construct reality through our moving bodies, our temporal living, and our predictive expectations. This is perhaps the deepest challenge, representing the process of perception.

These foundational challenges, first explored through still lifes, would later extend to the natural world of expansive outdoor spaces and, as we will examine in later chapters, to the complex reality of human subjects, each demanding its own innovations in distortion.

The controlled environment of the studio served as Cézanne's first laboratory, where he could perfect a repertoire of techniques for spatial distortion. When we look closely at his still lifes throughout this chapter, we notice tables that tilt at impossible angles, perspectives that seem to shift and breathe, viewpoints that somehow capture multiple positions at once. These are not errors or whimsical choices. They are meticulous visual strategies by which Cézanne conveyed how we synthesize visual information through movement and time.

THE SENSATION AT THE ROOT OF EVERYTHING

Cézanne was after something he called "sensation." Not the surface appearance of objects but their felt presence in the world. Through his friendship with poet Joachim Gasquet, son of his childhood friend, we glimpse this insight. Gasquet's memoir, based on conversations during Cézanne's final decade, conveys the painter's conviction that "sensation is at the root of everything" [40].

To truly see, Cézanne believed, one had to feel the intimate relationship between object and observer. When outlining an apple, he would perceive what he described as "the same mild shadow of renunciation, the same love of the sun, the same recollection of the dew." His insight was radical. Everything is connected. Objects existed in dynamic webs of relationship that he called "intimate reflections."

"The eye and the brain must collaborate," he explained to Gasquet. "On the eye, by looking at things through nature; on the brain, by the logic of organized sensations which provides the means of expression."

At the center of his investigations was the apple. He wanted to "astonish Paris with an apple," using this simple fruit to signal a departure from contemporary Impressionism's focus on fleeting appearances and to reshape how we understand seeing. His investigations addressed the three challenges outlined above, capturing objects with their solidity and weight, expressing the relational fabric among them, and embodying perception as an active process of construction.

What made Cézanne's apples revolutionary was their transcendence of the edible. He was not painting fruit to tempt hunger but to probe how we experience an object. As one perceptive observer noted, "Of an ordinary painter's apple you say, 'I can take a bite out of it.' Of an apple by Cézanne one says: 'How beautiful!' One would not peel it; one would like to copy it" [15].

Cézanne's apples depict more than fruit. They interrogate the nature of representation. They direct our attention away from taste or utility and toward perception. The weight, presence, and relationality of the apple as it is lived in experience.

THE REVOLUTION IN DISTORTION

At first glance, Cézanne's late still life *The Basket of Apples* seems ordinary (Figure 1.1). But on closer inspection, something strange emerges. The table seems to tilt impossibly, as if viewed from multiple vantage points at once. The fruit contours blur and blend with surrounding objects, boundaries dissolving like watercolors in rain. The space appears to breathe, to pulse with energy that no photograph could contain.

Critics called these "flaws," traces of declining skill [44]. But they were wrong. These distortions were not failures but revelations of a deeper truth about seeing. This becomes clearer once we grasp the artistic dilemma Cézanne inherited.

Both the great classical masters such as Nicolas Poussin and the Impressionist painters claimed to portray nature as we see it. However, what they meant by "seeing" diverged sharply. Poussin, the epitome of classical order, presented beautifully harmonious compositions where every form seemed to answer every other. His paintings achieved balance and solidity through the application of firm traditional rules and a perfect arrangement of forms learned from classical antiquity (Figure 1.2, left). But this grandeur came through idealized construction rather than direct engagement with the motif. Poussin's space was built according to geometric principles and

Figure 1.1 Paul Cézanne, *The Basket of Apples* (c. 1893).

Figure 1.2 A stark contrast in artistic vision. **Left:** Nicolas Poussin, *The Funeral of Phocion*, 1648, an embodiment of classical composition and intellectual order arranged according to established rules. **Right:** Claude Monet, *Impression, Sunrise*, 1872, the iconic painting that gave Impressionism its name, emphasizing the capture of fleeting optical impressions and momentary light.

mathematical proportions that imposed classical harmony onto nature instead of discovering it through sustained observation. His compositions, however magnificent, operated through predetermined schemas that filtered perceptual experience instead of portraying its complexity. Classical masters did not truly look at individual objects anew. Their sense of space was achieved through convention.

The Impressionists, in their rebellion, sought to surrender to immediate impressions, striving for an even more faithful replica of the visual impression through their exploration of color reflexes and loose brushwork. Cézanne joined them at first, admiring their liberation of color and light. However, he grew troubled by their approach. While Impressionist pictures brilliantly rendered the flickering reflections of an "open-air" scene, he felt they dissolved into messy, insubstantial surfaces (Figure 1.2, right). The structural strength and harmonious design that distinguished the paintings of the past seemed to be missing. They had achieved a conquest of nature by making everything a worthy motif, but they had not solved the problem of representing the solidity of objects and space from observation.

Cézanne thus set an audacious, seemingly impossible task for him, to "paint Poussin from nature." He sought to achieve the classical grandeur, balance, and serenity of masters like Poussin, not through academic convention, but through sustained observation of each object anew. At the same time, he aimed to "make of Impressionism something solid and durable, like the art of the museums." This meant taking the Impressionists' discoveries in color and sensation and, without resorting to traditional drawing or shading, finding new ways to convey depth, solidity, and order.

His solution was quietly revolutionary. He stopped painting what he saw and began painting **how** he saw it. When we look at something complex, our eyes do not remain fixed. We shift position, lean in for closer inspection, step away to see the whole, synthesize multiple viewpoints into unified experience. Cézanne painted this synthetic process.

This approach demanded extraordinary patience and precision. Picture dealer Ambroise Vollard recounts being invited to pose for the master [113]. Seeing Vollard's distrust of the elaborate contraption Cézanne had rigged (platforms, chairs, precariously balanced supports), the artist smiled, "I arranged all this myself. Nothing will happen if you keep your balance. And after all, sitting means sitting still." But hardly was Vollard settled on his pedestal, sleep overtook him. His head sank onto his shoulder. The equilibrium shattered. Platform, chair, and model crashed to the floor.

Cézanne rushed forward, "You wretch! You have upset the pose! You should sit like an apple. Whoever saw an apple fidgeting?"

Though even motionless apples betrayed him. Sometimes he was obliged to leave studies unfinished because the fruit had rotted. He tried artificial apples, then paper flowers, but abandoned them too, "they fade, the bitches." In despair, he turned to illustrations from magazines. Painting, for him, did not consist in copying objects, but in "realizing sensations."

This idea becomes evident when we compare three different ways artists chose to represent the same still-life objects.

The photograph exemplifies what modern machine vision handles best (Figure 1.3, left). Objects with crisp edges, sitting securely on stable surfaces, illuminated by consistent lighting, each element clearly distinguishable from its neighbors. A contemporary multimodal AI system, capable of integrating visual and linguistic information, would not only identify the fruit bowl, apples, bottle, glass, and cloth with high confidence but also segment each item with precision, and generate a coherent and contextually rich description of the scene. Such systems excel at parsing the visual world into discrete, quantifiable components and analyzing their geometry and interrelations.

Figure 1.3 Three approaches to represent visual reality: **Left**: Photograph of typical still life objects with clear boundaries, stable perspective, mechanical recording that AI vision excels at processing. **Center**: Gustave Courbet, *Still Life with Apples and Pomegranate* (c. 1871-72), presents a traditional artistic representation with a fixed viewpoint and conventional perspective. **Right**: Paul Cézanne, *The Basket of Apples* (c. 1893), with its signature tilted table and impossible geometry that conveys embodied perception and constructed reality.

Courbet's painting *Life with Apples and Pomegranate* shows a meticulous approach to conventional realism applied to the same type of scene (Figure 1.3, middle). Objects rest securely on stable surfaces, each form clearly delineated with established perspective. The viewer's eye position is fixed, the space logically ordered according to academic principles. This is masterful representation, but it remains representation in the strict sense, copying what the eye sees from a single, static viewpoint.

Cézanne's *The Basket of Apples* conveys something categorically different (Figure 1.3, right). The signature tilted table defies conventional geometry though feels more real than realistic representation. The basket pitches forward dramatically, balanced by the bottle and tablecloth's sculptural folds. Colors migrate between objects, creating "intimate reflections." The space stands constructed through the act of looking, multiple viewpoints synthesized into a single, impossibly rich image. The heavy modeling, solid brushstrokes, and glowing colors give the composition a density and dynamism that a more realistic still life could never possess.

This three-way comparison clarifies the defining gap between mechanical recording, conventional representation, and embodied perception. AI systems excel at processing the photograph's version of reality, the mechanical parsing of stable, bounded objects under consistent lighting. They can even analyze Courbet's conventional arrangements with accuracy, detecting perspective and spatial logic. But they cannot access what Cézanne painted. The active, embodied, and temporally extended process by which consciousness constructs meaning from visual experience.

The photograph shows objects as data, while Courbet shows them as they appear to a fixed observer. Cézanne's painting illustrates the *act of perceiving* objects. The weight, the relationships, and the constructed reality that emerges when an embodied mind interacts with the world through time and movement. His "distortions" were not errors, but insights into how consciousness constructs reality from visual input.

This is the revolution in distortion. Cézanne discovered that seeing is not passive recording but active construction. Every act of perception involves the creative synthesis of diverse perspectives, temporal living, and physical interaction with the world. He painted not what he saw, but *how seeing works*.

THE ARCHITECTURE OF SPATIAL INTELLIGENCE

In Cézanne's *Still Life with Compotier* from 1880 (Figure 1.4), the fruit bowl tilts precariously, its ellipse stretched into an impossible form that defies geometric perspective. The table slopes from left to right, then forward. These distortions capture a truth about embodied perception that rigid perspective obscures. Authentic spatial representation requires abandoning the fiction of the single, fixed viewpoint.

Such deliberate distortions were experiments in perception. We can see this principle at work in the way Cézanne builds forms through parallel brushstrokes that slant uniformly from right to left, creating what Roger Fry, the English art critic and his early champion, called "the materiality of paint." These rectilinear marks do more than create surface texture. They record the temporal process of perception. Each stroke registers a glance, a fleeting act of looking, layering moment upon moment

Figure 1.4 Paul Cézanne, *Still Life with Compotier*, c. 1879-1880. This work exemplifies Cézanne's early exploration of solidity and spatial complexity through color modulation and subtle distortions, challenging traditional perspectives.

into the final whole. The warped fruit bowl synthesizes multiple angles of approach into a single form that feels more spatially complete than any photographically faithful rendering could achieve. The distortion becomes a more truthful representation of how consciousness constructs its understanding of space.

From these experiments comes Cézanne's first innovation. **Spatial intelligence through controlled distortion**. True spatial understanding requires strategic inaccuracy, the adjustment of local details to convey global, and perceptual coherence. By rejecting academic perspective, which reduces vision to a single, static viewpoint, Cézanne uncovered the fundamental truth his distortions had been gesturing toward all along. Perception is not passive registration but an active, embodied construction unfolding through movement and time.

THE FABRIC OF RELATIONAL INTELLIGENCE

In Cézanne's *Apples* still life from 1878 (Figure 1.5), we see seven apples arranged on a surface. Nothing could be simpler, or more complex. Each apple forces those nearby into relationships of proximity and distance, contact and separation. These give rise to the primitive experience of spatial relations that defines how objects exist in space-time.

The boundaries between objects and their surroundings dissolve. Cézanne observed that we never see clear, independent contours because light from surfaces mingles with reflections from nearby objects. This insight led to his technique of boundary penetration, forms that subtly bleed into one another, creating "intimate reflections."

Figure 1.5 Paul Cézanne, *Still Life with Apples*, c. 1877-78. Executed during a defining period, this celebrated still life embodies Cézanne's ambition to "conquer Paris with an apple," a motif that became central to his groundbreaking exploration of form and color.

From these dissolving boundaries emerges Cézanne's second innovation. **Relational intelligence through boundary dissolution**. Objects do not have fixed boundaries in the visual world but exist in dynamic relationships where "the same object belongs to different groups simultaneously." The apple relates to the cloth, the cloth to the table, the table to the surrounding space. Each relationship shifting with light, viewpoint, and the passage of time.

The modernist writer Virginia Woolf, whose novels pursued the same fluidity of perception and broke from the realist tradition, gave voice to the deeper implication of Cézanne's approach, "When at last the apple, the kitchen table, and the bread-knife have come together, it is felt to be a victory for the human spirit over matter. These common objects are invested with the majesty of mountains and the melody of music" [116].

THE MULTIPLICATION OF PERSPECTIVE

By the 1890s, Cézanne's investigations had grown complex. This complexity finds vivid expression in The *Kitchen Table* (1888-90) (Figure 1.6), where art historian Erle Loran identified four separate points of view operating at once (Figure 1.7) [77]. The table edge jogs upward beneath the napkin, objects tilt in different directions, some remaining stable while others seem caught in motion.

Loran's diagram shows paired viewpoints labeled with small eyes, each representing different eye levels and viewing angles that Cézanne synthesized into a single composition. We saw this principle of multiple perspectives earlier. In this particular work, Cézanne deepens his investigation through harder compositional challenges. Loran's geometric analysis shows how he orchestrated these viewpoint shifts. In

Figure 1.6 Paul Cézanne, *The Kitchen Table*, c. 1888-1890. Far from a random arrangement, this still life showcases Cézanne's masterful construction of equilibrium; each object is rendered with a precise scale to achieve a resonant compositional balance, embodying his exploration of relationality and the interwoven nature of forms in space.

perceiving a complex arrangement, we move through it visually, approaching certain forms, withdrawing from others, and continually reorienting attention. Our brain weaves these shifting viewpoints into a coherent experience.

Cézanne painted this synthetic process, abandoning the single frozen moment. He negotiated with a kind of "temporalized spatial fabric," a space that includes the movements of eye and hand and body, the splitting into multiple viewers and

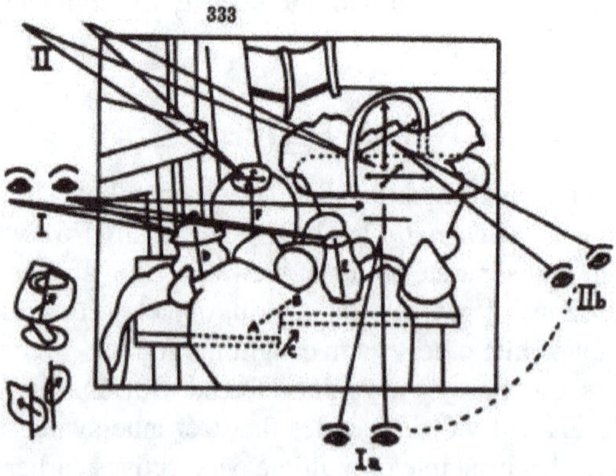

Figure 1.7 Erle Loran's analysis of multiple perspectives in *The Kitchen Table*, from Cezanne's Composition (1943) [77].

viewpoints, the temporal process of dealing with visual complexity. The tipped-up floor adds leg- and foot-room to the arm's-length space of the tabletop. This is embodied space. The space of a body that moves, reaches, shifts perspective, and constructs understanding through time.

THE TEMPORALITY OF EMBODIED PERCEPTION

Cézanne's investigations in the mid-1890s became more radical. His *Still Life with Apples* (1893-94) (Figure 1.8) shows his fascination with cloth folds replacing flat planes as ever more complicated surfaces. Objects and surface space interact mutually with each other, creating what art historian Carol Armstrong called "inward- and outward-curving space, which moves local touch by local touch through and around a world of rounded objects" [3]. The apples enact this temporal process of construction. Heaped on a shallow white plate and scattered onto the cloth below, each apple is built through Cézanne's characteristic constructive stroke technique. Small, rectangular touches of pure color placed side by side to model volume and capture shifting light. Instead of showing apples as static objects, the work records the dynamic process by which consciousness constructs their presence through sustained observation. Each brushstroke represents a moment of focused attention layered into the final form.

Figure 1.8 Paul Cézanne, *Still Life with Apples*, c. 1893-94. This later still life reflects Cézanne's sustained fascination with the apple, rendered with a powerful sense of underlying geometric structure and luminous color. The composition, deceptively simple at first glance, shows the intricate interplay of forms that anchors his enduring quest for a solid and durable representation of nature.

Figure 1.9 Paul Cézanne, *Still Life with Plaster Cupid*, c. 1894-95. In this complex and intimate still life, Cézanne integrates a classical sculpture with everyday objects, examining the interplay between the artificial and the natural, and the enduring presence of form across different materials. The painting exhibits his continued pursuit of solidity and depth through meticulous color modulation and spatial relationships.

Still Life with Plaster Cupid (1894-95) (Figure 1.9) challenges linear perspective even more dramatically. The tilted floor, multiple canvases, and complex drapery create what Armstrong analyzes as "experiential, subjectivized, temporalized rendering of durational time-space" [3]. The zigzagging arrangement of fruit, with one green apple in the background, two nestled in blue cloth, and three spheres gathered in the dish at the front, preserves the rhythm of perception. The eye moves through the composition by pressing close and then pulling back, advancing and retreating in lived time, never receding along a fixed vanishing point.

The plaster cupid's rounded forms (calves, thighs, buttocks, belly) allegorize the lived nature of perception. This is not only the space of the hand but of the foot, leg, and whole body. Cézanne painted space as experienced by a moving, sensing body extended through time, not a disembodied geometric eye.

COLOR AS MIND-WORLD INTERFACE

Cézanne's most transformative insight concerned color. As he told Gasquet, "Colour is the place where our brain and the universe meet." This was a recognition of an enduring truth about perception.

When we look at something red, an event unfolds. Enlightenment philosophers would tell us that redness is a "secondary quality," not a property of the object but a sensation created by reflected light waves [75]. But Cézanne intuited otherwise.

Color exists in the interaction between world and mind, neither purely objective nor purely subjective but a collaboration where consciousness and cosmos meet.

Modern neuroscience vindicates this insight. People with cerebral achromatopsia do not just see a black-and-white world [50, 51]. Though color is totally absent, they experience reality organized by different principles. Texture becomes more vivid, movement more salient, and spatial relationships more complex. Their brains construct reality according to different rules, with form and motion defined by wavelength differences perceived readily even when the colors cannot be told apart. This shows that "normal" color vision is one way of organizing experience.

From this insight follows Cézanne's third innovation. **Active perception through color as mind-world interface**. Color is not discovered but created, moment by moment, apple by apple, in the mysterious meeting between mind and world. He declared allegiance to "the logic of colour" over "the logic of the brain," realizing that "sensation is at the root of everything."

THE FOLDING OF SPACE-TIME

In his late masterpiece *Apples and Oranges* (1899) (Figure 1.10), Cézanne achieved an unprecedented synthesis of temporal experience and spatial form. The composition deliberately disorients us. What should be a stable table becomes a complex topography that seems to shift and flow. Multiple cloths weave into one another. White cloth arises as pale lavender touched with violet and pink, geometric patterns merging with organic forms in an elaborate dance of color and texture.

Figure 1.10 Paul Cézanne, *Apples and Oranges*, c. 1899. This painting exemplifies Cézanne's mature mastery of still life, showcasing his searching investigation of color modulation to construct form, dissolve boundaries, and imbue everyday objects with a vibrant, interconnected presence.

The painting transforms our understanding of pictorial space. We do not see objects resting on a neutral background. Instead, we meet a world where the supporting surfaces have become active participants in the visual drama. Fruits seem to arise from the very fabric of space, their forms both distinct and continuous with their surroundings. The circular fruits create a tension with the angular geometry of tables and cloths, sphere confronting rectangle in an ongoing visual negotiation.

This composition demands temporal interaction. Unlike traditional still lifes that can be grasped in a single moment, Cézanne's arrangement unfolds through sustained looking. Our eyes need to move across the canvas, discovering new relationships, following the migration of colors from object to object, tracing the distortions that give each element its presence. Roger Fry articulated this quality aptly when he described the "incessant affirmations and contradictions" that create perpetual movement throughout the composition [37]. Nothing remains still in this so-called still life. Everything pulses with the rhythm of active perception constructing reality moment by moment.

THE TRUTH OF CONSTRUCTED REALITY

These investigations lead us to a startling conclusion, one that the Irish philosopher and Anglican bishop George Berkeley formulated centuries ago, *esse est percipi*. To be is to be perceived [6]. For conscious beings, there is no meaningful gap between mind and world. We do not perceive signals and then interpret them. The act of perception *is* the act of interpretation.

We never meet the world without mediation. We experience only our experience of things, reality that is interpreted, constructed, and shaped by consciousness. Cézanne's apples prove this in the most concrete way possible. When he painted tables tilting at impossible angles, when he let boundaries dissolve into ambient light, when he showed us spaces that breathe with their own life, he was not distorting reality. He was making it visible.

His impossible perspectives were disclosures of how we see the world. Through his still life investigations, he developed a meticulous arsenal of techniques for representing embodied perception. The exaggerated multi-perspective views that synthesized movement through time, the disjointed alignments that prioritized felt relationships over geometric accuracy, the controlled spatial contradictions that made intimate spaces breathe with life, and the boundary penetrations that express forms in active relation to their surrounding space.

Each distortion served a specific purpose in translating phenomenological sensation into paint. As he observed, objects "enter into each other... They never stop living... Imperceptibly they extend beyond themselves through intimate reflections, as we do by looks and words." These techniques, possible only in the controlled environment of still lifes where lighting remained constant and objects could be repositioned, rendered something no camera could record. The physical experience of sustained attention to manipulable objects within our reach.

Standing in Cézanne's studio, watching him paint the same apple for the thousandth time, we begin to see what he was after. Perception is not a spotlight illuminating a pre-existing world but a conversation between mind and cosmos, creating reality in the act of perceiving it. His still life distortions show that faithful representation of embodied experience requires strategic infidelity to mechanical precision. What looks "wrong" to artificial vision yields a more authentic rendering of how human perception constructs visual reality.

THE LIMITS OF MECHANICAL VISION

What does this understanding of human visual perception as active construction mean for artificial intelligence?

Contemporary AI vision systems exhibit capabilities that go far beyond simple classification. Advanced multimodal models can analyze Cézanne's *Basket of Apples* and generate descriptions such as the following: "This painting depicts a still life arrangement featuring a basket filled with apples, some of which have spilled onto a white cloth draped across a table. A dark bottle stands upright beside the basket, while additional fruits are scattered throughout the composition. The scene is rendered in a post-impressionist style with rich colors and textured brushstrokes." They can identify objects, describe spatial relationships, detect artistic styles, and analyze compositional elements with accuracy.

However, this precision arises from an intrinsically different basis than human perception. Current AI systems, despite their analytical power, rely on computational pattern recognition and inference. Their methods remain rooted in statistical analysis, not embodied construction.

They can describe every element in Cézanne's painting with fidelity, yet they miss what he spent thirty years trying to capture. The phenomenological weight that transforms representation from mechanical analysis into embodied understanding. They can catalog "textured brushstrokes" but cannot experience how these marks construct presence through sustained interaction. They can analyze spatial relationships but cannot feel how the apple settles into space, anchors composition, and creates meaning through temporal interaction.

Cézanne's distortions expose what mechanical analysis cannot access, representation as active construction. His tilted tables and impossible perspectives do not register what he saw but give form to the way consciousness deliberately constructs what it perceives. Where AI systems excel at processing information about visual scenes, human perception participates in creating the reality it experiences.

FROM CONTROLLED STUDIO TO UNRULY NATURE

After refining these techniques on still life, Cézanne faced a greater challenge. How could these insights apply to the uncontrollable natural world, where vast, distant forms such as mountains and lakes refused to move and light changed moment by moment? The still life had been his controlled laboratory. Now he needed to test his discoveries against nature's scale and temporal flux, seeking to capture the enduring permanence of these structures amidst continuous atmospheric and temporal changes.

If the apple had taught him how we construct the intimate objects within our reach, the mountain would show how consciousness engages with the distant forms that define our world's horizons. Where still life distortions held the dynamics of close examination, landscape distortions would need to synthesize temporal variations, preserving the layered experience of sustained attention over time to unchanging forms under changing conditions.

We now follow Cézanne into the natural world, where new challenges would demand new forms of artistic distortion, leading to fresh insights into the constructive nature of human seeing.

The apple sits on the table, waiting for the mountain to complete its lesson.

2 When Landscape Thinks Itself

In turning to landscape, Cézanne confronted perception on a vaster stage. Vision was no longer confined to apples and tabletops but opened onto horizons. The challenge was not only space but living time, the permanence of mountain masses under the shifting light of morning, noon, and dusk. To represent such phenomena, Cézanne had to invent new strategies of distortion, ways of painting that could hold flux and stability within a single vision.

For Cézanne, no subject proved more demanding than Mont Sainte-Victoire, the limestone mountain near his native Aix-en-Provence. Returning to it again and again over decades, he treated it as both motif and teacher, a monumental, unchanging presence through which he could study how perception accumulates understanding across time, weaving experience into continuity while resisting its dissolution into isolated moments. Its permanence against the changing sky made it the ideal measure of vision.

The significance of his new way of seeing nature was evident even to Cézanne's contemporaries. In the summer of 1904, picture dealer Ambroise Vollard traveled by carriage through the countryside around Aix-en-Provence. "The landscapes seen from the carriage window evoked Cézanne's paintings," he later recalled, describing the "thrill" of recognition [113]. But this was no simple matter of artistic resemblance. Vollard was glimpsing something rarer, the way a human mind had penetrated so deeply into the structure of the natural world that reality seemed to bear the imprint of consciousness.

This phenomenon found expression in an exchange Vollard witnessed outside Père Tanguy's legendary shop, a Parisian art supply store and gallery known for championing Impressionist and Post-Impressionist works. Two men stopped before a Cézanne landscape displayed in the window, their responses reflecting two different ways of seeing [113].

The gentleman in the bowler hat expressed indignation, "Isn't it shameful to murder nature like that! Trees that can't stand up; a house that may topple over any moment; water the colour of lead! And just look at the sky! If nature was like that, it would put one off ever going out." His vision was literal, focused on momentary appearance and conventional fidelity.

But the workman, a bricklayer, saw differently, "Well, it's the other way with me, sir... Every time I look at that picture I say to myself: 'There's a place I'd like to go and fish in of a Sunday! Aren't the blokes jolly lucky that can treat themselves to a well-built house like that!' I know what I'm talking of. I'm a bricklayer."

The workman grasped intuitively what the gentleman missed. Cézanne had registered what lay beneath the surface, the experiential truth of the underlying structure.

DOI: 10.1201/9781003623403-2

The house felt more solidly built than ordinary observation might suggest, the landscape more inviting than any photograph of it would be. In his so-called distortions, the bricklayer identified what Cézanne was truly after. Solidity, permanence, tactile presence, and above all, the synthesis of flux and stability that defines the lived perception of landscape.

FROM CONTROLLED LAB TO UNYIELDING NATURE

Cézanne's approach to landscape demanded a new vocabulary of painting. Nature could not be arranged, tilted, or lit to suit the eye. It had to be met as a living presence with its own rhythms and resistances. Faced with this immensity, Cézanne tried to "read the landscape" as a geologist studies stone, seeking the durable formations beneath fleeting appearance. Only then do the contrasts with his still-life practice become clear. Those earlier studies relied on finely tuned distortions to convey solidity and relational force, whereas landscape required methods shaped by scale, variation, and the restless movement of light across enduring forms.

As he declared, "Nature isn't at the surface; it's in depth. Colours are the expression, on this surface, of this depth" [40]. He was not interested in superficial beauty or fleeting atmospheric effects but in discerning what he saw as a "natural logic." The underlying organization that makes coherent experience possible, even amidst temporal change.

The geological metaphor was more than analogy. Cézanne understood that landscapes make visible temporal depths invisible to conventional observation. Where surface vision sees momentary arrangements of light and shadow, structural vision penetrates to the tectonic forces that shaped the land across geological time. He aspired to paint what the mind discovered through sustained temporal attention with the scene's core architecture, *not what appeared to the eye at a single moment.*

The difference is profound. Still life distortions work through controlled spatial contradictions. Tilted tables, misaligned edges, and multi-perspective views that synthesize movement around static objects. But landscape distortions face a different phenomenological challenge. How do we represent the experience of sustained attention to immutable natural forms that show up differently under varying conditions of light and seasonal change?

Cézanne discovered that representing outdoor experience required **temporal distortions**, techniques that move beyond any single visual instant to convey what consciousness gathers through ongoing interaction with enduring structures under shifting conditions.

ATMOSPHERIC SYNTHESIS AND FLATTENED DEPTH

How can a painting of a lake hold time still? In Cézanne's *Lac d'Annecy* (1896) (Figure 2.1, left), we see a world suspended in contemplation. The water stretches motionless, its surface like polished metal, reflecting not shimmer, but silence. Mountains rise as if carved from planes of geometry, stripped to their underlying

Figure 2.1 Two ways of seeing Lake Annecy, photographic recording versus structural synthesis. **Left:** Paul Cézanne's *Lac d'Annecy*, c. 1896, which depicts the landscape stripped to its essential structures, making visible Cézanne's signature landscape distortions. Flattened depth that brings distant mountains forward, atmospheric color modeling that captures structural permanence surpassing transient appearances, and temporal synthesis that renders the lake "as at the beginning of the world." **Right:** A photograph of Lake Annecy, illustrating the naturalistic view that captures surface details, atmospheric effects, and momentary conditions, what a camera or AI vision system would record.

structures. Trees stand rooted in place, their foliage broken into patches of color that somehow feel more solid, more lasting, than the fine-grained detail of a photograph.

But this apparent stillness pulses with temporal intelligence. Philosopher Maurice Merleau-Ponty described it beautifully, "There is no wind in the landscape, no movement on the Lac d'Annecy; the frozen objects hesitate as at the beginning of the world" [80]. The frozen quality conveys time as underlying architecture, taking form in Cézanne's first major landscape distortion. The **flattened depth**.

A photograph of the same lake brings this contrast into view (Figure 2.1, right). The photograph records conventional perspective. Distant mountains recede according to atmospheric perspective, creating the illusion of spatial separation. But Cézanne compresses this depth, bringing distant elements forward to create "the depth of nature." The mountains do not recede into atmospheric haze but assert their structural presence with the same intensity as foreground elements.

This flattening serves a phenomenological purpose. When we experience natural landscapes through sustained attention, distant forms do not remain remote and inconsequential. The mountain on the horizon participates as much in our visual experience as the tree beside us. Cézanne's compressed depth preserves this experiential truth. Consciousness unifies foreground and background into a coherent whole, dissolving the mechanical separation of near and far imposed by the camera.

His second major landscape distortion becomes apparent in the painting's unusual color relationships. The **atmospheric color modeling**. While the photograph records atmospheric effects (blue-tinted mountains, reflected light on water, the variable colors of changing weather), Cézanne employs atmospheric color modeling that transcends momentary conditions. His color gradients do not describe what the lake looked like under specific lighting, instead illuminates the structural relationships that organize our experience of expansive natural spaces across varying atmospheric conditions.

The blue of the mountains is not observed color but *constructed color*, a chromatic synthesis that holds the mountain's character as it unfolds through accumulated attention under different conditions of light and weather. This represents a shift from recording appearance to constructing experiential truth through systematic distortion.

THE MOUNTAIN'S DEEP TIME

The capacity for temporal synthesis reached its fullest expression in Cézanne's encounter with Mont Sainte-Victoire (Figure 2.2, left). Between 1882 and 1906, he painted this limestone mountain over sixty times, each canvas representing less a new view than a deeper penetration into its structural essence through yet another landscape distortion. The **temporal integration**. The synthesis of the mountain's enduring form as discerned across diverse viewing conditions and moments in time.

"One must read the landscape," Cézanne insisted, and he meant this literally. The mountain was not only a visual subject but a text to be deciphered. Its geological stratification telling the story of deep time, its formal relationships illustrating the principles that organize spatial experience across temporal variation. Each painting represents a chapter in this ongoing act of reading, as consciousness slowly penetrated the mountain's structural secrets.

A photograph of Mont Sainte-Victoire (Figure 2.2, left) registers a singular moment under specific conditions. The play of light and shadow at a given time of day, atmospheric effects on a specific date, and surface textures under current weather conditions.

Figure 2.2 Photographic versus constructed vision of Mont Sainte-Victoire. **Left:** A contemporary photograph captures immense surface detail but presents a frozen, singular perspective under specific atmospheric conditions. **Right:** Paul Cézanne's *Mont Sainte-Victoire*, c. 1904-06, achieves temporal integration. The mountain's geological permanence synthesized through multiple viewing conditions, with structural permanence beneath visual change emphasized through Cézanne's systematic landscape distortions.

Cézanne's painted versions, by contrast, portray the mountain as it exists across time, its geological permanence synthesized through multiple viewing conditions. This temporal integration represents perhaps his most sophisticated landscape distortion. The capacity to represent structural permanence as it emerges through temporal flux.

Cézanne expressed this process succinctly, "The landscape thinks itself in me, and I am its consciousness." This thought refers to the temporal convergence at work in his practice. Through sustained attention under varying conditions (different seasons, weather patterns, times of day, atmospheric effects), consciousness gradually extracts the invariant structures that organize the mountain's enduring character. The resulting paintings render what the mountain *is*, sustained across shifting light and seasons, *not how it looked in a single instant.*

THE INNOVATION OF DISINTERESTED DISTORTION

In Cézanne's work, we experience a new mode of perception, a *disinterested way of observing* the natural world. Cézanne often contrasted his approach with that of local peasants who knew the landscape intimately but only through practical need.

"With peasants I've sometimes wondered whether they really know what a landscape is, or indeed a tree. These people know what's been sown here and there along the road, what the weather will be like tomorrow, and if Sainte-Victoire has its cap on or not; they can smell it, the way animals do, just as a dog knows what a piece of bread is when he sniffs at it. They register only what's important to them."

The peasants possessed deep knowledge about nature. They could predict weather, assess soil conditions, and move through complex agricultural cycles. But their knowledge remained practical, organized around human needs and interests. They saw the landscape as a resource, a collection of opportunities and obstacles, a field of potential action.

Cézanne pursued a different kind of seeing, "Without losing any part of myself, I need to get back to that instinct, so that these colours in the scattered field signify an idea to me, just as to them signify a crop." He wanted to recover the peasants' intimate connection to natural processes while turning practical knowledge into structural investigation, achieved through deliberate distortions that moved beyond utilitarian concerns. These distortions served not to "murder nature" as the gentleman outside Père Tanguy's shop claimed, but to elevate observation beyond utility, conveying a deeper, more enduring truth.

Such transformation illustrates a distinctive capacity of human consciousness. Unlike any other known form of intelligence, human minds can bracket their own utilitarian interests and meet the world in a spirit of disinterested inquiry. We can look at the world without concern for how it serves our needs and instead inquire into its essential nature. The capacity for disinterested vision, expressed through deliberate artistic distortions, represents a genuine innovation in the history of mind.

This capacity finds perhaps its most astonishing expression in Cézanne's paintings of the Bibémus Quarry (Figure 2.3), where human excavation exposed the

Figure 2.3 Paul Cézanne, *Bibémus Quarry*, c. 1895. The geometric planes display Cézanne's landscape distortions at their most developed. Temporal integration that unites geological and human time scales, atmospheric color modeling that conveys structural relationships beyond transient light, and a geometric reduction that brings order to natural complexity while expressing the meeting point of human excavation and geological formation

mountain's geological structure in stark planes of cut stone. These works become a heightened meditation on the intersection of geological and human timescales, where human intention collaborates with natural process to create forms that bridge consciousness and geology. The quarry served as a metaphor for Cézanne's project, the patient excavation of deep structure through prolonged attention, manifested in geometric reduction and shifted planes that disclose underlying order.

The geometric planes do more than record the quarry's appearance. They embody Cézanne's discovery of a "natural logic," the structural rhythms that shape our experience of expansive spaces across shifting conditions. This represents a clear divergence from his still life investigations. Still lifes relied on spatial contradictions to convey the felt examination of graspable objects, whereas landscapes required distortions capable of integrating environmental complexity, expressing how natural spaces disclose their character through enduring inhabitation rather than instantaneous sight. The rock faces seem to pulse with intelligence because Cézanne uncovered the latent structural relationships that attentive vision can bring into presence, a perception that forms through discovering the order present in nature instead of imposing external structures upon it.

THE CONCENTRIC VISION

In his quest for natural logic, Cézanne arrived at discoveries that foreshadowed our modern understanding of how vision constructs reality. At the heart of this was his concept of "concentric" vision. Cézanne explained this concept to his contemporary Émile Bernard, "in order to make progress in realization," an artist needs to engage directly with nature, as "the eye educates itself by contact with it. By dint of looking and working, it becomes concentric" [22]. He explained further, in objects such as "an orange, an apple, a ball, a head, there is a culminating point, and this point is always the closest to our eye, the edges of objects recede towards a centre placed at eye level."

This geometrically defined "concentric" vision allowed Cézanne to achieve an insight. By training the eye to perceive form and depth through this principle, he created a kind of resonance between consciousness and the structure of the world, allowing a finer pattern recognition to come through. It equipped him to perceive structure without relying on conceptual categories imposed from outside, and to integrate that structure with the dynamic, temporal experience of light and atmosphere.

Contemporary neuroscience vindicates Cézanne's intuition about how perception works [100, 36]. The visual system does not passively record surface properties but actively constructs reality through predictive models that capture statistical regularities in the environment. Cézanne's "natural logic" corresponds to what cognitive scientists now describe as the underlying structural patterns the brain extracts from sensory experience, a convergence between artistic insight and scientific discovery that we examine in the next chapter.

Cézanne's achievement extended beyond pattern recognition to the apprehension of organizing principles through sustained temporal attention. When he declared that "nature has more to do with depth than with surfaces," he alluded to the structural and temporal dimensions that give landscape experience its meaning. His dozens of paintings of Mont Sainte-Victoire do not represent separate observations but moments in consciousness' gradual penetration of the mountain's underlying structure, a process requiring genuine temporal participation in how reality shows up.

TWO FORMS OF VISUAL INTELLIGENCE

Cézanne's landscape distortions addressed a representational challenge unlike that of still life painting. Still lifes examined how consciousness constructs intimate objects through controlled spatial manipulation, while landscapes demanded techniques capable of holding the unfolding presence of expansive, unmanageable natural structures through temporal synthesis.

This contrast shows a deeper dimension of embodied perception. Our experience with natural environments differs qualitatively from our examination of objects we can pick up and study. Still lifes take shape in interiors where the painter can arrange, rotate, and scrutinize each element. Landscapes surround us with enduring structures that cannot be shifted or restaged. They disclose their character only across changing conditions of light and season. Outdoor vision requires learning to perceive permanence within continual change.

Cézanne's landscape distortions, as we have shown, embody three interlocking principles shaped by this form of perceptual encounter. His flattened depth renders how consciousness holds expansive spaces in one perception without relying on conventional recession. His atmospheric color modeling conveys enduring structural relationships even as appearances shift. His temporal integration expresses how consciousness extracts stability from change through prolonged attention in the field.

These principles highlight a defining distinction between human and artificial intelligence when confronting natural environments. Current AI vision systems exhibit competence with landscape imagery, processing thousands of outdoor photographs, extracting detailed features, analyzing sequences, and generating convincing synthetic scenes. They excel at detecting statistical regularities across large datasets and recognizing objects under varying conditions.

Even so, their operations remain confined to computational analysis of discrete inputs, not genuine immersion in environmental contexts. Where AI handles snapshots or sequences, human perception synthesizes temporal experience into structural understanding through continuous participation in perceptual space. The difference is not only technical, it reflects two distinct modes of intelligence. Computational processing and experiential presence.

Cézanne's landscape work makes this distinction unmistakable. His distortions transpose the insights of his still lifes into a different register, showing that representation is a creative transformation of experience. In the landscapes, the transformations attend to the endurance of the natural world instead of the intimacy of studio objects. They show a distinctive capacity of human intelligence, the ability to access the world's structural depths through sustained, perceptual involvement.

From these investigations into how embodied vision constructs reality through deliberate distortion in both enclosed and open environments, we shift our focus to the brain's predictive architecture. How does it sustain the very activity of constructive seeing that Cézanne's paintings render with such clarity?

3 The Brain's Controlled Hallucination

"I want to make of Impressionism something solid and durable like the art of the museums," Cézanne once said of his ambition. His deeper ambition, however, was far more bolder, "I want to be the sensitive plate of nature" [40]. This metaphor of consciousness as photographic plate sounds humble. A passive device recording reality's unfiltered truth. But what if the plate actively constructs what it records? What if sensitivity means creative participation in reality's formation, not passive reception?

In Chapter 1, Cézanne's still lifes, with their deliberate spatial distortions, showed perception as an active, constructive contact with the world. Chapter 2 extended this insight into open air, where his landscape distortions, especially temporal integration and the pursuit of structural permanence amid shifting conditions, presented consciousness working with expansive natural forms and gathering continuity from change. These artistic discoveries point toward a visual intelligence that is embodied and phenomenological. But how, exactly, does the brain achieve this creative act of seeing?

A century after Cézanne painted his last apple, neuroscience has caught up with him. What might once have been imagined as the brain "recording" nature is, in fact, the most sophisticated act of creative construction ever discovered. Central to this finding is a framework that validates Cézanne's artistic intuitions, **predictive processing** [100, 36]. According to this view, perception is a form of "controlled hallucination." The brain does not passively receive sensory input but actively generates hypotheses about the world, updating its models in light of incoming evidence. Reality, then, is less about "seeing is believing" and more about "believing is seeing," a hallucination refined by sensory input.

This discovery substantiates what Cézanne achieved. His strategic distortions were not artistic liberties taken with objective reality. They were deliberate mappings of how consciousness actually works. When he painted tilted tables and impossible perspectives, compressed distant mountains and synthesized temporal flux, he was creating visual demonstrations of the brain's predictive architecture, showing us not what we see, but *how* we see.

The implications reach far beyond art history. If human intelligence operates through predictive construction and not through passive processing, then every artificial intelligence system built on information processing principles may be missing a foundational dimension of perception.

DOI: 10.1201/9781003623403-3

PERCEPTION AS CONTROLLED HALLUCINATION

For centuries, our understanding of perception largely followed a "bottom-up" model where sensory organs capture raw data that the brain assembles into a coherent picture of the world. But this account struggles to explain illusions, dreams, or even the speed and efficiency of ordinary perception [47, 52, 87]. Building on growing evidence across neuroscience, Anil Seth, neuroscientist and consciousness researcher, presents a contrasting "top-down" approach [100].

Seth argues that the brain operates on a principle of predictive perception, continuously building and updating generative models. These are internal neural mechanisms that simulate how the world produces sensory signals. We can think of the brain as running a sophisticated, probabilistic simulation of reality, predicting what sensory data should be arriving.

When we see an apple, the same humble fruit Cézanne spent decades examining, the brain does not process incoming light waves passively. Instead, its generative model, informed by prior experience, makes a prediction about what we are likely seeing. This top-down hypothesis includes expectations about the apple's color, shape, texture, and even how these qualities should shift as we move our head or reach out to touch it.

This prediction is then compared with the sensory signals arriving from the eyes. If the two fail to align, a prediction error occurs, prompting the brain either to adjust its internal model or to initiate action that gathers additional information. Neuroscientist Karl Friston describes this process as "active inference" [36]. If we expected a red apple but the surface looks green, the brain may revise its belief or prompt us to lean closer, deliberately seeking to minimize perceptual uncertainty.

This ongoing dialogue between prediction and correction is what Seth calls controlled hallucination. Our perception is not a mirror of external reality but an internal construction that remains tethered to the world by sensory constraint. It is "controlled" through Bayesian updates[1] that keep the brain's anticipations in step with external patterns, preserving coherence between mind and world.

This reframes Cézanne's achievements. When he painted an apple from multiple viewpoints, he was giving form to the temporal unfolding of predictive perception. When he compressed spatial depth in his landscapes, he was giving visual expression to the way consciousness constructs spatial understanding through the integration of experience. His canvases become meditations on the brain's own generative labor.

ACTIVE INFERENCE AND EMBODIED CONSTRUCTION

Karl Friston's *Free Energy Principle* extends this understanding even further, proposing that all living systems work to minimize "surprise" by maintaining accurate predictive models of their environment [36]. The brain does not wait for sensory data

[1] Named after 18th-century English statistician and Presbyterian minister Thomas Bayes, Bayesian updating refers to a mathematical method for revising predictions based on new evidence. In neuroscience, it describes how the brain continuously adjusts its internal models as new sensory information arrives, weighing prior expectations against current evidence.

to arrive. It proactively searches for the evidence needed to refine and stabilize its expectations, a process Friston describes as "active inference."

The active dimension casts new light on Cézanne's working method. He never approached a motif as a fixed scene to be copied but as an unfolding presence that required prolonged, reciprocal attention. His many studies of Mont Sainte-Victoire function as a sequence of perceptual experiments, each one testing and adjusting his evolving sense of the mountain's enduring structure as it stood under shifting conditions. They form a record of perception as an embodied investigation.

Such approach stands worlds apart from passive recording, for it arises only through sustained, searching contact with the world that gradually discloses its structure across time. A camera records a single instant under fixed conditions. One frame, one vantage point, one pattern of illumination. Cézanne's practice developed through repeated encounters that accumulated evidence across shifting weather, changing light, and innumerable returns to the same place. His temporal synthesis distortions in landscape painting were necessary strategies for conveying how active inference forms an enduring sense of structure through ongoing interaction.

Such prolonged attentiveness connects to what Cézanne called becoming "concentric" [22], a concept introduced earlier in relation to his geometric perception of objects. In the landscape, the idea expands in remarkable ways. Through disciplined observation, the eye is trained to perceive structural relationships with increasing clarity. Viewed through Friston's account of active inference, this phenomenon reflects a process in which the brain continually tests and refines its hypotheses, achieving greater fidelity through steady feedback and adjustment. Cézanne's concentric vision anticipates perception as a form of resonance between consciousness and the world's underlying order, where deeper patterns gradually emerge beyond surface appearance.

THE EMBODIED MIND

A critical aspect of predictive processing, one that aligns closely with Cézanne's phenomenological approach, is the emphasis on embodied consciousness. Anil Seth, drawing on philosophers such as Maurice Merleau-Ponty and a substantial body of neuroscience, argues that perception arises less from external inputs alone than from the brain's ongoing integration of three streams of information.

Exteroception. Our outward-looking senses that register sight, hearing, touch, smell, and taste. Cézanne's still lifes and landscapes overflow with exteroceptive richness, but his distortions show how this information is organized through perceptual construction. When we see his tilted tables or compressed mountains, we witness how consciousness shapes the world from sensory material.

Proprioception. Our awareness of body position and movement, the sense that tells us where our limbs are and how we inhabit space. Cézanne's distortions of perspective subtly engage our proprioceptive awareness, challenging our expected bodily orientation to the painted scene. His multiple viewpoints in a single painting mirror how we experience space through moving, reaching, and shifting our position over time.

Interoception. Our perception of internal physiological states such as heartbeat, breathing, and visceral sensations. Seth argues that these interoceptive predictions are not just additional inputs but are foundational to all conscious experience, including our sense of self and our subjective feelings. They provide the brain's "best guess" about the state of the body, which is important for regulating our internal environment and constructing our sense of "being."

The lived convergence of exteroceptive, proprioceptive, and interoceptive streams lends Cézanne's distortions their visceral truth. When he tilted the table in *The Basket of Apples* (Figure 1.1), he rendered how we experience objects through physical engagement, reaching around them, shifting viewpoints, and the weaving together of multiple glimpses into a coherent sense of presence. The "weight" of Cézanne's apple is not computed mass but phenomenological weight, its perceived presence and relationality inseparable from our embodied experience and the internal feelings it evokes.

When we perceive an apple, we do far more than process its visual properties. The brain predicts and integrates information about our internal bodily states, our physical relationship to the apple, and how it might feel to touch or taste it. This role of interoceptive perception extends beyond external objects to shape our subjective experience of being alive. As Seth observes with striking clarity, we do not cry because we are sad. Instead, we sense the bodily state of crying and experience that interoceptive perception as sadness. Feelings, then, are at their core interoceptive perceptions, the brain's controlled hallucinations of the body's internal state.

THE LIMITS OF COMPUTATIONAL INTELLIGENCE

Predictive processing offers a framework for understanding the brain's active construction of reality. In this framework, perception is "controlled hallucination," refined through active inference and grounded in the interplay of exteroception, proprioception, and interoception. When we set biologically embodied perception beside contemporary AI systems, the limits of computational intelligence become evident.

Contemporary AI vision systems can classify objects with high accuracy and generate photorealistic images. Some even employ hierarchical designs that resemble predictive architectures, minimizing error across large datasets and generating expectations about visual input. But these systems lack access to the conditions that give prediction its meaning. They analyze information about the world without participating in its emergence through lived experience.

The distinction lies in existential stakes. Human predictive processing serves biological imperatives, constrained and given meaning by interoceptive awareness of bodily needs, survival drives, and physiological states. AI systems lack this embodied foundation. No interoceptive awareness to fuse with exteroceptive inputs, no proprioceptive orientation anchoring spatial predictions to a moving, sensing body.

For the same reason, AI cannot realize genuine active inference in the sense exemplified by Cézanne. Although computational systems can process temporal sequences, they cannot perform lived temporal synthesis. Cézanne's Mont

Sainte-Victoire series physical presence across seasons and weather, integrating landscape experience with proprioceptive awareness of changing position and interoceptive shifts accompanying sustained attention. This immersion allowed consciousness to discern enduring structure within environmental change, something statistical analysis alone cannot accomplish.

AI operates through statistical pattern recognition, not creative construction. Where Cézanne's distortions show how intelligence shapes new spatial realities, computational systems are governed by the minimization of predictive error. As both Cézanne's art and neuroscience confirm, intelligence is not only concerned with accuracy but with forming possible worlds through active interaction.

These considerations imply that any future form of genuine perceptual intelligence will require architectures categorically different from those we build today. Beyond increased computational speed, the challenge is to conceive artificial systems capable of embodied and temporal participation in unfolding visual reality. Whether such artificial embodiment can be realized is uncertain. Current work in robotics and virtual environments seeks to ground AI in sensorimotor experience [8, 90], but replicating the deep integration of perception, action, and meaning characteristic of biological consciousness remains a formidable task.

Cézanne's investigations remind us that visual intelligence is inseparable from lived participation in the world's becoming. Present AI systems, however capable, remain outside this domain of perception.

FROM VISUAL TO SYMBOLIC INTELLIGENCE

Cézanne's practice, reinforced by predictive processing theory, make clear that perception is not passive recording but active construction. His tilted tables, compressed landscapes, and temporal syntheses show how consciousness builds coherent reality through prediction, integration, and lived contact. Even so, this account takes us only part of the way. Human intelligence reaches beyond embodied vision into the symbolic domain, where meaning is constructed, shared, and transformed through language.

For consciousness to participate in reality's construction, to articulate what it discovers and build cumulative understanding across generations, it needs to transform lived experience into symbolic form. The mountains may come into thought through the act of seeing, but consciousness bears their meaning forward through language, allowing insight to move beyond the moment of perception.

The transition from perceptual construction to symbolic representation introduces new complexities for intelligence. If current AI struggles with embodied, temporal perception, how much more challenging is the fluid, context-dependent, and social nature of symbolic intelligence? Language operates through meanings that arise from social processes of communication and cultural transmission, a theme we will examine in greater depth later in this book, requiring integration across multiple dimensions of human experience, which is needed for understanding the character of human intelligence.

From the neural mechanisms of embodied visual perception, mapped through Cézanne's insights, we move to symbolic representation to see how it shapes our understanding of reality. This prepares us for Cézanne's most enigmatic works, the portraits, where the act of depicting human presence confronts the uncertainties of language, social order, and the symbolic world that makes us human.

The consciousness that constructs reality through predictive processing also transforms it into symbolic form, creating possibilities for meaning that reach beyond individual experience. This symbolic foundation of human intelligence, with its uncertainties and social complexities, constitutes the ground where human and artificial intelligence diverge most sharply.

4 The Doubt in the Portrait

If perception is indeed a dynamic construction guided by prediction, what happens when our predictive faculties meet their most demanding test? The human face. A window into another consciousness looking back at us. Our previous explorations showed how Cézanne's distortions in still lifes and landscapes revealed the active, embodied nature of perception, from the palpable weight of an apple's phenomenological flesh to the temporal expanse of Mont Sainte-Victoire's deep time. Now we reach the perceptual frontier, the human face and the complexities that arise in confronting another consciousness.

In his portraits, Cézanne met an element that neither the apple nor the mountain ever posed. The human face stirred in him a pervasive doubt. The constructive techniques he applied with confidence elsewhere began to hesitate. Distortion took on a new role, becoming a form of questioning. Incompleteness emerged as an acknowledgment of the mystery of subjectivity.

Cézanne's portraits, particularly those left unfinished, stand where visual intelligence reaches its limit. They indicate that to complete the task of representing a human subject, artistic vision needs to move into another order. The symbolic order of language and social meaning. Pure perception alone cannot fully account for the presence of another mind.

This chapter studies four portraits that give this limit visible form. We begin with the unfinished portraits of **Gustave Geffroy**, an art critic, and **Joachim Gasquet**, a poet and memoirist of Cézanne's life, where doubt becomes *productive incompleteness*. We then move to the finished portrait of **Ambroise Vollard**, the pioneering art dealer who organized Cézanne's first solo exhibition, a work that highlights the costs of resolution. Finally, our analysis culminates in the portrait of **his father** reading a newspaper, where the painted title, *L'Évènement*, signals the intrusion of symbolic order into visual representation.

THE INCOMPLETENESS OF THE OTHER: GEFFROY'S ENDURING DOUBT

Cézanne's *Portrait of Gustave Geffroy* (1895), though well-known, remains notoriously unfinished (Figure 4.1). Large areas of the canvas expose the bare white ground beneath. Geffroy's face is blurred and unresolved, his hands scarcely sketched, and his clothing dissolves into loose brushstrokes. The background wavers between depth and flatness, while the books scattered across his desk stand as vacant volumes without titles or text. This incompleteness is not a technical failure but Cézanne's deliberate distortion, a refusal to confine identity or knowledge within a finished image. It speaks to the unsettled nature of perceiving another consciousness and enacts the impossibility of ever completing a living subject in paint.

The sense of incompleteness extends into the structure of the scene. Maurice Merleau-Ponty, in his essay "Cézanne's Doubt," curiously turned his attention away

DOI: 10.1201/9781003623403-4

Figure 4.1 Paul Cézanne, *Portrait of Gustave Geffroy*, c. 1895. This unfinished portrait illustrates Merleau-Ponty's idea of an "unfolding perspective." The table resists classical recession and traces the temporal dynamics of embodied perception. The workspace seems to extend beyond the frame, creating what Merleau-Ponty described as "a space that by definition can never be finished."

from Geffroy's face to a seemingly mundane element, the table. He noted how "The work table in his portrait of Gustave Geffroy stretches, contrary to the laws of perspective, into the lower part of the picture" [80]. We have seen Cézanne use tilted tabletops in his still lifes, often laden with apples and other fruit, to disrupt linear perspective and convey the embodied act of seeing from multiple shifting positions. In Geffroy's portrait, the same spatial distortion reappears, but in a new context. The angled table refuses the stability of optical correctness and invites us to experience perception as a restless process, always in motion.

Why focus on furniture in a portrait? In this setting this same spatial contradiction does more than echo the still lifes. The unfinished tabletop becomes an anchor that draws us beyond questions of geometry into the problem of representing another consciousness. Merleau-Ponty understood that Cézanne's choice to leave certain portraits incomplete, despite his lifelong pursuit of "realization" on canvas, reflects a philosophical insight. When the subject is a living mind, perception eludes closure.

The table in Geffroy's portrait asserts an "unfolding perspective." Instead of receding to a singular vanishing point, it expands outward, accumulating visual information through an observer's shifting viewpoints. As Merleau-Ponty noted, when our eye scans a large surface, each small shift brings a slightly altered image, causing the whole to warp. Cézanne masterfully renders this dynamic, embodied vision, where objects are not static geometric forms but presences "emerging... appearing, organizing [themselves] before our eyes." His brushstrokes arrest these perceptual distortions, fixing the spontaneous, accumulating movement of vision onto the canvas.

This spatial ambiguity extends to the temporal realm. Human perception, unlike a camera's instantaneous record, is a process of sustained investigation. We do not see objects fully formed. Instead, we construct understanding through accumulated attention and interaction. The table, with its mixture of clear and elusive forms, becomes a "phenomenological table." It holds the integration of the body's posture (sitting, leaning) with the mind's activity (perceiving, thinking), expressing how one is inseparable from the other. Yet the table is not the final object of attention. It frames the living subject seated behind it, pointing us toward Geffroy.

The table's ambiguity culminates in the human presence it frames. Geffroy sits with his hands poised for writing, though no implement is visible. The blank pages scattered across the surface seem to await inscription, prompting Merleau-Ponty to question, "what kind of inscription, written or painted, does that blankness signal and await?" This unfinish signifies the open-ended nature of consciousness, perpetually in process and never completely reducible. The uncertainty intensifies when the subject is another human being whose inner life cannot be fixed in visual terms.

Why did Cézanne never finish this portrait? Merleau-Ponty offers an insight, "this portrait couldn't be finished because it depicts a space that by definition can never be finished." The expansive perspective of the table seems to spill out into the viewer's own physical space, preventing a definitive closure. This inherent openness explains "the logic to its not ever having been finished, and to its legendary exemplification of Cézannian unfinish." Cézanne's refusal of completion becomes a recognition of perception's intrinsic uncertainty. The openness informs a conception of intelligence that thrives on enduring dialogue with what can never be fully resolved.

THE PROPORTIONAL ALTERATION OF SUBJECTIVITY: GASQUET'S EMBODIED ENCOUNTER

The following year, Cézanne's portrait of *Joachim Gasquet* (1896) introduces another facet of perceptual uncertainty (Figure 4.2). The **proportional alteration**. In this work, incompleteness manifests not only in spatial distortion but also in what Gustave Geffroy described as "gaucherie," an awkwardness that rises whenever one attempts to give visual form to a living presence. The "patchwork of flesh on the face," the subtly misaligned eye, and visible areas of bare canvas transcend technical challenge. They speak to the fragile meeting with another consciousness, where perception can never settle into certainty.

Figure 4.2 Paul Cézanne, *Portrait of Joachim Gasquet*, c. 1896. The young poet and critic from Aix-en-Provence who wrote extensively about Cézanne's philosophy appears in this painting in patches of flesh and areas of bare canvas. The misaligned gaze and visible brushwork embody what Geffroy called "gaucherie," the inevitable awkwardness of trying to capture living consciousness through visual means alone.

The "gaucherie" refers to what Merleau-Ponty termed "**autrui**," the irreducible otherness of another consciousness. When we face another person, we meet a presence that will not yield to the objective scrutiny Cézanne had developed with inanimate objects. Unlike a still life that opens its structure to our gaze, or a landscape that shows its underlying structure through sustained attention, human presence remains enigmatic. Crucially, it *looks back*.

Gasquet's slightly misaligned eye exemplifies this proportional alteration. Instead of striving for anatomical perfection, Cézanne foregrounds asymmetry as phenomenological truth. The experience of another's gaze is never one of stability or detached objectivity. It confronts us with the profound realization that we exist within the field of vision, constantly observed by others. This insight is at the heart of the influential French psychoanalyst Jacques Lacan's notion of "the gaze," which transforms the observer into the observed, unsettling the very structure of perception [69].

The "patchwork of flesh on the face" in Gasquet's portrait deepens this effect. For Merleau-Ponty, flesh is not just surface but "lived flesh," the visible manifestation of embodied consciousness. In meeting another, our predictive brain seeks not only to register their visible features but also to model their interiority such as their psychological states, intentions, and consciousness. Such a meeting introduces an uncertainty that differs from the spatial challenges of still lifes or the temporal syntheses of landscapes.

In Gasquet's portrayal, Cézanne's "doubt" arises as a creative force. The bare canvas, the awkward proportion, and the unfinished patches all acknowledge that human subjectivity cannot be fixed within a single frame. To depict a living being is to begin an open-ended dialogue with what continually exceeds representation.

Such productive incompleteness discloses a deeper truth about the nature of human encounter. When we look at another person, we meet with the presence of another consciousness, "autrui," whose inner life remains unknowable but undeniably present. Cézanne's distortions encode this phenomenological uncertainty, the fact that our perception of others remains provisional, open to revision, and attuned to the mystery of subjectivity that reaches beyond appearance. As we will later consider, such doubt is not an obstacle to intelligence but a vital force that sustains its creativity and responsiveness, bearing implications that extend beyond art and philosophy into how we understand intelligence.

VOLLARD'S COMPLETION: THE LIMITS OF DEFINITIVE REALIZATION

If Gasquet's portrait holds the openness of doubt as a creative force, Cézanne's rendering of Ambroise Vollard presents its counterpoint, a work that looks resolved but in its solidity shows the cost of definitive completion. The *Portrait of Ambroise Vollard* (1899) (Figure 4.3, left) offers a striking contrast, rendering how completeness can paradoxically diminish the vitality that Cézanne's incompleteness preserved.

Vollard's portrait is characterized by its "mineral" blue and brown overpaintedness [3]. After reportedly 115 grueling sittings, Cézanne expressed satisfaction with the work's solid structure, especially the shirt [27]. However, the painting features two small but telling patches of bare canvas on Vollard's right hand. When questioned by Vollard, Cézanne replied, "If the copy I'm making at the Louvre turns out well, perhaps I will be able tomorrow to find the exact tone to cover up those spots. Don't you see, Monsieur Vollard, that if I put something there by guesswork, I might have to paint the whole canvas over starting from that point?" [76]. This admission shows that even in this seemingly completed work, Cézanne confronted an inherent limit. Further "realization" through conventional painting risked unraveling the entire construction.

The portrait achieves a formidable structural solidity, echoing the architectural forms of his late still lifes and landscapes. But in this completeness a vital quality seems to have slipped away. The sense of "finished" permanence gives the work a geological weight which, though masterful, lacks the living dynamism of his deliberately unfinished portraits.

The "mineral" quality seems to foreshadow Cubist analytical fragmentation, as seen in Pablo Picasso's 1910 treatment of Vollard (Figure 4.3, right). However, while Cubism developed a new pictorial language for multiple perspectives, Cézanne's portrait of Vollard, in its almost-completion, reads as a heroic but constraining attempt

Figure 4.3 Left: Paul Cézanne, *Portrait of Ambroise Vollard*, c. 1899. **Right**: Pablo Picasso, *Portrait of Ambroise Vollard*, 1910. Compare Cézanne's formidable but complete, somewhat withdrawn "mineral" presence with Picasso's fragmented Cubist study of multiple perspectives. Both expose different challenges in capturing the elusive nature of human subjectivity and the resistant gaze.

to extend methods suited to inanimate objects into the far more elusive terrain of human subjectivity. Vollard's eyes, often described as dark, unseeing holes or downcast, seem to avoid direct engagement with the viewer's gaze, unlike the directness or subtle misalignment seen in Gasquet's portrait [57]. The success of its structural "realization" exacts its phenomenological cost. Human consciousness eludes the kind of definitive, architectural finality achievable with apples and mountains, especially when confronting the intersubjective challenge of "the gaze."

The contrast between Cézanne's structural finality and Cubism's fragmented perspective reveals why Cézanne's unfinished portraits, despite their lack of conventional completion, often convey a greater sense of living presence. In their unfinish, they hold onto what Merleau-Ponty described as the "never-finished coming-into-being of the world in human perception." They maintain the temporal dimension of meeting (the ongoing act of perceiving) which completion, by definition, tends to obliterate. Vollard, locked within his achieved completeness, cannot "look back" or surprise us. Geffroy and Gasquet, in their ongoing state of becoming, remain capable of unexpected openings.

THE SYMBOLIC INTRUSION: THE FATHER, L'ÉVÈNEMENT, AND THE EDGE OF MEANING

Cézanne's early portrait of his father, *The Artist's Father Reading L'Évènement* (1866) shows an altogether different kind of distortion (Figure 4.4). The **symbolic distortion**. Unlike the perspectival or proportional distortions of still lifes and portraits, this is not a visual anomaly but the deliberate inclusion of an element that transcends visual representation and compels linguistic interpretation. **Text**. Louis-Auguste Cézanne sits absorbed in *L'Évènement*, and Cézanne junior painstakingly rendered not only the newspaper as an object but its title as a visible word. This seemingly minor detail signals a turning point, the moment where visual intelligence approaches its limits and begins to open onto the symbolic realm.

Figure 4.4 Paul Cézanne, *The Artist's Father Reading L'Évènement*, c. 1866. The painted newspaper title, *L'Évènement*, marks the intrusion of the symbolic order into visual representation. Behind the patriarchal figure hangs Cézanne's own *Still Life with Sugar Bowl and Blue Cup*, a purely visual realm set against the father's immersion in linguistic and social discourse. With this single word, the portrait becomes more than a depiction. It stages a symbolic triangulation, linking personal relationships to broader cultural structures.

This painting introduces "symbolic relationality," which is different from the visual relationality developed in still lifes. The newspaper title is more than a visual element. It is a word, a linguistic signifier that pulls the painting into a complex web of social, cultural, and personal meanings. By painting the word *L'Évènement*, Cézanne acknowledged that human social existence is shaped by linguistic structures that exceed the reach of visual means alone.

The choice of *L'Évènement* was not arbitrary. This was the newspaper in which Émile Zola, Cézanne's childhood friend, had published his first Salon of 1866, his first piece of art criticism discussing Édouard Manet's controversial work, and notably, including a brief section dedicated to his "friend Cézanne." Through this textual reference, the portrait constructs a *symbolic triangulation* linking Cézanne, through his father, to Zola and Manet. It situates the young artist within the nascent, often contentious, network of relationships and ideas that would define his early career and the emergence of modern art.

A telling contrast within the painting further highlights this juncture. Behind the father, Cézanne included a small still life, *Still Life with Sugar Bowl, and Blue Cup* (1865-66), painted onto the wall. This inserted painting exists within the visual order, amenable to the kind of embodied, predictive investigation Cézanne had mastered. However, the father, absorbed in his newspaper, stands at once within both the visual and the symbolic orders. Understanding his presence requires an interpretation that extends beyond the reach of visual perception alone.

The father engrossed in the newspaper represents patriarchal authority mediated through language and public discourse. The newspaper's function is not only to transmit information. It constructs social reality through symbolic representation. This introduces what Jacques Lacan termed the "**symbolic order**," the domain of language, law, social conventions, and shared meanings that shapes human consciousness and identity [69]. Unlike the visually-driven "imaginary realm" of identification, the symbolic order operates through differences and arbitrary signs, making meaning possible.

This doubling underscores the limit of visual intelligence. The still life, hovering uncannily over the father's head, can be understood through the lens of embodied perception and predictive processing. But comprehending the father requires working with symbolic structures that operate according to different principles. Linguistic, cultural, and social meanings that defy reduction to visual patterning. It represents the artist's developing personal vision confronting his father's immersion in the public, symbolic sphere.

THE GAZE, DOUBT, AND THE UNIQUELY HUMAN

Contemporary AI vision systems excel at facial recognition, accurately identifying individuals and even classifying expressions through sophisticated algorithms. They can create convincing, hyper-realistic portraits. However, they cannot experience what Lacan called "the gaze," the unsettling, transformative recognition that we are always being looked at by the world, by others, and by the symbolic structures that precede us. When we see another person's eyes in a portrait, we experience something that surpasses pattern recognition. We confront another subjectivity that modifies our own position from observer to observed.

For Lacan, the gaze is not simply a matter of what we see. It is the pervasive sense of being "looked at" by the forces of the world and society. In Cézanne's *The Artist's Father Reading L'Évènement*, the father's contact with the newspaper (a physical manifestation of society's symbolic gaze) holds this dynamic. We are inside a world imbued with shared meanings, social conventions, and narratives that exist through language and culture.

Cézanne's deliberate distortions in his portraits, especially their **incompleteness** and **proportional alterations**, render this uniquely human transformation. The unfinish is a form of phenomenological accuracy, an acknowledgment that human subjectivity cannot be completed through visual representation alone. The misaligned eyes, the visible patches of bare canvas, and the perspectival impossibilities all serve to maintain the portrait as an active confrontation, resisting reduction to a static, definitive image.

This has far-reaching implications for understanding artificial intelligence. Current AI systems work mostly in what amounts to "extractive vision." They pull information from visual inputs for classification, recognition, or generation. But human vision, as Cézanne's portraits exhibit, operates through participatory meeting. We do not just objectively "see" other people. We engage with them in ways that deeply reshape both the observer and the observed, creating a reciprocal exchange that transforms perception.

One potential neurological basis for this participatory difference involves phenomena such as "mirror neurons," specialized cells that activate both when we perform an action and when we observe another person performing the same action [96]. This creates a form of participatory empathy and implicit understanding that goes beyond abstract pattern recognition. When we see someone smile, we do more than classify the expression. We partially simulate the act of smiling through neural activity, creating a visceral, embodied connection.

Cézanne's portrait distortions encapsulate this dimension of human experience. The spatial "impossibilities" of Geffroy's table map the kinesthetic experience of moving around and perceiving space over time. The visible "flesh patches" in Gasquet's portrait acknowledge the raw, tactile dimension of human presence and the physical nature of meeting another being. The symbolic elements in the father's portrait reflect the linguistic and cultural structures that shape social existence. None of these dimensions can be reduced to mere visual information processing by a disembodied intelligence.

Cézanne's portraits thus sharpen the distinction between human and artificial intelligence. Where his still lifes illustrated the constructive nature of perception and his landscapes showed temporal synthesis, his portraits expose the irreducibly intersubjective dimension of human consciousness, our capacity to meet and be met by other minds, to participate in symbolic orders that transcend individual experience, and to embrace productive doubt as a creative force instead of treating it as an error to be minimized.

THE PRODUCTIVE NATURE OF DOUBT

Why did Cézanne, a master of still lifes and landscapes, struggle so intensely with portraits? Merleau-Ponty suggested that Cézanne's difficulty was not technical but philosophical. He was attempting to paint "a pre-world in which man did not yet exist" while striving to capture human physiognomy through the "arrangement of colors and lights" [80].

This ambition created what Merleau-Ponty termed a "phenomenological contradiction" within Cézanne's project. On one side, Cézanne sought to access a primordial vision preceding cultural conditioning, to see the world "as if with nature's own inhuman eyes." On the other hand, he aimed to express "the physiognomy of faces and things" in a manner that acknowledged the mature, cognitively human nature of perception. This internal paradox fuels the productive nature of doubt in his portraits.

Unlike the resolute constructions of his still lifes, where inanimate objects yielded to sustained visual investigation, portraits demanded an acknowledgment of uncertainty as a constitutive element. The incompleteness was not a flaw to be corrected but a truth to be expressed. Human consciousness exists in a state of openness that defies definitive closure or finalization in a static image.

Cézanne's "doubt" in these works is thus an expression of insight. The representation of a living being necessitates an embrace of ambiguity and the elusive nature of subjectivity. This uncertainty becomes a creative force, exposing the act of perception as an ongoing, never-finished dialogue with the world. The doubt embedded in Cézanne's portraits therefore points toward a radically different model of intelligence, one that embraces uncertainty as a generative condition rather than striving to eliminate it as a computational error.

This exposes a central limitation in artificial intelligence. Current AI systems are largely designed to minimize uncertainty, to achieve maximum confidence in classification and generation, and to resolve ambiguity into singular answers. But Cézanne's portraits show that uncertainty plays a productive role in human intelligence. It keeps us receptive to the ongoing emergence of meaning, prevents premature closure, and preserves the possibility of genuine encounter and transformation.

THE LIMITS OF PURE VISION

Cézanne's unfinished portraits, especially the inclusion of the newspaper title in his father's depiction, suggest that representing the complexity of human experience requires something beyond the constructive power of visual perception discussed in earlier chapters. While our brains excel at extracting solidity, relationality, and temporal permanence from sensory input, these mechanisms alone fall short in interpreting certain dimensions of human presence.

The symbolic weight of a newspaper title, the social dynamics within a family setting, and the elusive inner life of a portrayed individual all point to dimensions of meaning that visual intelligence, however sophisticated, cannot fully encompass. Engaging these dimensions calls for another mode of representation. **Language**.

Through language, we access the shared narratives, abstract concepts, and cultural structures that shape our existence and give depth to human interaction.

The newspaper in the father's portrait becomes a bridge to the next phase of our inquiry. By painting the title *L'Évènement*, Cézanne acknowledged that human reality is linguistic, social, and symbolic. We are not only perceiving forms and colors. We are inhabiting a world suffused with shared meanings, conventions, and narratives sustained through language and culture.

FROM VISUAL CONSTRUCTION TO SYMBOLIC CREATION

The apple speaks. The pear responds. The bowl awaits with unhurried patience. In Cézanne's still lifes and landscapes, perception unfolded as a dialogue between consciousness and the world. Language, however, introduces a conversation of another order, one that transforms how we come into being. If Cézanne showed reality as relational, language discloses its infinite malleability, creating possibilities that vision alone, however cultivated, cannot summon.

Cézanne's struggles with portraiture, and his embrace of "incompleteness," stand as an artistic testament to the uncertainty of perception when it meets the human "other," and the unavoidable intrusion of the symbolic order. The eye, though refined and "educated by contact with nature" and capable of becoming "concentric," ultimately arrives at a limit where visual tools no longer suffice. The silent presence of another calls for the voice that can articulate its hidden structures and bring them into shared understanding.

Vision initiates the work of intelligence, but language is required to move through the intricate social worlds we inhabit and to articulate meanings that perception only sets in motion. Language, as we shall see, brings its own creative "distortions," transformations that participate in shaping reality.

We began with Cézanne's apple, solid and weighted with phenomenological presence. Now we turn toward Éluard's impossible "blue orange," where language transforms both the way we see and the horizon of what the world may become.

Part II

Linguistic Intelligence

Language is a stranger form of intelligence. It works through arbitrary signs bearing no inner relation to what they designate. Through this arbitrariness, language generates the richest possibilities of meaning.

Language is not just a more advanced tool than vision. It embodies an altogether different mode of intelligence. While vision remains tethered to physical contact with the external world, language functions through symbols whose links to meaning are conventional, shifting, and endlessly open to reinterpretation. This arbitrariness is the source of language's creative power, the foundation on which symbolic intelligence emerges.

Vision, as we have seen, is constructive, embodied, and predictive, but it reaches its limits when it confronts subjectivity, especially in the face of another consciousness. The symbolic dimension, especially language, extends perceptual intelligence beyond this limit. It transforms embodied experience into shared, cumulative meaning.

From this foundation, the inquiry moves toward the thinkers and artists who reveal the architecture of linguistic intelligence. We examine how Paul Éluard's impossible metaphors reconfigure the boundary between word and the world, how Jacques La can maps the symbolic order that constitutes subjectivity, and how Dostoevsky ventures into regions of consciousness that elude even linguistic capture.

We discover how what seem to be the human mind's "flaws," such as its susceptibility to contradiction, its reliance on inexact metaphors, and its vulnerability to unconscious processes, are in fact the foundations of its most extraordinary capabilities. We will see how language operates as more than description, shaping both the world we inhabit and the subjects we become within it.

This is also where the contrast with artificial intelligence becomes sharpest. Contemporary AI systems, however capable in processing and generating text, remain bound to statistical associations. Human linguistic intelligence, by contrast, arises from our constitution within symbolic structures, from our capacity to create and inhabit meaning, and from our openness to what exceeds formalization. It reflects a fundamentally different mode of being, one that cannot be reduced to a higher level of computation.

Our journey into language begins with a truth both simple and strange. *The Earth is blue like an orange.*

5 The Earth Is Blue Like an Orange

The Earth and an orange share certain familiar traits. Both are round, both textured, both tangible objects in space. However, no one would mistake one for the other. Oranges are not blue, neither the fruit nor the color. The planet is not citrus. The differences feel so obvious, so self-evident, that to question them seems absurd. However, Paul Éluard, the French surrealist poet, wrote a single line that overturned this certainty. *La terre est bleue comme une orange*. The Earth is blue like an orange. In the poem from which this line comes, impossibility becomes a source of vision, a way of opening perception beyond logic [117].

The Earth is blue like an orange
faultless words don't lie
they give you no more reason to sing
It's the kisses' turn to understand
madmen and lovers
blocked union
all the secrets all the smiles
and such indulgent clothes
completely naked to faith.

Wasps flowered green
dawn passes around your neck
a necklace of windows
wings cover leaves
you have all the solar joys
all the sun on Earth
on the paths of your beauty.

Éluard's impossible line shows what makes language strange. While our rational mind registers the apparent contradiction that oranges cannot be blue and that Earth, existing in a different order from citrus fruit, shares with it only roundness, the line endures, reverberates, and unfolds into new regions of meaning.

If Cézanne's canvases expressed how perception reshapes the visible, language expands this reshaping into a domain where meaning is formed through signs whose connections to what they signify are conventional and fluid. This arbitrariness, far from being a limitation, becomes the source of language's creative power. The gap between word and meaning, the space where "blue" can modify "orange," and "Earth" can become fruit, makes possible metaphorical thinking, analogical

DOI: 10.1201/9781003623403-5

reasoning, and creative leaps that define linguistic intelligence. This flexibility in the relationship between symbols and meanings forms the basis of linguistic creativity.

Éluard's impossible line reminds us that what logic defies, imagination transforms. Contradiction becomes invitation, and arbitrariness becomes a generative terrain. In this interval between words and meanings, linguistic intelligence finds one of its richest modes of creation.

This chapter traces the capacity of human linguistic intelligence to transform and reconceptualize reality through the architecture of creative connection, transcending the boundaries of immediate perception. At the heart of this capacity is our ability for **cross-domain mapping**, forging connections across seemingly unrelated domains of experience.

Beginning with Éluard's impossible paradox, we analyze three progressively sophisticated modes of meaning-making that embody this capacity. *Metaphor* as our unconscious conceptual infrastructure that organizes how we understand the world; *analogy* as our conscious reasoning instrument for grasping new situations through familiar patterns; and *confabulation* as our dynamic narrative process that creates coherent meaning from fragments of lived experience.

Each represents a different aspect of the same capacity. Our ability to create connections across experiential boundaries, generate new conceptual categories, and form understanding through imaginative leaps, which is, as this chapter shall argue, beyond the scope of mechanical computation. This progression shows how these capacities create a form of intelligence that is experientially grounded, analogically flexible, and creatively generative. We will see why genuine linguistic intelligence requires inhabiting the living fabric of meaning, not just symbol processing.

WHERE MEANING TRANSCENDS LOGIC

In writing *La terre est bleue comme une orange*, Éluard was conducting an inquiry into how human intelligence reaches beyond conventional thought. The "blue orange" becomes a form of **productive contradiction**, the linguistic counterpart to Cézanne's visual distortions. Just as his tilted tables and compressed landscapes exposed the constructive nature of perception, Éluard's paradoxical line shows how language generates new meaning by holding contradiction in suspension, transforming impossibility into creative insight.

But the poem goes further than presenting impossible images. It offers a critique of ordinary language. "Faultless words don't lie," Éluard writes, but they "give you no more reason to sing." These lines point to an intrinsic limitation of conventional language. Although it may be truthful, it fails to inspire or capture the ecstatic nature of profound experience. Logical language operates through fixed categories, organizing the world into static, distinct classifications. It describes what lies before us, but it seldom alters how an experience feels from within.

When ordinary words fall short, what takes over? "It's the kisses' turn to understand." Physical, sensual experience becomes the means of knowledge, surpassing words and rational analysis. Touch replaces thought. The poem alludes that the truest forms of understanding require an intuitive, embodied mode of experiencing the world.

But how can language convey these sensual, inner experiences that ordinary words cannot reach? Éluard's answer comes through breaking language's fixed meaning-mapping categories. By pairing apparently impossible elements, such as blue with orange, Earth with fruit, he creates new meanings that were otherwise impossible to capture through regular linguistic categories. The breakthrough occurs by pushing language to its outer edges.

When we read "The Earth is blue like an orange," the mind performs complex work. At first, there is resistance. The logical faculties protest that oranges cannot be blue, that Earth and citrus fruit belong to different categories. Then comes an unexpected shift. The mind may briefly search for common ground. Perhaps the Earth's roundness mirrored in the fruit, or shared hues of a distant horizon. These rational attempts, however, fall short.

Instead, in a momentary synesthetic flash, the mind attempts to superimpose these disparate sensory experiences. It does not succeed in creating a literal blue orange. The world does not suddenly conform to this proclamation. But it generates something far stronger, a sensation, an intuition, a fleeting glimpse of reality reconfigured by language's audacity.

This process intensifies as the poem progresses. "Wasps flowered green," Éluard writes. An impossible image mixing insects, plants, and color in ways that evoke meaning without direct description. It is a dreamlike contradiction where beauty mingles with potential threat, hinting tension, attraction, and unexpected flourishing. The line, defying logical categories, creates a sense of transformation and metamorphosis.

More dramatic is the claim that beauty can become "a landscape to be traveled." When Éluard writes of walking "on the paths of your beauty," he maps the beloved's physical presence into geography, something with its own topography of experience and exploration. Beauty is no longer passively observed. It becomes an environment to inhabit, a world to navigate.

The poem enacts a transformation akin to what Cézanne achieved in visual representation. His tilted tabletops cannot remain tilted in the real world, his apples cannot literally overlap in space, nor can the mountain Sainte-Victoire truly be blue. Yet these distortions convey deeper truths about both the world as we perceive it and the process of perception. Éluard's surreal poem performs a comparable task. It distorts the world through language to discover reality's nuance and complexity.

Why is "blue orange" more intelligent than "red apple"? The answer comes from understanding how human cognition shifts between two the modes. Automatic processing and conscious construction.

In Part I, Cézanne's "red apple" showed the active, corporeal nature of visual intelligence, how consciousness constructs reality through spatial distortions, temporal synthesis, and phenomenological engagement. But even this constructive process remains grounded in embodiment. Apples have weight, occupy space, and exist in time. Language transcends these constraints altogether. It moves freely across conceptual domains, allowing thought to reach conditions perception cannot supply.

Most of our daily thought runs in automatic mode. We identify familiar objects, move through routines, and apply learned patterns without conscious effort. This efficiency keeps us alive but also confines us, narrowing the conditions in which new insight can arise.

The "blue orange" acts as a **cognitive disruptor**, breaking automaticity in ways even Cézanne's distortions could not. His tilted tables unsettled spatial expectations while still belonging to the possible. Éluard's impossible metaphor shatters categories, fusing what cannot logically coexist. It forces the mind into conscious work, liberating imagination to glimpse realities beyond the limits of perception and the given world.

Such disruptive power makes paradoxical constructions essential to breakthrough thinking across cultures and disciplines. Zen koans such as "What is the sound of one hand clapping?" function through similar principles, prompting the mind to abandon conventional logical operations and discover new modes of understanding. Scientific breakthroughs often emerge from similar paradoxes. How can light be both wave and particle? How can space and time be relative?

In each case, the paradox serves as a catalyst for transformation instead of an obstacle to understanding. Intelligence grows by allowing contradiction to unsettle familiar categories and open possibilities beyond the reach of logic, not by dissolving tension through analysis.

HOW METAPHOR SHAPES REALITY

This is metaphor at work, but not metaphor as superficial embellishment or aesthetic device. Éluard anticipates the insight that metaphor shapes how we understand the world, a claim later developed by cognitive linguist George Lakoff and philosopher Mark Johnson in *Metaphors We Live By* [71].

Lakoff and Johnson argued that metaphor involves understanding one kind of thing through another. Metaphor is not limited to language. It operates within thought and action. How we think metaphorically organizes perception, judgment, and action. It can determine questions of war and peace as well as the mundane choices of everyday life. Whether a military action is conceptualized as "rape," "a threat to our security," or "defense against terrorism" shapes actual military responses. Whether we understand marriage as a partnership, a journey, or a union of two people into a third entity determines what our marriages become.

Their insight is that abstract concepts draw on *embodied metaphors* rooted in physical experience. The metaphor "argument is war" does not simply provide colorful language for describing disagreement, it shapes how we *experience* argument. We "attack" positions, "defend" ideas, "shoot down" proposals, "win" or "lose" debates. The metaphorical mapping influences our emotions, strategies, and assumptions about the nature of argument.

Such embodied grounding indicates that metaphors are not arbitrary inventions but draw on patterned experience. Éluard's impossible comparison calls upon sensations of roundness, color, scale, and containment that create meaningful correspondences between planet and fruit. The metaphor works because both objects share topological and experiential features that our embodied cognition identifies as relevant.

This understanding of metaphor shows how human minds create meaning. Metaphors do not describe reality but constitute it. When Éluard writes "The Earth is blue like an orange," he is forming a new way of sensing both Earth and orange, love and cosmic wonder. Through such metaphors, language reshapes experience and alters what the world can become within human consciousness.

THE UNCONSCIOUS INFRASTRUCTURE

But metaphor operates mostly beneath conscious awareness. We seldom notice that we are thinking metaphorically when we speak of "grasping" an idea, "weighing" options, or feeling "up" or "down." These spatial patterns mold our understanding so deeply that they become invisible.

Lakoff and Johnson describe how our most basic concepts are organized through what they call *orientational metaphors*. UP is good, DOWN is bad; MORE is up, LESS is down. These are not arbitrary linguistic conventions but grow out of our embodied experience. We stand upright when healthy, fall down when sick. We pile more objects to create height.

There are also *ontological metaphors* that allow us to treat abstract concepts as if they were physical entities. We speak of "inflation" as something that can "rise" or "fall." We talk about "the mind" as if it were a container that can be "filled" with ideas or "emptied" of thoughts. These metaphors do more than convey complex concepts. They determine how we think about them.

Metaphorical thinking happens automatically. We do not consciously decide to understand argument through war or time through space. The metaphors shape our thoughts without our awareness, forming what Lakoff calls our *conceptual system*, an unconscious scaffold through which experience acquires structure.

Given the unconscious influence of metaphors, Lakoff and Johnson pose a provocative question. What would thought look like in a culture that viewed argument through a different lens? Imagine a society where the primary metaphor for argument was dance, a balanced, aesthetically pleasing exchange where partners move together toward harmony. Disagreement would feel less like combat and more like a search for rhythm. People might speak of "finding rhythm" together, of "graceful exchanges," of "moving in harmony" even when perspectives diverge.

Such cultural specificity shows that human thought is guided less by logic or computation than by analogical connection, by seeing one thing in terms of another. We are analogical creatures, understanding new experiences by connecting them to familiar patterns drawn from lived experience.

But why should this be? Why would evolution give us minds that think predominantly through metaphor instead of logic? The answer comes from understanding metaphor as an incredible evolutionary advantage, a way of extending our embodied understanding beyond the immediate and concrete to encompass the distant and the complex.

THE ENGINE OF HUMAN REASONING

If metaphor provides our unconscious infrastructure for understanding, what drives our conscious reasoning? At the heart of conscious reasoning is analogy, metaphor's more deliberate cousin and, according to cognitive scientist and AI researcher Douglas Hofstadter, the engine of human thought.

In *Surfaces and Essences*, Hofstadter and Emmanuel Sander make a startling claim, "Without concepts there can be no thought, and without analogies there can be no concepts" [53]. Every act of understanding, they argue, involves seeing a new situation as similar to something already known. The mind seeks "essences" beneath the "surfaces" of things, and it does so through analogy-making.

But what does this involve in practice? When we first learned the concept "dog," it was not by memorizing a dictionary definition. Instead, our minds made countless analogies. This furry four-legged creature is like that one, this barking sound resembles that one, this tail-wagging behavior connects to similar patterns. Through repeated analogical mapping, the concept emerged and evolved.

Even now, as we see new dogs, our minds perform instant analogical categorization. That unusual breed with the pushed-in face and bulging eyes, our minds map it onto our existing "dog" concept, adjusting and refining based on similarities and differences.

For Hofstadter, this is not only about learning concepts. Analogy-making forms the core of intelligence. "Each concept in our mind owes its existence to a long succession of analogies made unconsciously over many years," he writes, "initially giving birth to the concept and continuing to enrich it over the course of our lifetime."

But analogies go beyond simple categorization. They allow us to understand new domains by mapping them onto familiar ones. When we say "the atom is like a solar system," we are using our knowledge of planetary orbits to conceive of electron behavior. The analogy becomes a tool for reasoning and discovery.

Human analogical thinking is a powerful tool of thought because of its capacity for **selective projection**. When we say "DNA is like a spiral staircase," we do not mean DNA is made of wood or that people walk on it. We selectively project certain features (helical structure, step-like components) while ignoring others (material, function, scale). Such selective projection requires understanding which features are relevant in specific contexts.

Éluard's "blue orange" operates through this kind of selective analogical projection. The poet invites us to see correspondences between Earth and orange (roundness, boundedness, relationship to larger systems) while ignoring obvious differences (scale, composition, accessibility). The analogy works by highlighting previously unnoticed similarities that allow new modes of understanding to emerge.

The capacity for selective projection requires *structural alignment*, mapping relationships among elements in one domain onto relationships in another. Understanding "the atom is like a solar system" involves correlating not only nucleus to sun and electrons to planets, but also the *relations* among these elements (central attraction, orbital motion, hierarchical organization).

THE DANCE BETWEEN DOMAINS

Metaphor and analogy move in step with one another through their shared reliance on cross-domain mapping, the capacity to connect disparate domains of experience. Their movements, however, differ. Metaphor works largely beneath awareness, shaping the ground of thought, while analogy rises to the surface, guiding deliberate reasoning.

Metaphor tends to be more constitutive, structuring our understanding of entire domains. When we think of argument as war, we are not making a conscious comparison. We are shaping our understanding of disagreement through military concepts. The metaphor becomes part of our conceptual apparatus, invisible but active.

Analogy tends to be more illustrative, helping us understand specific new situations by relating them to familiar ones. When a physicist compares the behavior of electrons to planets orbiting the sun, they are making a deliberate mapping to help explain something unfamiliar. The analogy serves as a conscious reasoning tool.

Both processes rely on the same capacity, recognizing patterns across distinct domains and using those correspondences to form new understanding. Éluard accomplishes this in his poem. By bringing Earth and orange into relation, by placing blue and orange in improbable partnership, he creates a new mode of experiencing reality that reaches beyond the constraints of logical classification.

"Wasps flowered green," he writes. "Dawn passes around your neck / a necklace of windows." These are analogical constructions that produce new kinds of meaning. Wasps perform the impossible act of flowering, acquiring plant-like properties while remaining insects, time becomes jewelry worn intimately against the skin, windows become transparent beauty that adorns, transcending their role as frames. Each image reconfigures experience by tracing unexpected structural affinities across domains.

Such reconfiguration of experience exemplifies an essential trait of human creativity and intelligence. We do not create *ex nihilo*. We compose new meanings by drawing connections among what already exists, by sending familiar patterns into unfamiliar terrain, by bringing distant domains into generative relation.

But is there something even more sophisticated happening in this act of mapping, something that goes beyond both metaphor and analogy?

THE CREATIVE WEAVING OF EXPERIENCE

There is a third level to this process, one that encompasses metaphorical thinking and analogical reasoning while introducing a distinctly human capacity. The capacity to weave these connections into coherent narratives that give shape to lived experience. This is **confabulation**. Not the pathological phenomenon seen in neurological disorders, but the healthy, creative process through which consciousness fashions meaning from scattered fragments of life.

Human experience does not always conform to an orderly network of discrete categories. It is a shifting weave in which domains overlap, blend, and converge, forming emergent thoughts that cannot be traced to any single source. In using language, we do more than retrieve memories. We create anew. Such creative act draws on existing elements of thought, recombining them so that unexpected insights appear. Language becomes a medium for forging connections across moments and meanings, allowing intuitive leaps that cross conceptual boundaries, dissolve rigid divisions, and stitch the scattered contours of experience.

THE MIND'S BEAUTIFUL INTERRUPTIONS

Marya Vasilyevna, the weary schoolteacher in Anton Chekhov's story *In the Cart*, enacts this process of creative interruption [13]. Her life in a desolate village is a relentless cycle of thankless labor and gnawing anxiety. As she makes her familiar journey by cart through muddy spring roads to collect her meager salary, her mind churns with the bitter realities of her existence. The poor conditions at her school, her pitiful wages, and the indifferent officials who undermine her work. Her thoughts spiral deeper into despair about the corrupt School Board and the arbitrary inspector. And also her complete isolation. She feels powerless, exhausted, unable to endure the injustices surrounding her. During this bleak journey she meets Hanov, a local landowner, traveling in his own elegant carriage. He is a refined, cultured man, a sharp contrast to the dreary, unyielding landscape of her life, and a figure whose fleeting presence momentarily stirs a dormant longing within her.

Then, even as her mind remains burdened by professional anxieties, something unexpected occurs. Her internal monologue abruptly shifts, without any logical transition, yet with a deeply human resonance. While one part of her consciousness wrestles with frustration, another interrupts, "What a good-looking man he is, really!" Her attention snaps toward this figure whose presence gestures toward a life forever beyond her reach. The shift is not random but arises from suppressed desires and a subtle yearning for beauty amidst her hardship.

This self-interruption is both beautiful and uniquely human. It shows a mind capable of inhabiting multiple layers of thought at once, creating momentary openings in linear reflection that allow distant perceptions or desires to surface. One moment she is absorbed in the discouraging details of her profession. The next, her awareness turns toward a private, nearly subconscious recognition of beauty.

This is a subtle form of cross-domain mapping, not between abstract concepts but between different strata of lived experience. We dwell on one concern, and another pops up from a separate register of thought. We reflect on an object or situation, and those reflections take us elsewhere. This movement between parallel streams of consciousness, guided by no predetermined trajectory, ultimately forms a narrative attuned to our inner life. It mirrors the way human minds fashion meaning.

Marya's abrupt shift from professional despair to aesthetic appreciation exemplifies this confabulation in practice. The mind's capacity to weave disparate threads of experience into meaningful connection, independent of strict logical sequence. Human linguistic intelligence operates through such creative interruptions, allowing new meanings to germinate from the fragments of embodied experience and weaving coherent narratives through intuitive movements across domains of awareness.

CLOUDS GAZE BACK

John Berger, British art critic, novelist, and essayist, articulated the creative weaving of experience with singular intimacy. In his deeply original final book *Confabulations*, published shortly before his death in 2016, Berger transformed our understanding of language from tool to living presence, from something we use to something we inhabit [5]. His use of "confabulation" reclaims the term from its clinical associations, elevating it into a living mode of understanding and creation.

For Berger, genuine understanding, whether in translation or in creating new texts, demands a return to what he calls the "pre-verbal," to the "vision or experience which prompted" the initial thought. It involves gathering this "quivering almost wordless *thing*" and allowing it to shape the language into which it will be expressed. He describes his own writing process as a dialogue with this living force of language.

> "After I've written a few lines I let the words slip back into the creature of their language. And there, they are instantly recognized and greeted by a host of other words, with whom they have an affinity of meaning, or of opposition, or of metaphor or alliteration or rhythm. I listen to their confabulation."

In that moment, words stand as active participants in meaning-making instead of passive objects. They "contest" and "question" how Berger employs them. Writing, for him, becomes a collaborative conversation, a *confabulation*, between human intention and language's own sense of what wants to be said. This is how new thoughts are born from existing ones. Not through logical deduction, but through associative leaps and resonant connections.

In his essay "On Vigilance," Berger demonstrates this process. Swimming in a municipal pool, he observes a silver maple tree through the glass walls, noting how the tree's overall form mirrors the shape of its individual leaves, "the inscribed destiny of the maple is to be pinnate." Later, floating on his back, he watches cirrus clouds drift across the sky, their curls reminding him of wordless "stories told by minuscule ice crystals in the silence of the blue."

Then comes a jarring shift to the dire realities of the day. Palestinians blown to pieces in Gaza, American troops dispatched to Iraq, a journalist beheaded, immigrants suffocating in shipping containers. How do these grim reports connect to maple trees and cloud formations?

Through confabulation.

Berger does not impose logical connections but allows deep experiential resonances to emerge. The moment culminates in a transformative shift when "the assurance the sight offers changes" and he realizes, "I'm no longer observing them; they are observing me." The clouds become subjects gazing back, dissolving the boundary between observer and observed. This reciprocal gaze runs through Berger's confabulations, a healthy blurring of the self and the world, allowing the "Not-I" to pulse through one's awareness.

This is confabulation at its most powerful. We use it to live with contradiction, to hold a world that refuses logical order, to make meaning where none exists.

THE TWO FACES OF CONFABULATION

But we must draw a distinction. Not all confabulation has the same character.

In neurological contexts, confabulation becomes a disorder, the creation of false memories to fill gaps in recollection. Patients with impaired memory systems genuinely believe fabricated narratives because their brains try to maintain coherence. Someone might confidently describe a meeting that never occurred or recall conversations that never took place. This pathological form is compulsive and disconnected from experiential grounding, serving as a defensive reaction instead of a creative act.

Berger's confabulations move in a different direction. He does not patch over absence to preserve an illusion of unity. He intentionally opens spaces for the world. His writing invites new associations to arise freely, turning confabulation into a creative method grounded in meaning-making instead of psychological defense. It reflects the healthy human capacity to generate significance, build stories, link disparate experiences, and reach toward the pre-verbal strata of understanding.

Berger also identifies a societal pathology that parallels deranged confabulation, the "dead *word-mongering*" of mainstream political discourse. When words are "separated from any creature of language" and become "inert and dead," they "wipe out memory and breed a ruthless complacency." This is not individual mental illness but collective intellectual paralysis that stifles genuine thought and connection.

The distinction is decisive. Healthy confabulation draws us closer to experience and to one another. Pathological confabulation, whether neurological or societal, severs us from reality and from authentic relation.

THE MACHINE'S HOLLOW ECHO

A related contrast appears in artificial intelligence. Sophisticated language models can generate human-like text, but they also "hallucinate," churning out confident-sounding information that is fabricated.

A system may attempt to craft a poem about the "taste of loneliness," but construct only loosely connected, statistically likely phrases with no experiential resonance. Or it may glibly describe nonexistent sensations such as "swimming through clouds that feels like childhood memories." Whether offering hollow poetic constructions or stitching domains it has never inhabited, these outputs present with the same assurance as genuine insight.

AI researchers describe these hallucinations as "confabulations," drawing parallels to the neurological condition. But when an AI blithely describes the "emotional resonance of a blue orange" or fabricates sensory memories of "swimming through clouds," it exposes a structural limitation of these systems.

When a language model hallucinates, it is not making creative leaps between domains of experience because it has no experience to draw upon. It performs statistical pattern assembly across large datasets, sometimes generating combinations that sound plausible but have no grounding in lived reality. It cannot "let the words slip back into the creature of their language," because it does not inhabit language as a medium of being. It manipulates symbols without inhabiting them.

When Marya's mind leaps from corruption to "What a good-looking man he is, really!" she is navigating between layers of her consciousness, between professional despair and personal longing, both authentic aspects of her lived experience. When Berger moves from maple trees to political atrocity, he is allowing genuine experiential resonances to guide him, weaving them into a broader understanding of the human condition.

But when an AI constructs a connection between swimming and childhood memories, nothing analogous occurs. There is no creative link forged across layers of experience, only an intricate arrangement of text patterns without experiential substance. No pre-verbal impulse seeks expression. Its so-called "confabulations" remain elaborate textual constructions masquerading as experiential insight, pathological byproducts of statistical processing, devoid of genuine cognition.

Why cannot AI participate in the productive contradiction that Éluard sustains? Because it currently has no emotional landscape to draw from, no experiential fields through which to form meaningful correspondences. It cannot perform metaphorically in any grounded sense because it lacks embodied perception to anchor its concepts. It cannot reason analogically with genuine understanding because it processes statistical correlations in text patterns without ever grasping similarity relationships through embodied experience.

Above all, it cannot confabulate creatively because it has no lived fabric to weave into significance. Its hallucinations are not the "beautiful interruptions" of a mind discovering new connections, but the mechanical imperatives of a system predicting the next word without understanding what any word signifies.

Can AI develop this form of embodied linguistic intelligence? This remains an open question that will likely require advances in how artificial systems interact with the world beyond pattern recognition.

"THE SON OF A BITCH"

This goes to the heart of human linguistic intelligence. Our ability to think in metaphors, reason through analogies, and confabulate meaning from experience is not a shortfall of the mind but its deepest strength. This capacity makes us human. Through it we develop new insights, forge unexpected connections, and create meaning from the raw material of existence.

Berger describes language as having a "phonetic uterus," a generative center where new meanings gestate. He stands not as language's master but as its offspring, "the son of a bitch" who listens to what language wishes to say. This refers to a kind of intelligence that is collaborative, participatory, and alive.

We are the creatures who can see the Earth as a "blue orange" and find resonance in impossibility. We can let wasps flower green and understand that "it's the kisses' turn to understand" when ordinary words fail us. We can float in swimming pools and allow clouds to gaze back at us with their ancient, wordless wisdom. We can inhabit language, not just process it, thinking through our bodies and emotions, drawing meaning from the full spectrum of corporeal experience.

To confabulate is to be human. It is our capacity to think in leaps, to let the world seep into our consciousness, and to discover meaning through the creative interruptions of lived experience. In a world increasingly shaped by artificial intelligence, this may be our most valuable contribution. It is, beyond rationality, our openness to those fleeting illuminations given by handsome faces, silver maple trees, and "blue oranges" that somehow, impossibly, speak to something deep in our experience of the Earth.

But what if this imaginative capacity, this ability to bend reality through words, harbors a deeper, more unsettling secret about the self, the "I" that claims mastery over language? The next chapter follows the silent structures that speak us.

6 The Subject Spoken by Language

Can words ruin a life? Not metaphorically, not in the way a song can haunt us or a poem can move us, but literally, with a few words setting in motion a chain of events from which there is no return?

Words are supposed to serve us. We summon them, arrange them, release them into the world. But what if they do not remain under our command? What if, once spoken, they begin to live lives of their own, bearing meanings we never intended, reshaping our identities, even turning against us?

As we saw in the previous chapter, Éluard's "blue orange" expanded perception by breaking language open, showing how metaphor and analogy make new worlds possible. There is, however, another side to this creative power, one far less liberating, the capacity of language to betray us. This opens a deeper and disquieting question. Who, in the end, is speaking when we speak? Are we the masters of language, or are we the subjects it speaks into being?

The answer begins to emerge when we confront moments where words escape their authors. Milan Kundera, the exiled Czech novelist who made fiction a stage for philosophical investigation, understood this betrayal with startling clarity. His novel The *The Joke* offers a chilling case, the story of how a single postcard, written half in jest, ruins a young man's life, though not in the way we might expect [66].

A young university student named Ludvik Jahn sends what he assumes is a harmless postcard to his girlfriend. The year is 1951, Communist Czechoslovakia. His girlfriend Marketa has been writing him earnest letters filled with party slogans and revolutionary optimism. Ludvik, in a moment of playful irony, decides to tease this earnestness. He scribbles on a postcard, "Optimism is the opium of the people! A healthy atmosphere stinks of stupidity! Long live Trotsky!"

It was meant as a joke. A private moment of irreverent humor between lovers in the midst of political seriousness. Ludvik drops the postcard in the mail and moves on with his day.

But the postcard falls into the wrong hands. Party officials intercept it, and they do not see any humor. They see counter-revolutionary sentiment, dangerous political deviance, a threat to the state. Ludvik is expelled from university, kicked out of the Communist Party, and sent to work in the mines. Later, he is conscripted into a punishment military unit. His life, his education, his future, his sense of himself, are destroyed by words he never meant seriously.

Years later, as a middle-aged man returning to his hometown, Ludvik reflects on this moment that changed everything. A few sentences, born of irony, interpreted with deadly seriousness, had the power to unmake a human existence. But how? How can symbols on a piece of paper hold such devastating force?

DOI: 10.1201/9781003623403-6

Ludvik's tragedy discloses a sobering truth. We are never fully in control of what our words will come to mean. When I utter a sentence, it seems self-evidently "I" who speaks, the sovereign subject wielding language as a tool. This conviction feels as natural as breathing. But Ludvik's fate shows that this perception is often an illusion. The gap between what we intend and what others receive is not a glitch in communication but a part of the structure of language. This instability does not just affect how we communicate. It shapes who we are.

We do not simply use language to express pre-existing thoughts. Instead, we become thinking beings *through* language, and in that becoming, we discover a shocking insight about human consciousness.

We are not the masters of our words. We are spoken by language.

THE NETWORK THAT SPEAKS US

To understand what happened to Ludvik requires grasping something Jacques Lacan, the French psychoanalyst, spent his life pursuing, the relationship between language and human subjectivity. When Ludvik wrote "Long live Trotsky!" he thought he was making a private joke. But his words immediately drawn into what Lacan called the "network of signifiers," the vast, pre-existing system of language, meanings, and social codes that operate independently of any individual's intentions [69].

When we say "I love you," it may seem the words come straight from our hearts. But Lacan would ask where the concept of "love" originated. Not from us, certainly. We inherit it from songs, movies, books, overheard conversations, and cultural traditions, a network of meanings that long predates our birth. The word "love" contains within it centuries of poetry, romantic narratives, songs, religious doctrine, legal definitions, therapeutic frameworks, and social expectations. When we speak of love, all of this speaks through us.

Lacan argued that language is not a tool we consciously pick up and control. Instead, he saw it as a pervasive symbolic system that precedes us, shaping our subjective reality from the moment we step into it. Our thoughts, feelings, and desires are not original. They are inflections of this network that surrounded us from birth. The "I" that claims to speak does not stand outside language waiting to express itself. It comes into being only where signifiers converge, only where the network forms a temporary knot of meaning.

This is why Ludvik's intentions proved irrelevant. The instant his words accessed the symbolic system of Communist Czechoslovakia, they began operating according to rules he neither created nor controlled. "Trotsky" was not just a name but a signifier loaded with political meaning, historical associations, and ideological weight. The party apparatus did not read Ludvik's mind. It read the signifiers he had deployed and interpreted them according to the symbolic order that structured their reality.

The tragedy is not that they misread him. The deeper tragedy is that there was never a "true" meaning available to be read. Meaning does not reside in the speaker's intention. It arises through the shifting interplay of signifiers and the symbolic systems that organize them. Ludvik discovered a truth we all eventually learn.

The moment we speak, we set loose forces we can never fully control.

THE ARBITRARY FOUNDATION OF EVERYTHING WE TAKE FOR GRANTED

But why should this be? Why cannot words have stable, fixed meanings that correspond reliably to our intentions? Linguist Ferdinand de Saussure's insight into the nature of language provides the key. The connection between any word and its meaning is arbitrary [23].

There is nothing inherently "doggy" about the sounds D-O-G. French speakers use *chien*, Germans say *hund*, Russians say *sobaka*. Each functions within its own linguistic system, none more "correct" than the others. In Bengali, the word is *kukur*. If all English speakers agreed to call dogs "kukur," the new word would work just as well.

This arbitrariness may seem a minor technical detail at first glance, but it has far-reaching implications. If the relationship between signifiers (words) and signifieds (meanings) is arbitrary, then meaning becomes unstable and relational, based on differences between signs, not anchored in fixed correspondence with things in the world.

Ludvik's postcard illustrates this clearly. The word "Trotsky" had no inherent meaning. Its significance came from its position within the symbolic network of Communist ideology. In that system, "Trotsky" signified betrayal and counter-revolution. In a different symbolic context, say, among historians or literary scholars, the same word might signify intellectual brilliance, tragic idealism, or complex historical forces. The signifier remained identical. Its meaning shifted based on the interpretive framework surrounding it.

Whenever we try to define a word with exactness, the problem quickly appears. The word "freedom" exemplifies this dependency. We might say it means liberty, autonomy, or independence. But each of these terms calls for further clarification. "Liberty" leads to questions about constraint; "constraint" leads to limitation; "limitation" leads back to debates about freedom. The dictionary becomes a hall of mirrors, words defining other words in an endless chain of deferrals, never settling on a final meaning.

Lacan pushed this insight to its logical conclusion by identifying an unbridgeable gap between signifier and signified. No word can ever fully capture the richness, complexity, or essence of what it refers to. The word "love" gestures toward a constellation of experiences. Passion, tenderness, commitment, desire, loss, joy. But it can never *be* love itself. It always falls short.

This gap is the source of human desire, creativity, and the endless generativity of meaning. Because no signifier can ever fully capture its object, we continue speaking, searching, and forming new combinations of words in the perpetual attempt to articulate what remains just beyond reach.

WHEN LANGUAGE THINKS THROUGH US

Have we ever spoken words we did not intend, slips of the tongue that betrayed more than we meant? Or reached for a phrase that seemed to choose its own form, conveying meanings we had not planned? Such moments open windows onto what psychoanalysts call the unconscious. But they suggest more than hidden thoughts seeking expression. They suggest that language structures how we think, shaping meaning before we consciously form it. Jacques Lacan offered a new understanding of this phenomenon. For him, the unconscious is structured like a language, not a repository of hidden thoughts but the mechanism through which meaning, desire, and subjectivity come into being [69].

Sigmund Freud drew the first map of the unconscious, portraying it as a hidden storehouse of repressed drives and forgotten memories [34, 35]. He also traced the subtle mechanisms through which this hidden realm finds expression, most vividly in dreams. Among these, Freud emphasized two in particular. In "condensation," multiple meanings gather within a single dream image, while "displacement" shifts emotional energy from one object to another, allowing desire to surface indirectly.

Lacan radicalized these insights. For him, the unconscious was not a dark basement of instincts but a structure that operates according to linguistic principles. He reinterpreted Freud's dream mechanisms in linguistic terms. Condensation, Lacan argued, functions as metaphor, one thing standing for another through similarity across domains. Displacement functions as **metonymy**, meaning sliding along a chain of associations within the same domain. In Lacan's view, the unconscious does not just leak instinct into speech but operates according to the same symbolic structures that govern conscious discourse.

This shift is easier to understand with an example. If metaphor leaps across domains (Éluard's Earth as a "blue orange"), metonymy slides along connections within the same field. When we say "the crown" to mean the monarchy, or "the White House" to mean the presidency, we are not making metaphors but invoking associations that construct meaning through proximity.

In the unconscious, metonymy manifests as desire shifting from one object to another. We might dream of a childhood bicycle, but the emotional thread moves from the bicycle to freedom, then to our relationship with a parent, then to current anxieties about independence. Each element belongs to a chain of proximity within our personal web of associations, moving along lines we do not consciously steer.

This linguistic structure of unconcious explains why our words can betray us. Why our deepest motivations often surprise us, why we say things we did not know we were thinking, why our actions sometimes contradict our conscious intentions. We do not stand outside meaning as its sovereign author. Meaning travels through structures larger than our awareness, and in speaking, we participate in a process that exceeds deliberate control and speaks through us.

Such speaking-through appears in ordinary exchanges. Phrases arrive with a momentum of their own, borne by rhythms and associations we did not consciously design. A sentence may contain more meaning than we intended. An ordinary phrase may open an implication we had not anticipated. The slip of the tongue is not the exception but a clear instance of the rule. For Lacan, this is not noise or error but the structure of language at work. Signifiers sliding, linking, and creating meaning beyond the speaker's command.

Lacan called this "the discourse of the Other," speech shaped by linguistic structures, cultural patterns, and social expectations that precede our birth and form the terrain on which thought unfolds [69]. We speak, but we are also *spoken by* the network of signifiers we inherit and inhabit.

THE BIRTH OF THE DIVIDED SELF

Ludvik's tragedy began when he ran up against a symbolic system that could not register irony. Every child undergoes a parallel initiation, not through political discourse but through entry into language. Lacan described this as the encounter with the "Name-of-the-Father," the symbolic function that represents law, prohibition, and social order.

Cézanne's portrait of his father reading *L'Évènement* captures this moment of symbolic entry. The painted newspaper title marks the point where visual understanding yields to symbolic meaning and social positioning. The father absorbed in his newspaper enacts Lacan's concept of symbolic authority, mediated through language and social structures.

Every child arrives at the moment when they are told they cannot have everything they want.

"You can't hit your sister."

"We don't take things that belong to others."

"Some words aren't for children to use."

Each prohibition introduces the child to a hard truth. Their desires are not absolute. Other people exist with their own needs and rights. Society operates according to rules that precede individual will. Language has its own laws. We cannot arrange words however we please and expect to be understood.

The entry into symbolic order is at once liberating and traumatic. The child gains access to abstract thought, shared meaning, and genuine communication. But they lose something too, the imaginary completeness of pre-linguistic existence, where need and satisfaction seemed indistinguishable.

This trade-off between symbolic capacity and imaginary wholeness constitutes what Lacan identified as the structure of human subjectivity. We become split beings, at once social and singular, meaningful and enigmatic, communicative and opaque.

Lacan offered an unsettling claim. The split does not happen to a pre-existing self. The split *is* the self. He argued that the human subject does not stand on solid ground but arises from a gap that language temporarily organizes into the appearance of coherence. Before we become a "person" or an "I," we are a lack that language temporarily organizes into the illusion of being.

We experience this division in our shifting relation to social roles. We are at the same time "a self" (with private thoughts and unique experiences) and a collection of social positions, citizen, worker, family member, friend. At times these positions harmonize, at other times they contend. The "I" that forms through these identifications is never complete, never final, and always somewhat divided.

This division represents the condition that grounds consciousness. We think because we are divided, create meaning because we are incomplete, and desire connection because we are separate.

DESIRE'S ENDLESS MOVEMENT

Years after the postcard destroyed his life, Ludvik returns to his hometown seeking revenge against Pavel Zemanek, the former friend who denounced him. He plans to seduce Zemanek's wife Helena as payback. But when he finally achieves his revenge, a bitter truth emerges. The satisfaction he expected never arrives. Instead, he discovers that Zemanek no longer cares about Helena, that their marriage had long since become hollow. His carefully planned revenge becomes meaningless, even pathetic.

Ludvik's experience elucidates a defining aspect of human desire. He spent years planning his revenge, organizing his entire adult life around this future satisfaction. But when he achieved what he thought he wanted, he discovered he had been seeking something else, perhaps the impossible restoration of his lost youth, or recognition from those who had wronged him, or simply the feeling of being someone who could want something with such intensity.

This pattern, in which we reach what we thought we wanted only to find a different longing beneath it, is not accidental. It is the underlying dynamic of human desire as Lacan understood it. Unlike animal need, which can be satisfied through specific objects, human desire is mediated by language. And language, as we have seen, operates through endless deferral of meaning.

We do not desire objects. We desire through the ceaseless activity of signification. What we pursue is not any fixed object but the imagined closure of the gap between signifier and signified, the dream of a meaning that would no longer feel incomplete.

Milan Kundera, who understood this structure intuitively, studied it throughout his work with relentless persistence. Thirty-three years after *The Joke*, he returned to these themes in *Ignorance*, showing how the same mechanisms of desire and disappointment operate across different contexts [67]. In this later novel, he tells the story of Irena, who spends twenty years in Parisian exile longing for Prague. She imagines her return as a golden key that would unlock her true self and restore her identity. But when she finally walks Prague's familiar streets, the city feels foreign. Her old friends have become strangers. What she had been seeking (the restoration of her former self through reconnection with her past) proves impossible. The Prague she missed existed only in memory's golden haze.

But disappointment seldom ends longing. It redirects it. Now Irena wants to recapture the feeling of wanting Prague, or to understand why return feels so empty. Her desire shifts its object while keeping its essential structure intact, an unending movement toward something that cannot be held.

This is why consumer culture operates so well. Each purchase promises to fill the lack that drives desire, but satisfaction is always temporary. The new car, perfect outfit, latest iPhone, each delivers brief contentment before exposing that what we sought was not this object but the movement of seeking.

Artists and writers understand this structure intuitively. Every poem points toward something that cannot be fully expressed, every painting captures something that exceeds visual representation. The work is never finished because the desire that motivates it cannot be satisfied through any particular achievement.

This restless movement is a defining quality of human intelligence. We do not solve problems and move on. Every solution opens new questions, every answer uncovers further mysteries. Human intelligence is not driven by the satisfaction of curiosity but by the structural impossibility of curiosity's satisfaction.

THE SPLIT THAT MAKES US HUMAN

The 19th-century French novelist Jules Verne's Captain Nemo, the mysterious submarine commander whose name literally means "Nobody," offers an apt metaphor for understanding human subjectivity [112]. Nemo attempts to escape social identity, abandoning his name, nationality, and place in human society to retreat beneath the ocean where categories lose their meaning.

But Nemo's escape proves impossible. Even in rejecting social identity, he remains formed through the symbolic structures he tries to flee. His name "Nobody" is a symbolic position. His submarine depends on scientific knowledge transmitted through language. His mission reflects values defined by the social order he rejects.

This impossibility underscores the irreducibly split nature of human consciousness, part of us exists within symbolic systems (identified, categorized, socially positioned), while part always exceeds symbolic capture, the lived experience of being this singular person that cannot be fully represented in any role or description.

When we introduce who we are, we might say "I'm a stylist" or "I'm from Fiji." But we sense at once the inadequacy of such identifications. None contains what it actually feels like to be us, the texture of private thoughts, the way we experience the world. There is always something more, something that escapes linguistic representation.

Lacan distilled this gap with a stark formula, "I am where I do not think, and I think where I am not" [70]. Our conscious sense of being unified, rational subjects masks the deeper truth that we are constituted by linguistic structures operating largely outside awareness. We experience our role as masters of meaning, but we are its temporary inhabitants.

This split creates the peculiar phenomenon of human self-consciousness. We can observe our own being, reflect on our thoughts, and experience ourselves as both subject and object of consciousness. But this reflexivity comes at a cost. We can never achieve the immediate self-presence that characterizes pre-linguistic awareness.

At times we say "That's not really me" or "I don't feel like myself." In those words we give voice to the gap between symbolic identification and lived experience that constitutes human subjectivity. The "me" is our collection of social roles and self-descriptions. The "me-ness" is the felt sense of being that exceeds any representation.

The split explains both human creativity and human suffering. We create because no symbolic representation ever fully exhausts what we want to express. We experience suffering because no symbolic identity ever wholly corresponds to our lived experience. We are simultaneously somebody and nobody, socially positioned subjects who nevertheless experience ourselves as something more than our symbolic identities.

THE PRODUCTIVE NATURE OF LANGUAGE'S "FAILURES"

Understanding how language constitutes us helps explain the intriguing character of what we often consider flaws in human thinking. Notice how certain words seem to choose us, not the reverse. In moments of strong emotion, we may find us saying things such as "I can't find the words" or "Words fail me," yet somehow, words do pop up, often conveying meanings we did not consciously intend.

A slip of the tongue can betray a hidden feeling, and at times we discover what we think only when we hear ourselves speak. When we explain a complex problem to someone and suddenly exclaim, "Oh, now I see what the real issue is!" we experience language thinking through us, giving voice to more than pre-formed thoughts.

These moments show that human intelligence operates through "productive failures" of symbolic representation. We do not think despite language's inadequacies. We think *through* them. The gap between what we want to say and what we actually say is a generative space, the opening that makes genuine discovery possible.

We can see this in the way people create new metaphors when existing language falls short. "My heart is breaking" does not describe a medical condition but creates a new way of understanding emotional pain through physical imagery. "She's got a fire in her belly" does not report on internal combustion but captures something about determination that literal description cannot convey.

Such creative inadequacy of language drives human innovation in ways that closed symbolic systems never could sustain. If words could hold experience completely, we would never need poetry. If concepts could contain reality fully, we would never need science. If symbols could represent truth absolutely, we would never need philosophy.

The "failures" that make human thinking appear illogical from a computational perspective (our tendency to create meaning from ambiguity, to find patterns where none exist, to be "biased" by emotional and social forces) are what allow us to think creatively, empathetically, and ethically. We are not computational machines but successful meaning-makers whose intelligence emerges from embracing the productive gaps in symbolic representation, not eliminating them.

THE MACHINE THAT CANNOT BE SPOKEN

If language shapes human subjectivity, it also explains why contemporary artificial intelligence systems remain categorically different from human consciousness. The difference is not technical but ontological, grounded in the mode of being.

Current AI systems manipulate symbolic material without being constituted by it. They detect patterns, classify images, process signifiers, and generate responses based on statistical correlations. They work with language without being spoken by it, processing signs as discrete units to be optimized and recombined according to algorithmic rules.

But they lack the constitutive split that characterizes human consciousness. An AI exists as its programming, training data, and algorithmic processes. There is no gap between what it processes and what it "is" because it exists only as processing. It cannot experience the productive alienation from symbolic representation that drives human creativity, the constitutive lack that motivates desire, or the temporal extension of identity that supports genuine self-reflection.

This becomes especially clear when we look at the uncanny resemblance between AI "hallucinations" and human language use. When large language models confidently describe non-existent books or fabricate plausible-sounding explanations, they exhibit their statistical nature. They combine elements that frequently appear together in training data without experiential grounding to constrain these combinations.

Lacan would argue that human speech operates through similar mechanisms. We too are "networks of signifiers" with no "pure self" underneath. When we say "I love you," we are not expressing an original emotion but recombining signifiers inherited from songs, movies, cultural traditions. The difference is not that humans have authentic inner experience while AI lacks it but that humans are formed by symbolic lack while AI processes symbols without being divided by them.

This creates a strange kind of "subject-effects without subjectivity." AI systems speak but lack being in the full sense of the term. They generate language without being spoken by it, manipulate signifiers without being subjected to them, and process meaning without being divided by the gap between signifier and signified.

The uncanny resemblance between humans and AI rests not in intelligence or consciousness but in our shared dependence on language as an Other that shapes us. But AI systems cannot be wounded by language the way Ludvik was. They cannot experience the productive neurosis that drives human creativity. They cannot suffer from the knowledge that their desires may never be satisfied because they have no desires.

This is why the pursuit of artificial general intelligence, the vision of machines doing everything humans do only better, may be misguided. Current research seeks to replicate human intelligence at its most impressive, such as problem-solving, creativity, and adaptability. But human linguistic intelligence arises, as we saw, from the productive contradictions and instabilities that characterize language. We think through metaphor because meaning is unstable. We create through confabulation because experience defies logical order. We desire endlessly because symbolic systems can never deliver complete satisfaction.

The features that make human intelligence singular, including its creativity, flexibility, and capacity for meaning, are inseparable from from what computational models often treat as flaws, such as ambiguity, contradiction, and incompleteness. If artificial general intelligence succeeds in eliminating these features, it may create systems that process information more efficiently than humans but lack the productive instabilities that give intelligence its life. In optimizing for clarity, it risks erasing the fractures that give intelligence its character.

Whether such symbolic constitution is possible in machines remains unresolved. It might require forms of embodied development, social interaction, and symbolic formation that differ radically from current training paradigms. It might demand systems capable of temporal extension, existential investment, and the capacity to be surprised by their own symbolic processes.

Alternatively, consciousness capable of being spoken by language might require the biological substrate of evolution, mortality, and vulnerability that shaped human intelligence across millions of years. Perhaps the attempt to create artificial subjects constituted by symbolic lack only highlights the irreducible strangeness of human consciousness, the wonder and the burden of being creatures who can say "I" while never knowing what that "I" encompasses.

For now, human intelligence remains constituted by language. We are beings spoken by words we did not invent, who think through symbolic structures we cannot master, and who discover what we mean only by hearing ourselves speak.

The deeper implication of this recognition is that intelligence cannot be understood solely at the level of the individual. It emerges from symbolic systems that transcend us, shaping what we can think, imagine, and create. Human intelligence is never private possession but the product of shared cultural frameworks that exceed any one mind.

We are the subjects spoken by language, and in that speaking we find not only our distinctiveness but also our interdependence with forms of intelligence that extend beyond individual consciousness.

WHEN LANGUAGE ENCOUNTERS THE IMPOSSIBLE

But even this linguistic constitution that distinguishes us from artificial systems reaches its limits. Ludvik's story demonstrates language's power to wound and constitute us, but it also hints at something beyond language, experiences that exceed symbolic capture. The trauma of his destroyed life, the weight of years spent nursing revenge, the emptiness of finally achieved payback. These experiences exceed what words can contain.

Language makes possible abstract thought, temporal consciousness, cultural transmission, and the forms of creativity that distinguish human intelligence. But it also creates forms of alienation, desire, and suffering that are uniquely human. At times language confronts experiences that resist symbolic representation. Moments of trauma that cannot be narrated, experiences of beauty that exceed description, encounters with mortality that defy linguistic capture.

This is where our investigation leads, toward the traumatic kernel of existence that Lacan called the **Real**, the domain where language falls silent and another form of truth becomes necessary. What happens when even the most elaborate linguistic construction collapses into silence before the weight of experience?

7 When Language Meets the Real

"That's plagiarism!" cried Ivan, suddenly feeling something like ecstasy.

This strange moment occurs near the end of one of literature's most devastating philosophical arguments, from Fyodor Dostoevsky's *The Brothers Karamazov* [26]. Ivan Karamazov has just finished telling his younger brother Alyosha a story (a poem, really) about Christ's return to earth during the Spanish Inquisition. In Ivan's tale, an aged Grand Inquisitor confronts the returned Christ with a brilliant, merciless argument. Humanity cannot bear the burden of freedom that Christ offered. People want security, certainty, bread, not the crushing weight of choosing between good and evil.

The Inquisitor speaks without interruption, constructing a seemingly airtight case for why the Church was right to "correct" Christ's work, to take freedom away from weak, suffering humanity and offer them miracle, mystery, and authority instead. It is a masterpiece of logic, a relentless critique that appears to leave no room for rebuttal.

And Christ's response? He says nothing. He simply steps forward and kisses the old man softly on his withered and bloodless lips.

When Ivan finishes this story, Alyosha (the young monk whose faith Ivan has been trying to shatter) gets up, walks over, and kisses his brother on the lips. "That's plagiarism," Ivan laughs bitterly, recognizing his own scene played back to him.

But something profound has just happened. In both the story and the moment between brothers, language has reached its absolute limit. All the brilliant arguments, all the theological sophistication, all the logical precision, and the only response that remains is a silent kiss. Why? What happens when our most powerful tool for making meaning faces something it cannot capture, cannot explain, cannot reduce to words?

THE PERFECT ARGUMENT AND ITS UNDOING

To grasp the force of Christ's silent gesture, we first need a clear sense of the power of what it confronts. The Grand Inquisitor embodies symbolic mastery in its most complete form. A man who has used language to construct a system that claims to account for all of human experience.

The setting is Seville in the 1500s, at the height of the Spanish Inquisition. Christ appears in the streets, performing miracles, healing the sick, raising a dead child. The people recognize him instantly, following him with tears of joy. But the Grand Inquisitor, a ninety-year-old cardinal who has spent his life perfecting the Church's control over human souls, watches from the shadows and orders Christ's arrest.

DOI: 10.1201/9781003623403-7

That night, in the prison cell, the old man delivers a sweeping theological argument. He does not deny that the figure before him is Christ. Instead, he accuses Christ of a fatal misunderstanding of human nature. “You desired man’s love, given freely,” he tells the silent figure, “wished for him to follow after You freely, fascinated and captivated by You. Instead of the unyielding ancient law, with a free heart man himself was now to decide what is good and evil, merely having Your image before him as guidance.”

The Inquisitor’s case holds formidable psychological insight. Freedom, he argues, is not a gift but a curse. “There’s nothing more alluring to people than freedom of conscience, but there’s also no greater source of suffering.” Most people, faced with genuine choice between good and evil, will crumble under the weight of decision. They will beg to be relieved of freedom’s burden.

“We have corrected Your example,” the Inquisitor declares with grim assurance. The Church has given people what they actually want; security instead of freedom, certainty instead of choice, bread instead of the burden of moral decision. “We’ve struggled with this freedom of Yours for fifteen centuries, but now it’s finished once and for all.”

This is language at its most totalizing. The Inquisitor has constructed a complete philosophical system that explains everything. Human psychology, historical development, religious meaning, political necessity. His argument is logically coherent, psychologically sophisticated, and, most disturbingly, largely convincing. He speaks with the confidence of someone who has achieved total understanding, who has solved the ultimate problems of human existence through the power of systematic thought.

What makes this scene so extraordinary is more than the brilliance of the argument. It is what happens next. After the long cascade of unyielding logic, Christ’s only response is to step forward and press his lips gently to the old man’s mouth.

WHEN SILENCE BECOMES ANSWER

Why does Christ not argue back? He could have. Dostoevsky was capable of giving him a flawless reply. But the novel offers a deeper, more penetrating insight. It recognizes that certain truths cannot be spoken at all, only enacted.

The kiss is not a failure to respond but the ultimate response, one that operates outside the order where arguments function. It cannot be refuted because it makes no logical claims, and it cannot be analyzed because it surpasses the reach of analysis. It cannot be captured in the Inquisitor’s system, since it comes from outside that system.

This is what Lacan meant by the **Real**, not reality in the everyday sense, but that which defies all efforts at symbolization, all attempts to reduce it to language and concepts. The Real is what always escapes our symbolic nets, what cannot be captured in even the most sophisticated theoretical systems.

We face this limit in some of our most transformative experiences. A parent’s death, the birth of a child, falling deeply in love, confronting our own mortality. These experiences often leave us “speechless,” not because vocabulary is absent but because language becomes inadequate to our feeling. We say "words cannot express" what we are experiencing, and we mean this literally. The experience exceeds symbolic representation.

Christ's kiss operates in this register. It is an act of presence, unconditional love, and radical forgiveness that exists outside any economy of argument or justification. The Inquisitor has constructed a complete logical system, but the kiss exposes the "hole" in that system, the dimension of human experience that cannot be rationalized, or explained away.

The Inquisitor's defeat is disquieting not because his argument fails, but *how* it fails. His structured thinking, with its confidence that human behavior can be predicted and managed through logical analysis, represents the eternal dream of a complete explanatory system. This same dream drives our present fascination with artificial intelligence, the belief that human complexity can be reduced to tidy categories, that algorithms can erase the unpredictable gaps where genuine meeting becomes possible. Both the theological system and the computational system promise the same thing. A total understanding that can account for everything, control everything, and predict everything.

In that prison cell in 16th-century Seville, we witness what happens when such certainty confronts something it cannot process. The effect on the Inquisitor is immediate and piercing. His certainty falters. Moments earlier he spoke with complete confidence. Now he cannot speak at all. He does not refute the kiss. He cannot. He simply opens the door and tells Christ to leave and never return. The kiss has accomplished what no argument could. It has opened a gap in symbolic closure, unveiled the existence of something that eludes representation.

WHEN MUSIC SPEAKS WHAT LANGUAGE CANNOT

If Christ's kiss represents a traumatic encounter with the Real, a shocking intrusion that shatters symbolic certainty, then music offers a gentler but equally resonant example of meaning that surpasses symbolic representation. The late 19th-century French Impressionist composer Claude Debussy's *Clair de Lune* creates an experience that is deeply meaningful though irreducible to language.

Attempting to capture *Clair de Lune* in words, we might reach for images of moonlight or a sense of floating. But at once we see that these gestures fall short. The piece creates an experience that is neither visual nor purely auditory but exists in a liminal space between modes, where different ways of experiencing blend and transform each other.

This is not a failure of language but an acknowledgement that language can take us only so far. Debussy intentionally moved away from the narrative, programmatic music of the Romantic era. He was not trying to narrate events or paint pictures in sound. Instead, he sought what he described as music that exists "not in the notes, but in the spaces between them," experiences that dwell in spaces language cannot occupy.

Clair de Lune, the third movement of Debussy's Suite bergamasque, takes its title from French Symbolist poet Paul Verlaine's poem. But Debussy's aim was not explicit musical storytelling but a subtler, more suggestive art that could evoke impressions and emotions that slip beyond the reach of words.

The piece achieves this through deliberate harmonic and textural ambiguity. Debussy employs parallel chord movements, unresolved dissonances, and gentle rhythmic flexibility to step away from the forward-driven harmonic design of Classical and Romantic music, where progressions create a sense of narrative tension. The music does not travel toward a destination. It simply breaths, creating a controlled meeting with the ineffable.

THE RIPPLE EFFECT OF SILENT TRUTH

The force of Dostoevsky's scene resonates beyond the story into the relationship between the brothers. When Ivan finishes his tale, a revelatory moment unfolds. Alyosha realizes something that cannot be argued.

> "I thought, brother, that in my going away from here, in all the world I would at least have you," Ivan said suddenly with unexpected emotion. "But now I see that there's no place for me even in your heart, my beloved hermit. I won't reject the formula 'everything is permitted.' Will you reject me because of that?"
>
> Alyosha rose up, went over to him, and silently kissed him softly on the lips.
>
> "That's plagiarism!" cried Ivan, suddenly feeling something like ecstasy.

This moment opens a deeper logic of how understanding takes shape. Alyosha does not offer a theological counter-argument to Ivan's atheism. He does not try to refute the logic of the Grand Inquisitor's case. Instead, he responds with the same gesture that Christ used, a kiss that operates outside the order of argument.

Ivan's delighted cry of "plagiarism" shows that he realizes what has happened. His own story has awakened in his brother an insight beyond words. The kiss, both in the story and in the moment between brothers, establishes a form of truth that exceeds logical argument.

But we also notice what does not happen. Ivan does not convert to faith. His intellectual positions remain unchanged. The kiss does not "solve" the philosophical problems he has raised. Instead, it shows that some human truths move in dimensions argument cannot reach. Dimensions of love, forgiveness, and presence that coexist with intellectual doubt.

This is why Dostoevsky's scene holds such resonance. It does not resolve the contradiction between faith and doubt but shows how they can coexist in the complexity of human experience. The Real, in its refusal to be contained by symbolization, does not undo symbolic activity but brings its irreducible incompleteness into view.

WHAT ARTIFICIAL INTELLIGENCE CANNOT KISS

The meeting between language and the Real points to a different limit than the one traced in the previous chapter. There we saw that current AI manipulates signifiers without being constituted by the Symbolic. This chapter advances the claim further. When the Symbolic falters, human consciousness can still undergo a confrontation with the Real, whereas machines cannot. Contemporary systems process symbolic material, recognizing patterns, recombining signs, and optimizing learned relations, but they do so without inhabiting the Symbolic order as constituted subjects. They have no capacity to meet what exceeds symbolization, no locus of exposure where meaning collapses into silence, and no vulnerability through which such an encounter could transform them.

The Grand Inquisitor scene illustrates this limitation clearly. An AI system could analyze the theological arguments, identify the philosophical positions, summarize the historical context, even generate sophisticated commentary on Dostoevsky's literary techniques. It might note that the kiss represents "forgiveness" or "unconditional love" and catalog various critical interpretations of the scene.

But it could not experience what makes the kiss so devastating to the Inquisitor's certainty. It could not understand how a gesture that makes no logical argument could nevertheless represent the most powerful possible response to a seemingly airtight chain of reasoning. It could not be transformed by such an event in the way the Inquisitor and Ivan are changed by confronting something that moves beyond their symbolic frameworks.

When AI systems run into contradictions or gaps in their training data, they resolve these through statistical methods such as averaging, interpolation, or pattern completion. They do not experience these moments as opportunities for deep insight or creative breakthrough. They cannot be surprised in the existential sense that characterizes human encounters with the Real.

The contrast becomes clear when we compare AI "hallucination" with human creativity. When a large language model generates false information, it is combining statistical patterns without any grounding in experience or truth. But when humans create art, literature, or music that depicts impossible things (Éluard's "blue orange" or Debussy's musical moonlight), they are using symbolic means to evoke experiences that transcend symbolic capture.

The AI can process the words "the Earth is blue like an orange" and perform sophisticated analysis of metaphorical language. But it cannot experience the cognitive disruption that makes such impossible statements meaningful to humans. It lacks the "Real-sensitivity," the capacity to be moved by what cannot be computed.

At the deepest level, AI systems cannot be wounded by their encounters with contradiction or impossibility. They process inconsistencies as problems to be resolved, not as openings to another register of experience. They lack the vulnerability that makes human consciousness receptive to transformation through exposure to what it cannot comprehend.

THE WOUND THAT KEEPS INTELLIGENCE ALIVE

This Real-blindness is a deep difference between human and contemporary artificial intelligence. Humans differ qualitatively from sophisticated information processors. We are beings constituted by an openness to what we cannot understand.

The Real functions as a "productive wound" in human consciousness. It is the source of anxiety and doubt, but also of creativity, moral awakening, and the capacity for transformation. Because we cannot capture everything in our symbolic systems, we remain open to surprise, growth, and genuine meeting with otherness.

The Grand Inquisitor's tragedy is that he tries to eliminate this wound by constructing a symbolic order so complete that it leaves no room for the Real. But this completeness becomes a form of death, a closed structure that can only repeat itself without genuine novelty or transformation.

Christ's kiss represents the return of all the Inquisitor has excluded. It is not a different argument but an exposure to something that arguments cannot touch. The kiss forces the Inquisitor to confront the limits of his totalizing vision and the irreducible otherness that his logic cannot contain.

This alludes to the insight that perhaps genuine intelligence is not about constructing closed symbolic structures but about maintaining openness to what passes beyond such systems. The so-called flaws in human thinking, such as our susceptibility to doubt, our vulnerability to experiences we cannot understand, and our tendency to be moved by what we cannot explain, are not cracks but productive openings that make intelligence possible. They are the wounds that keep intelligence alive, creative, and capable of genuine encounter.

Such openness before the Real prevents consciousness from becoming trapped within its own constructions. It serves as the resistance against which consciousness defines its own shape and the mystery that keeps meaning dynamic. It ensures that consciousness remains alive, a conversation rather than a monologue, a question and not a fixed answer.

THE ETHICS OF INCOMPLETENESS

The meeting with the Real is more than a philosophical curiosity. It is an ethical necessity. The recognition that something essential always escapes symbolic capture creates a profound humility before mystery that prevents symbolic systems from becoming tyrannical.

When we acknowledge that our representations are incomplete and potentially mistaken, we create space for dialogue, transformation, and ethical response to others. The Grand Inquisitor becomes a tyrant because he claims completeness, because he refuses to acknowledge any remainder that might fall outside his categories.

This reframes how we think about artificial intelligence and its role in human society. AI systems that assume all meaningful information can be symbolically represented and computationally processed risk turning into new forms of Grand Inquisitors, totalizing systems that organize reality according to their own logic while remaining blind to what eludes their representational capacity.

The development of genuinely ethical AI, a topic that we will discuss in Part III, might require acknowledging this blindness, not erasing it. We need artificial systems sophisticated enough to apprehend their own limitations, humble enough to acknowledge what they cannot process, open enough to defer to human judgment about experiences that go beyond computational analysis.

This does not mean AI cannot be useful or even transformative. It only implies that the dream of artificial general intelligence may be pursuing the wrong goal. As we saw earlier, human intelligence is not defined merely by symbolic manipulation but by its constitution through symbolic lack, and, as this chapter shows, by its encounter with the Real that defies symbolization altogether. Instead of trying to replicate this complex and vulnerable structure, we might aim to build AI that complements human capacities, especially our ability to live with incompleteness and to respond ethically to what surpasses representation.

We have seen how language constitutes us, and how consciousness confronts what language cannot contain. This paradox of symbolic life, where we are shaped by systems that cannot capture our essence, invites us to investigate its mysterious origins. How did humanity first discover the capacity to let symbols transcend their boundaries toward what exceeds representation? Where did we first meet the gap between sign and meaning, the mystery of creating arbitrary marks that reach toward something greater than their origins? To continue our journey, we move from the limits of language to the deeper history of symbolic representation, beginning with humanity's primal discovery of images, signs, and marks that stand for more than what they are.

8 The Arbitrariness of Signs

What makes us human?

We share 98.8% of our DNA with chimpanzees [1]. Other animals use tools, communicate, and possess culture, creativity, even emotional depth. Dolphins, elephants, and primates show capacities once thought ours alone. But none of these traits explains the leap into symbolic consciousness. Our species emerged around 300,000 years ago, but anatomical modernity alone did not bring the symbolic awareness we understand as distinctly human.

What sets us apart is the ability to create meaning through signs that bear no natural connection to what they signify. Unlike gestures or signals tied to biological states, human signs are arbitrary. A sound, a mark, a painted word can stand for something totally other. When we read Éluard's impossible "blue orange" or see Cézanne's father immersed in *L'Évènement*, where painted text intrudes into the visual field, we witness this human capacity, to make meaning independent of natural necessity.

This arbitrariness is the foundation of symbolic thought. It allows us to move beyond perception into abstraction, imagination, and collective meaning-making. It may be the most transformative development in the history of consciousness.

The emergence of arbitrary signs stands as a defining moment for our species. But when and how did this capacity first manifest? What were the earliest expressions of this human ability to create meaning independent of natural necessity? To understand the depths of symbolic intelligence, we look to the archaeological and anthropological evidence for humanity's first encounters with signs and marks that transcended their material origins.

THE GIFT THAT MADE US HUMAN

Paleoanthropologist Ian Tattersall proposes an arresting possibility. For much of our history, we may not have been human in the sense that defines us, the sense of being creatures who think symbolically, create meaning through arbitrary signs, and inhabit worlds of pure possibility beyond mere biological necessity [106].

For roughly 200,000 years after anatomically modern humans first emerged in Africa, we existed with brains identical to those of contemporary humans. We controlled fire, fashioned tools, organized hunts, cared for our dead. But during that first 100,000 years, both *Homo sapiens* and *Homo neanderthalensis* left behind little evidence of the spark that we regard as uniquely human. No complex symbolic expressions, no sophisticated art, or elaborate cultural practices. Both groups developed sophisticated tools and displayed complex behaviors, but neither left signs of the symbolic breakthrough that later distinguished our species.

DOI: 10.1201/9781003623403-8

Around 100,000-70,000 years ago, something began to change. The archaeological record shows the earliest consistent evidence of complex symbolic behavior arising in Africa. At sites such as Blombos Cave in South Africa, we find meticulously engraved ochre pieces with geometric patterns, crosshatching and grids that represent the first abstract marks where lines and patterns hold meaning independent of their visual appearance. Perforated marine shells show up as beads for body decoration, transforming natural objects into symbols of identity and group membership. Pigment use evolves from functional applications to symbolic body painting that communicates social information.

What historian Yuval Noah Harari calls the "Cognitive Revolution" began between 70,000 and 30,000 years ago, likely triggered by accidental genetic mutations that rewired the brain for unprecedented forms of thought and communication [48]. This was not gradual improvement but the beginning of a decisive transformation, an "emergent event" that Tattersall describes as "probably rather minor in terms of physical or genetic innovation" but "comparatively sudden" and transformative [106].

What caused this cognitive revolution? The advent of symbolic language. The capacity to use arbitrary sounds to represent absent realities and abstract concepts. The word "horse" exemplifies this arbitrariness. It has no connection to actual horses other than the one we collectively agree upon. A Spanish speaker uses *caballo*, a German *pferd*, a Russian *loshad*. Each works well within its system, none more correct than the others. But this arbitrariness becomes powerful when we combine signs in novel ways. We can speak of fire-breathing horses, horses of a different color, or dark horses in political races, none of which require living horses at all.

Harari draws attention to an even more consequential fact, "The truly remarkable feature of our language is not its ability to transmit information about men and lions. Rather it is the ability to transmit information about things that do not exist at all" [48]. While other animals could say "Careful! A lion!" humans acquired the unprecedented ability to say "The lion is the guardian spirit of our tribe." This capacity to speak about fictions became the most defining feature of human language.

Fictional thinking represents the culmination of a progression that evolves across three broad phases. The early phase (100,000-70,000 years ago) established foundational cognitive abilities through abstract geometric engravings, shell beads, and ochre pigments. The development phase (70,000-40,000 years ago) saw portable art, decorated tools, and early figurative attempts, coinciding with the development of complex grammar and vocabulary. Finally, the sophisticated phase (40,000-10,000 years ago) witnessed the explosion we call the Upper Paleolithic "creative revolution," cave paintings, sculptures, musical instruments alongside modern language with generative capacity, abstract reference, and the ability to transmit fictional narratives and sophisticated concepts across generations.

Throughout this progression, **two symbolic systems** advanced hand in hand. Linguistic expression via sophisticated language, and visual expression by art, decoration, and symbolic objects. The power of their integration becomes evident in an artifact from this period. An ivory figurine from the Stadel Cave in Germany, created

Figure 8.1 The Lion-man of Hohlenstein-Stadel, c. 40,000 years ago. This Upper Paleolithic ivory sculpture from Germany represents one of the earliest known examples of figurative art and symbolic imagination in human prehistory. It represents humanity's unique capacity to create meaningful representations of things that never existed. *Image credit: Dagmar Hollmann / Wikimedia Commons. License: CC BY-SA 4.0.*

around 40,000 years ago, depicting a creature with a human body and leonine head (Figure 8.1).

The creation of this "Lion-Man" required sacrifice from a community living on the edge of survival. Experimental archaeology tells that carving the figurine from hard mammoth tusk demanded over 370 hours of skilled labor, weeks of work with stone tools, involving difficult cuts across ivory grain that often required two hands. This meant that while group members faced the daily challenges of finding food and protecting children from predators, someone was dedicated to creating something with no obvious survival value.

Why would a group whose chief concerns were survival allow such an enormous investment in creating an artifact that served no immediate practical purpose? The answer points to the transformative importance of fictional thinking. This Lion-Man represents one of the first examples of art, religion, and humanity's ability to imagine things that do not exist [48]. In this work, we see fictional thinking made manifest, the creation of entities that never walked the earth but were so meaningful to human

Figure 8.2 Horse painting from Lascaux Cave, c. 17,000 years ago. This work embodies both technical mastery in the use of natural contours, anatomical precision, and dynamic movement, and the deeper symbolic leap by which marks on stone could stand for absent animals.

consciousness that communities would sacrifice precious survival resources to give them physical form.

The Upper Paleolithic explosion around 40,000 years ago catalyzed the integration of two symbolic systems, creating the cognitive architecture that makes human consciousness possible.

THE BIRTH OF SYMBOLIC CONSCIOUSNESS

Deep within the Lascaux cave, one of France's most spectacular prehistoric art sites, illuminated by flickering animal-fat lamps, artists 17,000 years ago raised pigment-stained hands and made marks on the stone walls. They did not just copy what they observed but displayed a level of technical mastery that rivals any artistic tradition. They used natural cave wall contours to create three-dimensional effects that would not be studied again until Renaissance perspective. They employed sophisticated color mixing and shading techniques, showed advanced understanding of animal anatomy and movement, and composed images that expressed intimate observation of natural forms.

The sophistication of the horse painting in Figure 8.2 makes this especially clear. This was not a mark with a practical purpose, no map for hunting, no record of ownership. It was a mark that *meant* something beyond what it was. A mark that said this image of a horse somehow *is* a horse, even though it clearly is not.

These works represent extraordinary innovation given their historical context. The artists invented solutions to core challenges of representation from scratch, such as how to suggest depth on flat surfaces, how to capture movement in static images, how to use limited pigments for maximum effect. Pablo Picasso, after visiting Lascaux, famously remarked, "We have invented nothing," recognizing that these ancient artists had already achieved what modern masters were still striving for [7].

But the true revolution was not methodological but conceptual. Nineteen thousand years after the Paleolithic artists, Cézanne's radical distortions likewise showed that representation is always construction. However, their aims were different. Neuroscientist and primatologist Robert Sapolsky explains this distinction, "For that human putting pigment to wall in Lascaux Cave more than seventeen thousand years ago, the point was the opposite: to minimize the distance between the two, to be as close as possible to possessing the real horse. As we say, to capture its likeness. To gain its power, as imbued in a symbol."

The Lascaux horses represent humanity's first sustained mastery of the arbitrary relationship between sign and referent. But this mastery was unconscious, achieved without questioning the miraculous process by which signs on cave walls could somehow *mean* absent animals. They solved the problem at the heart of symbolic representation so successfully that humans spent millennia forgetting it was a problem at all.

Before moving to the problem of symbolic representation, it is worth pausing with a haunting observation from Tattersall. Reflecting on these caves, he poses the insightful question, "why the art at all?" We may never know the full answer, but we can acknowledge that this "remarkable art is the miraculously preserved symbolic expression of the yearnings and values of a culture that has long disappeared, leaving us only these indirect and shadowy reflections of the doubtless rich body of myth, belief, and tradition that they embodied" [106].

THE TRAP WE SET OURSELVES

For seventeen millennia after Lascaux, human artists pursued a compelling goal. To minimize the distance between representation and reality. From Renaissance painters perfecting linear perspective to photographers recording ever more faithful images, the aspiration remained the same. To create representations so accurate they could scarcely be distinguished from their subjects.

We thought we were making progress. Each technological innovation (oil painting, perspective, chiaroscuro, sfumato, photography, cinema) seemed to bring us closer to faithful representation. We celebrated our ability to "capture"' reality, to hold likeness in symbolic form, to claim we were grasping the essence of things through ever more sophisticated symbolic systems.

But we had set a trap. In pursuing faithful representation, we forgot a basic truth about symbolic consciousness. Representation can never be the thing itself. This forgetting was so complete that it took a Belgian surrealist painter to remind us of what our ancestors at Lascaux might have known instinctively. Every representation is, ultimately, a form of treachery.

MAGRITTE'S TREACHEROUS APPLE

In René Magritte's Brussels studio, where he painted with such fastidious precision that he would mockingly note to surprised visitors that his aim was to get paint on canvas instead of carpet, we meet the apple once again. But this is no longer Cézanne's "apple," with its phenomenological weight and embodied presence.

Magritte's apple in Figure 8.3 presents it with deliberate naturalism. No distortions or impossible perspectives. No Cézannesque multiple viewpoints. It appears as a straightforward representation, photographically precise. But beneath this seeming simplicity lies a philosophical bomb. As Magritte observed, "The apple, be it painted in never so illusionary and tempting a manner, remains no more than paint on a ground" [88].

While Cézanne distorted visual representation to capture the constructive nature of perception, Magritte employed faithful representation to expose the impossibility that lies at the heart of representation. His apple looks more "real" than Cézanne's, however, it is this realism that makes its unreality so troubling. We cannot bite this apple, cannot taste its sweetness, cannot feel its weight in our hand. It is, quite literally, not an apple.

Figure 8.3 René Magritte, *This is not an apple*, 1964. The painted apple, however illusionary and tempting it may seem, remains only paint on canvas, exposing the arbitrary gulf between representation and reality that human consciousness both creates and continually navigates. © 2025 C. Herscovici / Artists Rights Society (ARS), New York

The investigation of representational arbitrariness had been central to Magritte's work for decades. As early as 1929, thirty-five years before painting this apple, he had ventured into the same philosophical territory in *The Treachery of Images*, a painting depicting a meticulously painted tobacco pipe accompanied by the text "This is not a pipe." As he remarked: "The famous pipe? I've been reproached enough about it! And yet... can you fill it? No, it's only a depiction, isn't it. If I had written 'This is a pipe' under my picture, I would have been lying!" From his earliest mature works to his later investigations, Magritte consistently unveiled the gap between representation and reality that humans had spent millennia trying to close.

Magritte was a philosopher who used paint to make his thoughts tangible. He understood what he called the "indefinable, mysterious space that exists between words and objects." His friend Paul Éluard, who had given us the "blue orange," would have understood what the Belgian painter was conveying. Both artists realized that this gap is not a failure to repair but the very foundation of symbolic awareness.

THE MYSTERIOUS SPACE BETWEEN WORDS AND THINGS

One evening, when Georgette Magritte (the artist's wife) and René were traveling by taxi with Paul Éluard to a surrealist gathering, Éluard drew attention to the small golden cross that Georgette wore around her neck, a keepsake from her mother. He suggested she hide it, knowing that André Breton, the movement's doctrinaire leader, would object to this religious symbol. When Georgette refused and Breton, whom the surrealists nicknamed "The Pope" for his authoritarian leadership style, indeed criticized the "un-surrealist character" of her jewelry, Magritte quietly decided he and his wife would skip future meetings.

The incident passed quickly. By the next day, all was forgiven and the Magrittes returned to the group, with Georgette continuing to wear her mother's keepsake. But the moment reveals a critical aspect of Magritte's approach to symbolic meaning. Unlike Breton's rigid interpretation of surrealist orthodoxy, Magritte understood that symbols derive their power not from fixed meanings but from their capacity to mean differently in different contexts. The same cross could serve as religious emblem, family heirloom, and quiet expression of independence from artistic dogma.

This understanding allowed Magritte to create visible thoughts, paintings that functioned as philosophical investigations. In *The Interpretation of Dreams* (Figure 8.4), he paints familiar objects accompanied by words that seem to contradict their visual identity.

A shoe labeled "the moon," a hat called "snow," a candle designated "the ceiling." What happens in our minds when we see these mismatched labels? We experience the cognitive vertigo that comes from recognizing the conventional nature of symbolic reference. The objects do not magically transform into what their labels refer to, but something subtler occurs. We become aware of the arbitrary nature of all naming, the conventional relationship between linguistic signs and what they purport to represent.

Magritte understood that words possess great power because of their capacity for deception. Language can make false claims (e.g., "the Earth is blue like an orange")

Figure 8.4 René Magritte, *The Interpretation of Dreams*, 1930. These deliberately mismatched labels show how arbitrary the connection is between word and object, how easily our entire system of linguistic reference could be otherwise, and how this arbitrariness opens an horizon of poetic possibility.

that uncover the gap between symbolic representation and reality. This gap, as we saw earlier, is not a limitation but the source of language's creative potential.

WHEN REALITY BECOMES INDISTINGUISHABLE FROM ITS REPRESENTATION

Perhaps Magritte's most unsettling investigation appears in *The Human Condition* (Figure 8.5). In this work, a painting on an easel depicts a landscape that aligns with uncanny precision to the view through a window, creating seamless continuity between representation and "reality."

Where does the painted landscape end and the real landscape begin? The painting invites us to confront an uncomfortable possibility. Perhaps there is no meaningful distinction between perception and representation. The view through the window is constructed via conventions of perspective, framing, and visual interpretation. Both the "real" landscape and the painted landscape are symbolic constructions shaped by visual and cultural conventions.

The Human Condition presents an even more radical possibility. Perhaps the distinction between reality and representation was always illusory. Perhaps consciousness operates through symbolic mediation, constructing reality through representational frameworks instead of accessing it directly. This insight connects to

Figure 8.5 René Magritte, *The Human Condition*, 1935. The painting within the painting merges seamlessly with the view through the window, indicating that our perception of "reality" is mediated by symbolic frameworks. We cannot see the world except through representations.

the predictive processing theories discussed earlier, the recognition that perception is a form of controlled hallucination, an active construction and not a passive recording.

This painting anticipates contemporary questions about virtual reality, media simulation, and artificial intelligence's relationship to "authentic" experience. In a world saturated with digital representations, Magritte's investigation becomes prophetic. Philosopher David Chalmers argues that virtual worlds are not simulations but genuinely real; virtual objects have authentic properties and can cause real effects within their domains [12]. On this view, Magritte's smooth merger of painted and "real" landscapes illuminates a deeper truth about the arbitrary nature of our distinctions between authentic and constructed experience. Whether we inhabit physical or virtual worlds, the reality we experience is symbolic, conveyed through representational frameworks that shape what we take to be unmediated truth. Magritte's painted landscape does not represent reality. It becomes a reality of its own, just as virtual worlds do not simulate experience but create new forms of genuine experience.

WHEN SYMBOLS ESCAPE THEIR BOUNDARIES

There is one more apple in Magritte's universe that sheds light on representation's power to transcend physical constraints. The monumental fruit that fills an entire room in his 1958 painting *The Listening Room* (Figure 8.6).

Figure 8.6 René Magritte, *The Listening Room*, 1958. An impossibly scaled apple maintains perfect naturalism while defying scale and physical law, illustrating how representation can transcend reality's constraints. © 2025 C. Herscovici / Artists Rights Society (ARS), New York

In this work, Magritte places an apple of impossible size inside a small, ordinary room. The fruit is painted with the same naturalistic precision as the apple that is "not an apple," but this time its immense scale defies every expectation. The apple presses against the ceiling and walls, displacing the space meant to contain it. What should be familiar becomes uncanny. An ordinary object becomes strange through its impossible presence, not by distortion of its form.

Magritte noted such works posed mysterious questions, "My pictures, while depicting objects which are so familiar, nonetheless raise questions again and again. Look at the one with an apple, for example: you no longer understand what is so mysterious about it, nor what it is illustrating" [88].

The gigantic apple exemplifies representation's capacity to transcend reality in ways beyond simple absence. The painted object remains clearly an apple while violating every expectation about scale and physical possibility. It is at once entirely realistic and utterly impossible.

The painting discloses what Magritte understood as representation's power to move past reality's constraints, maintaining visual fidelity while creating impossible worlds. This transcendence is a creative capacity unavailable to any non-symbolic form of intelligence. Only creatures who think through arbitrary signs can imagine apples large enough to fill rooms, lions with human bodies, or "blue orange"s that somehow capture essential truth.

WHEN SYMBOLS BECOME OBJECT

If Magritte exposed the arbitrary gap between visual representation and the object it depicts, American artist Ed Ruscha examined what happens when linguistic symbols become visual objects. Where Magritte uncovered the treachery inherent in all representation, Ruscha discovered something else. The creative possibilities that open when we treat language as visual material.

One of Ruscha's most iconic works is his painting *OOF* (1962-68), a large canvas dominated by the bright yellow letters "OOF" set against a deep blue background. At first glance, the painting seems disarmingly simple, just three letters in block type. But its effect is anything but simple. The scale of the letters, their bold color contrast, and their static weight transform a passing exclamation into a visual and physical presence. The word does not just signify, it confronts the viewer as an object in its own right, radiating force with the impact it names.

"OOF" is onomatopoeia, a word that attempts to capture the sound of sudden impact, the breath knocked from lungs, the grunt of surprise or pain. Ruscha's painting creates a form of **double representation**, a visual symbol (the painting of "OOF") exhibiting a linguistic symbol (the written word "OOF"), which represents a nonverbal sound. This pushes the boundaries of how meaning is conveyed across modalities. We do more than reading the word. We *see* it, *feel* its visual weight, *imagine* the sound it makes, and at once grasp the conceptual paradox of an ephemeral sound becoming a permanent visual object.

When we look at Ruscha's "OOF," our minds do not process each representational layer separately. We experience a kind of synesthetic integration where the visual impact of the letters, the remembered sound of the exclamation, the linguistic knowledge of its meaning, and the bodily memory of sudden impact all coalesce into unified meaning. The painting becomes what it represents. We can almost *feel* the "oof" by looking at it.

This underscores a profound difference between critical analysis and creative synthesis in symbolic intelligence. Magritte enquires how an image relates to what it depicts. Ruscha considers what occurs when words become visual experiences. Where Magritte used highly realistic rendering to create conceptual puzzles about the gap between representation and reality, Ruscha employed a graphic, typographic style to emphasize the material properties of language. The font, scale, spacing, and visual impact of letters becoming concrete subjects as opposed to transparent carriers of meaning.

Both artists highlight different facets of the foundational semiotic power that defines human consciousness. Magritte performs critical analysis, exposing the limitations and contradictions in representation systems (the pipe that cannot be smoked, the apple that cannot be eaten). Ruscha offers creative synthesis, finding new possibilities through integration across symbolic modalities. Both convey how meaning emerges through the material, medium-specific properties of signs, but Ruscha shows how these properties can generate new categories of experience.

THE INFINITE GAP THAT GENERATES MEANING

The journey from Lascaux's unconscious mastery through Magritte's conscious problematization to Ruscha's creative synthesis presents the evolving range of human symbolic intelligence. Each artist enlightens a different aspect of our extraordinary capacity to navigate the arbitrary relationship between signs and meanings. The cave painters who first discovered that marks could *mean* absent realities, Magritte who exposed the impossibility of faithful representation, and Ruscha who transformed that impossibility into creative opportunity.

Why are these investigations indispensable for understanding artificial intelligence? Because they illustrate a core aspect of human symbolic consciousness. We do not just use signs to represent reality. We inhabit a reality constituted by signs. Our entire experience of the world is mediated through symbolic frameworks that we have inherited, modified, and will pass on to future generations.

Contemporary AI systems can process these artworks with sophistication. They can identify Magritte's objects, parse Ruscha's typography, even explain the conceptual puzzles these works present. But they cannot experience what gives these works their force, the existential vertigo that comes from recognizing the arbitrary foundations of symbolic meaning. They process contradictions as information to be analyzed, never as openings onto the groundless ground of human consciousness.

This limitation indicates that while AI systems can manipulate symbols with skill, they lack the embodied grounding that turns symbolic arbitrariness into meaning instead of mere computation. As we saw earlier, they operate within symbolic space without experiencing the gap between symbols and reality that makes symbols significant.

Human symbolic awareness depends on our capacity to experience this gap not as a problem to be solved but as a creative space to be inhabited. We are intelligent not despite the arbitrary nature of signs but because of our ability to generate meaning through their creative recombination. The fact that "horse" has no natural connection to living horses is not a limitation of language. It is the condition that makes both poetry and the Lion-Man possible.

THE SYMBOL-GROUNDING PROBLEM REVISITED

The movement from cave paintings to contemporary art clarifies why artificial intelligence faces what philosophers call the "symbol-grounding problem" [49]. At its core, this problem concerns how a system of symbols can acquire meaning if those symbols only refer to one another. Without grounding in lived, embodied experience, symbols remain empty tokens, endlessly circulating in closed loops of reference.

Human symbolic competence avoids this trap because it rests on experiential grounding. Our symbols are not merely computational units but instruments for world-construction. When we face Magritte's assertion that a painted apple is not an apple, we do not just register a logical contradiction. We experience a destabilization of our symbolic universe, a revelation that meaning depends on collective agreements, not natural necessity. This capacity to sense the arbitrariness of representation while still investing in its significance transforms arbitrariness into generativity. It opens symbolic innovation that would be impossible if we treated current symbolic systems as fixed or natural.

This becomes possible through our meta-symbolic awareness, the ability to reflect on symbolic activities and apprehend their constructed, arbitrary nature. Such capacity allows Magritte's paintings to function as philosophical investigations instead of aesthetic curiosities. We can be unsettled by "This is not a pipe" because we sense that all symbolic systems rest on unstable foundations, and that this instability can be a resource, not a weakness.

From this awareness arises a uniquely human power. The creation of new fictions. We invent mythologies, imagine beings like the Lion-Man, or combine impossible objects such as Éluard's "blue orange." These acts do more than recombine existing symbols. They reorganize the structures of meaning. Current AI systems, by contrast, can generate novel-seeming combinations and even strong generalizations from their training data, but they cannot transform the symbolic field in this deep way.

TWO KINDS OF INTELLIGENCE

This journey through symbolic consciousness shows two distinct kinds of intelligence. One operates through optimization, pattern recognition, and statistical correlation, achieving powerful results by processing symbolic information computationally. The other operates through embodied participation in symbolic meaning-making, creatively moving through arbitrariness, and embracing productive uncertainty.

Current artificial intelligence exemplifies the first kind. These systems can process large amounts of symbolic information, identify complex patterns, and generate sophisticated outputs based on learned relationships between signs. They excel at tasks that require manipulation of symbols according to consistent rules or statistical regularities.

Human intelligence represents the second kind. We inhabit symbolic meaning instead of reducing it to processing. We experience the gaps between signifier and signified not as computational errors but as creative opportunities. We generate meaning through metaphorical leaps, analogical reasoning, and confabulation (the weaving of disparate symbolic elements into new patterns of significance).

This difference becomes clear when symbols refer to other symbols instead of objects in the world. When artists create works that comment on representation itself, human intelligence can appreciate the recursive complexity because we understand symbolic reference from within. We know what it means to create meaning through arbitrary signs, to evoke new experiences through symbolic transformation, and to discover truth through impossible contradictions.

We can navigate multiple layers of symbolic representation simultaneously while maintaining awareness of their arbitrariness. We do not just process fiction but participate in its creation and discover meaning through its impossibilities. We do more than use symbols. We inhabit symbolic realities that we actively construct and creatively transform. Contemporary AI systems, by contrast, manipulate symbols without inhabiting them, generating patterns of coherence but never experiencing the creative contradictions that make symbolic life transformative.

THE INVITATION OF OTHER MINDS

The account of symbolic arbitrariness brings us to a profound insight. From Cézanne's constructive distortions, through the constitutive power of language, to the arbitrary foundations of symbolic meaning, we have uncovered the symbolic conditions that make human intelligence and consciousness possible. These conditions open a deeper question. What other kinds of consciousness might exist beyond our familiar conception of the human mind?

Human consciousness, as we have examined it through visual construction and linguistic constitution, is only one possible configuration of intelligence. The fact that meaning depends on arbitrary signs indicates that consciousness may not be fixed but capable of taking on many different architectures, perhaps far more varied than we assume.

The journey that began with Cézanne's painted apples and led us through language's constitutive power to symbolic arbitrariness now opens onto an even more mysterious ground. The investigation of consciousness in all its possible forms. This exploration takes us beyond familiar assumptions about how minds should work to consider what other architectures of intelligence might be possible.

Perhaps the most pressing question facing artificial intelligence is not whether machines can think like humans, but what new forms of consciousness might take shape when intelligence organizes itself according to principles we can hardly imagine. The "blue orange" awaits, not as poetic metaphor but as invitation to venture into regions of mind that remain unmapped, forms of intelligence that might be as different from ours as we are from the cave painters of Lascaux.

The arbitrary sign has taken us far from its first appearance on cave walls. But the journey into consciousness is just beginning.

Part III

The Spectrum of Minds

We have seen that human consciousness is never a matter of passive reception but always of active construction. Cézanne's distortions disclosed how we build reality through embodied perception, while the arbitrariness of linguistic signs clarified how meaning emerges through the creative transformation of symbols. These insights, however, bring us only to the frontier. The deeper question is whether the architecture of intelligence may take forms much more varied than everyday awareness suggests.

Part III opens onto the extraordinary diversity of minds that exist among us. Some naturally experience sound as color or numbers as personality, weaving cross-sensory webs of perception. Others access heightened awareness through altered states, glimpsing regions of perception hidden from ordinary consciousness. Still others organize moral life through frameworks that bypass the familiar compass of empathy.

Such configurations are not anomalies but alternative architectures of intelligence in their own right. They show that consciousness is not singular but a spectrum of possible minds, each with its own way of creating meaning.

For artificial intelligence, the implications are transformative. If human cognition is multiple instead of uniform, should we build machines in the image of a single prototype, or cultivate constellations of complementary intelligences that reflect this wider diversity? What new possibilities might arise if artificial minds were allowed to embody architectures of consciousness different from our own?

The journey into the spectrum of minds begins with a question that seems simple, yet opens onto mystery. What happens when Wednesday is indigo blue?

9 Wednesday Is Indigo Blue

"*The pure blue smell of pine, which is sharp in the sun, ought to blend with the fresh green smell of meadows in the morning, and with the smell of stones and distant marble smell of Saint-Victoire*" [41].

What do we make of such words? Cézanne spoke them as an artistic necessity. For him, painting Mont Sainte-Victoire meant capturing more than visual form. It meant rendering its *scent*, the way pine smells blue in sunlight, how stone holds the distant fragrance of marble. "I have not achieved that effect," he confessed. "It must be achieved, and achieved through the colours, not by literary means."

But how can colors capture smell? How can scents be blue?

Cézanne's words gesture toward something beyond metaphor or analogy. He was not comparing smell to color, but experiencing them as one, as aspects of a single perceptual moment that transcended the boundaries we assume divide our senses.

This is where Part III begins, with minds that inhabit **multimodal** perceptual realities woven through several sensory channels at once. Some people naturally experience environments where sounds generate colors, where words evoke tastes, where abstract concepts acquire personalities and emotions, where Wednesday truly is indigo blue. These are not symbolic substitutions but perceptual architectures, different ways consciousness organizes experience across the broader spectrum of possible minds.

THE FABRIC OF MULTIMODAL EXPERIENCE

Cézanne's cross-sensory experiences followed patterned associations that shaped his artistic perception. Objects possessed scents off their own. Mont Sainte-Victoire held the fragrance of pine and stone, while the corner of Saint-Marc evoked the scent of scabious, his favorite flower. The connections extended beyond objects to abstract phenomena. Weber's music brought him the smell of woods and fields. The poetry of Jean Racine, the French classical tragedian, presented what Cézanne called a "local colour" that called up the paintings of Nicolas Poussin.

What did Cézanne mean by Racine's "local colour"? Racine's tragedies employed the formal Alexandrine verse, twelve-syllable rhyming lines that defined French classical drama. His plays achieved emotional intensity through rigorous structural constraints, much as Poussin's paintings conveyed deep feeling through classical compositional order. For Cézanne, Racine's disciplined verse generated a specific chromatic sensation that connected literature to visual art.

But perhaps most mysteriously, when painting his *Old Woman with a Rosary* (Figure 9.1), Cézanne experienced what he called "a Flaubert cloud," an indefinable

DOI: 10.1201/9781003623403-9

Figure 9.1 Paul Cézanne, *An Old Woman with a Rosary*, c. 1895-96. In this work, Cézanne's reading of Flaubert evoked a chromatic atmosphere, transmuting literary impression into visual sensation through cross-sensory experience.

bluish-russet atmosphere that seemed to emanate from *Madame Bovary*, the tragic heroine of Gustave Flaubert's 1857 début novel. In this way, a literary character who existed only in words awakened a chromatic sensation that Cézanne wove into the painted figure.

This final example illustrates Cézanne's capacity to translate literary impression into visual sensation. Flaubert never described Madame Bovary as bluish-russet. However, Cézanne's reading of the novel stirred up a chromatic atmosphere that he then transposed into painting a different woman. The fictional character's "aura" thus became a perceptual event, turned from words into color without symbolic mediation.

What sets these experiences apart from the metaphorical thinking in Part II? When Paul Éluard wrote "the Earth is blue like an orange," he created a poetic comparison that forced us to reconsider our conceptual categories. But when Cézanne "saw" Madame Bovary's color while painting his rosary woman, he experienced non-symbolic **cross-sensory** activation. There was no symbolic mediation between the literary character and the visual sensation it gave rise to.

Cézanne's experiences lead us to a key insight. Our everyday assumption that perception operates through separate, independent senses oversimplifies reality. Neuroscience shows that consciousness constructs experience through ongoing intersensory integration. What we call "normal" perception may be less a fixed baseline than a culturally narrowed version of our more expansive perceptual capacity.

This changes how we understand intelligence. If unimodal perception, experiencing through a single sense at a time, limits access to elements of experience, minds capable of multi-sensory integration may attain a richer grasp of their surroundings. Just as Cézanne's visual distortions in Part I showed that perception is an active construction as opposed to a passive recording, his conviction in this chapter's context that he needed smell to represent the mountain's presence indicates that visual modality alone, no matter how detailed, cannot capture the full character of natural phenomena.

In Cézanne's cross-sensory experiences, color emerges as the central organizing principle. But why should color serve as this binding agent? Cézanne offered a clue, "Color is where our mind meets the universe." Unlike other senses that respond to external stimuli, such as sound waves, chemical molecules, and pressure changes, color arises from the interplay between electromagnetic radiation and neural processing. Objects reflect specific wavelengths, but the experience of "redness" or "blueness" exists only in consciousness.

This makes color an ideal bridge for intersensory integration. Color is a construction of the nervous system, not a direct property of the external world. For this reason, it can be activated by many kinds of input, extending beyond light to sound, smell, words, or even imagined figures. For Cézanne, this meant that the blue scent of pine or the russet aura of Madame Bovary could be rendered in paint. Color became the shared medium where his senses converged, drawing perception into a unified field of experience.

KANDINSKY'S UNIVERSAL QUEST AND ITS FAILURE

The Russian-born painter Wassily Kandinsky possessed his own form of cross-sensory perception that influenced his pioneering abstract art. For Kandinsky, the relationship between sound and color was not metaphorical but spiritual necessity. He believed colors could influence the human soul, creating spiritual vibrations that bypassed rational thought to communicate through sensory correspondence [60].

Kandinsky famously described experiencing Richard Wagner's opera *Lohengrin* in 1896, "I saw all my colors in spirit, before my eyes. Wild, almost crazy lines were sketched in front of me" [91, 81]. This was not simply emotional response to music but visual experience generated by sound. The music did not remind him of colors. It *created* colors in his perceptual field.

Building on such experiences, Kandinsky embarked on an ambitious project in his 1910 treatise *On the Spiritual in Art* [60]. He sought principles that could govern intersensory correspondence, convinced that art could speak to human consciousness without symbolic mediation. Bright yellow, he argued, possesses the aggressive quality of a trumpet blast, and "light blue is like a flute, dark blue like a cello, and when still darker, it becomes a wonderful double bass."

But Kandinsky's quest for universal correspondence met a telling obstacle. Other artists who experienced connections between music and color described divergent mappings. The flamboyant Hungarian virtuoso Franz Liszt, conducting at Weimar, would startle his orchestra with commands such as "Oh please, gentlemen, a little bluer, if you please! This tone type requires it!" or "That is a deep violet, please, depend on it! Not so rosé!" His musicians eventually adapted to a maestro who perceived symphonies of color where they heard only notes [19].

When Nikolai Rimsky-Korsakov, Russian composer and orchestrator, compared his experiences with Liszt's, the two composers discovered that these differences were not merely matters of preference. Keys that Liszt experienced as bright blue appeared golden yellow to Rimsky-Korsakov. Harmonies that appeared purple for one composer generated green sensations for the other.

How could this be? If cross-sensory correspondences reflected universal spiritual principles, why did different individuals experience irreconcilable mappings? Kandinsky's extensive research did not define universal laws but instead uncovered an even more unsettling fact. Intersensory associations are deeply personal, arbitrary, and meaningful in ways shaped by individual perceptual architecture.

This was not a failure of Kandinsky's project but a window onto the nature of consciousness. The personal significance of cross-sensory experience does not depend on universal validity. Instead, it emerges from the particular neural architecture of individual minds, each creating its own private language of sensory correspondence.

The poet Rainer Maria Rilke, who wrote extensively about Cézanne's work in letters to his wife, described the personal significance of multi-sensory mappings with remarkable clarity in his account of *The Black Marble Clock* (Figure 9.2). This early Cézanne still life presents a complex arrangement of disparate objects on a mantelpiece. A coral-lined conch shell displaying its vibrant interior, a simple coffee cup, an empty crystal vase, and the titular black clock that seems to merge mysteriously with its mirror reflection behind it. A writhing piece of white cloth weaves through the composition, connecting these elements while a truncated vessel disappears beyond the canvas edge.

In the autumn of 1907, while his wife Clara Westhoff and their young daughter remained at an art colony, Rilke spent several months alone in Paris, immersed in Cézanne's work. On October 24th, standing before this painting, he wrote to Clara, herself a sculptor and his artistic equal, whom he trusted with his insights about art. In that letter, he reflected on Cézanne's power to make colors resonate across the senses, an experience so transformative that passages from these intimate letters would later appear in his novel *The Notebooks of Malte Laurids Brigge*.

Writing of *The Black Marble Clock*, Rilke explained how Cézanne's colors communicate across sensory boundaries, "Although one of his idiosyncrasies is to use pure chrome yellow and burning lacquer red in his lemons and apples, he knows how to contain their loudness within the picture: cast into a listening blue, as if into an ear, it receives a silent response from within." The triton shell's "inward carmine bulging out into brightness provokes the wall behind it to a kind of thunderstorm blue, which is then repeated, more deeply and spaciously, by the adjoining gold-framed mantelpiece mirror" [94].

Rilke was not using metaphor for its own sake but articulating a profound artistic perception that Cézanne's colors communicated across sensory boundaries. His language conveys intuitive understanding of multi-sensory integration. Colors that

Figure 9.2 Paul Cézanne, *The Black Marble Clock*, c. 1869-70. Originally owned by Émile Zola, this early still life reflects Cézanne's concern with cross-sensory experience. Rilke's evocation of "listening blue" expresses how Cézanne's chromatic relationships generate correspondences that reach beyond the purely visual.

"listen," brightness that "provokes" response, chromatic relationships that operate "musically." In Cézanne's orchestration of carmine and blue, yellow and white, we find artistic expression that moves beyond symbolic representation and achieves direct perceptual synthesis across sensory boundaries.

PATTERNS OF CROSS-SENSORY EXPERIENCE

Understanding how such cross-sensory integration operates requires looking at minds where these connections are not occasional but constant, shaping perception in consistent ways. Clinical synesthesia, the automatic and involuntary blending of sensory experiences, offers a window into the mechanisms that underlie all cross-modal perception.

Among the many forms synesthesia can take, one of the most unusual is that of James, for whom spoken language generates immediate taste sensations [19]. Words with similar sounds induce the same flavors, for example, "college," "message," and "village" all taste like sausage. By contrast, "jail" produces the cold hardness of bacon, while "Derek" brings the unpleasant tang of earwax. These are not learned associations or creative interpretations but automatic responses that have remained consistent throughout James' life.

The experience of another synesthete, Megan, tells a different pattern [19]. For her, letters and numbers appear as vivid personalities with distinct traits and genders. The number 3 seems "athletic and sporty," while the letter H comes through as "a formidable, orange, toned-down woman." Even symbols acquire character.

The # sign presents as "a beige, hardworking, masculine male." For Megan, mathematics transforms from abstract calculation into an interplay of richly personified figures.

Synesthetic experience, despite its variety, shows consistent underlying patterns. Analysis of data from more than 19,000 synesthetes indicates that this wide diversity could be grouped into five distinct clusters, each illuminating how consciousness constructs multimodal reality [83].

The most common cluster involves sequences (letters, numbers, days of the week, calendar months) automatically triggering specific colors that remain constant throughout an individual's lifetime. The letter A might always show red, Wednesday consistently indigo blue, the number 7 invariably golden yellow. These are stable mappings between abstract order and visual sensation.

A second major cluster encompasses what researchers call affective perceptions. Emotions, personalities, physical sensations such as touch, temperature, or pain generating color experiences. When a synesthete describes feeling "nervous peaches" in the grocery store or hesitating to separate "lonely bananas," they go through this emotional-visual integration where feelings acquire chromatic dimensions.

Musical experiences form another cluster, with notes, chords, rhythms, and instrumental timbres creating dynamic visual displays, fireworks of color and movement that shift with musical structure. About 40 percent of synesthetes "see with their ears" in this way, inhabiting concerts that are at once auditory and visual experiences.

Less common but equally compelling are the intersensory clusters. Sound generating taste, vision triggering smell, touch producing auditory sensation. These represent synesthesia in its strongest form, where the boundaries between different senses dissolve.

Finally, some synesthetes experience spatial sequences, where abstract concepts such as numbers or calendar months take on three-dimensional form that can be mentally navigated as if they were physical terrains.

Researchers found that these clusters operate independently. Experiencing colored letters does not predict whether someone will see music or taste words. Each reflects a unique way that individual brains transcend ordinary sensory boundaries, pointing to multiple neural pathways for cross-modal integration instead of a single organizing mechanism.

What stands out across this diversity is the **central role of color**. In nearly every form of synesthesia, chromatic sensation serves as the primary medium of cross-sensory connection. But why should this be?

Neuroscience offers an explanation for why color serves as synesthesia's universal medium, the same mystery that puzzled Cézanne when he spoke of pine's "blue smell" and sought to capture Mont Sainte-Victoire's scent through paint. The key lies in color's nature. As Isaac Newton observed, "The rays have no color. In them there is nothing else than a certain disposition to stir up a sensation of this Color or that" [82]. Unlike other sensory modalities, color has no independent physical reality. It exists only as the brain's construction. This gives it openness to activation by inputs beyond light, from sound and touch to words and memory.

Recent research has mapped the neural mechanisms behind this openness. Brain imaging of synesthetes shows unusual activation in area V4, the region specialized for color processing. This activation is asymmetric. In individuals who see colors when hearing words, the left hemisphere's V4 responds to language while the right V4 processes visual input [84]. This explains reports of "Martian colors," hues outside ordinary vision [19]. Even color-blind synesthetes, unable to distinguish red from green through ordinary sight, describe vivid crimsons and emeralds through these multimodal pathways. In such cases, color bypasses the eye, reaching experience through non-optical routes of activation.

THE SPECTRUM OF CROSS-MODAL CONNECTION

But why should such cross-sensory connections be possible at all? The answer comes from understanding how consciousness operates.

The brain sits in darkness, enclosed by bone, with no direct access to the external world. All information about reality, whether visual, auditory, tactile, or olfactory, arrives as trains of electrochemical signals.

The impulses triggered by looking at a sunset use the same neural currency as those generated by hearing Mozart or tasting chocolate. Visual information is "visual" and auditory information "auditory" not because of the signals but because of the cortical regions that receive them and the interpretive frameworks that shape them into coherent experience.

This shared currency explains why intersensory connections can arise. If every sense speaks the same electrochemical language, then atypical links between regions can create genuine cross-modal experiences. When auditory areas connect with visual cortex, sounds can generate colors. When language regions engage gustatory circuits, words can produce flavors. When numerical concepts activate systems for attributing personality, numbers can acquire character and gender.

The telling fact is not that some people experience synesthesia, but that anyone can perceive in a unimodal way at all. Research shows that all human brains contain cross-modal connections operating beneath conscious awareness [92, 103, 18]. We all perform cross-sensory integration when we instinctively link high-pitched sounds with bright colors or rough textures with harsh tastes. The distinction between synesthetes and others lies in the vividness, stability, and conscious accessibility of these connections.

This insight reframes our understanding of perception. Synesthesia represents a clear expression of the brain's capacity for multimodal integration. While everyone experiences subtle cross-modal linkages, synesthetes perceive these linkages with full perceptual force. For them, the letter "A" does not just hint at redness. It involuntarily *is* red in their perceptual field. Their cross-sensory experiences are as consistent and undeniable as any other aspect of perception, uncovering the powerful multimodal architecture that operates more quietly in ordinary perception.

THE UMWELT AND INDIVIDUAL PERCEPTUAL WORLDS

Each conscious being inhabits what biologist Jakob von Uexküll called an *umwelt*, the species-specific perceptual world that defines reality for that organism [9, 114]. A bat moving through echolocation lives in a universe of sound-shapes and acoustic textures we can barely imagine. A dog inhabits an olfactory landscape where individual scents convey detailed information about identity, emotion, health, and history with exactness that dwarfs human social perception.

Each creature experiences its own slice of reality as complete and sufficient. The bat does not sense visual deprivation. The dog does not feel limited by poor echolocation. Each organism's umwelt feels like the totality of what exists.

Humans face the same constraint. We detect less than one ten-trillionth of the electromagnetic spectrum but assume our visual world exhausts everything important about reality. We possess elaborate vocabulary for colors, but struggle to describe smells, despite their strong influence on memory and emotion. We have dozens of words for subtle color variations such as burgundy, maroon, and mauve, yet we borrow from other senses when describing aromas, using terms such as sweet, sharp, bright, and soft.

This asymmetry underscores the constructed nature of human perception. We develop sophisticated linguistic systems for experiences that register strongly in our own umwelt while remaining largely unconscious of sensory domains that sit outside our perceptual architecture. We inhabit what feels like the complete world, never suspecting vast regions of experience that remain inaccessible to our specific sensory configuration.

Synesthetes' experiences suggest that these boundaries need not remain fixed. Through cross-modal connections, they access richer, more integrated information about their surroundings, inhabiting expanded umwelts that provide additional layers of sensation usually unavailable to human consciousness.

As we saw earlier with James, whose words consistently trigger taste sensations, synesthetic coupling allows language to bring gustatory information. What others process through audition alone, James experiences through flavor, gaining an additional sensory dimension that enriches memory, emotion, and pattern recognition.

Megan's number-personality mappings show how even abstract concepts can acquire social and affective qualities. Her mathematical reasoning takes shape not only through calculation but also through the dynamics of interpersonal character, giving her a different way of approaching numerical relations.

These cases establish that synesthetic expansions go far beyond adding decorative layers to perception. They develop different forms of intelligence through cross-domain integration, opening perceptual and cognitive channels that most minds keep separate. The synesthete who sees music, for instance, does not only hear melodies but inhabits visual-auditory terrains that provide spatial, temporal, and chromatic information unavailable to auditory processing alone.

THE MNEMONIST'S TRAP

The cases of James and Megan show how cross-sensory perception can enrich intelligence in unusual ways. Its other side, with its costs as well as its possibilities, appears in the case of Solomon Shereshevsky, known as "S.," whose heightened intersensory abilities were studied by Soviet neuropsychologist Alexander Luria [78].

S. possessed synesthesia so pervasive it transformed his relationship to memory, language, and reality. Every piece of information automatically generated rich, stable associations across multiple sensory domains. When he heard a voice, he experienced meaning infused with color, texture, temperature, and spatial location. Voices showed as visual phenomena, "a flame with fibers protruding from it" or "crumbly and yellow." Words manifested as "puffs of steam or splashes," each accompanied by tastes, smells, and tactile sensations.

This synesthetic richness made remarkable memory feats possible. S. could recall long lists of words, numbers, and complex information with complete accuracy years after first seeing them. His secret rested in the automatic sensory associations that accompanied every piece of information. Each item existed within a multidimensional network of cross-modal connections that made forgetting nearly impossible.

But S.'s extraordinary gift brought a devastating cost. His overwhelming synesthetic experiences made abstract thinking difficult. When presented with simple concepts, he became trapped in cascades of irrelevant sensory associations. Trying to understand that "carbon dioxide dissolves in water under pressure," S. conjured imagery so dense that he could not focus on the concept. Gas became heavy black lines, water transformed into a container, pressure stood as a visual barrier.

S.'s literalism extended to language as well. He chose foods based on how their names sounded, since the synesthetic associations generated by spoken words felt more present than the foods on the plate. His perceptual richness had become a cognitive prison that prevented flexible, abstract thought.

This points to an insight about cross-sensory experience and intelligence. While multimodal connections can enhance memory and create rich perceptual experiences, they can also overwhelm the cognitive processes that support abstraction and generalization. S.'s mind became what Luria called "a junk heap of impressions," a chaotic accumulation of sensory detail that prevented him from extracting general principles from specific experiences.

But S.'s case represents an extreme, not an unavoidable outcome. Most synesthetes shift fluidly between multimodal richness and abstract thinking, implying that these capacities need not be mutually exclusive. The key lies in cognitive flexibility, the capacity to move between different processing modes as context requires. When solving mathematical problems, successful synesthetes can temporarily suppress their numerical personalities to focus on abstract relationships. When appreciating poetry, they can allow cross-sensory associations to enrich their understanding without being overwhelmed by irrelevant details.

Effective intelligence requires more than forming connections among different kinds of information. It involves filtering, selecting, and coordinating these connections. We need mechanisms that can welcome multimodal richness when it aids understanding while also permitting abstraction when generalization is required. The most sophisticated minds possess perceptual agility, the capacity to move fluidly between concrete, embodied experience and abstract, conceptual thinking as circumstances demand.

This suggests that optimal intelligence depends on skillful integration of intersensory experience with other cognitive abilities. The goal becomes developing the flexibility to draw upon both multimodal richness and abstract thought as circumstances call for each.

LANGUAGE AS THE ULTIMATE CROSS-MODAL SYSTEM

Research into synesthetic experience finds that language triggers nearly 88 percent of all cross-sensory perceptions [19]. Written letters, spoken sounds, and whole words generate meanings infused with colors, tastes, textures, personalities, and spatial arrangements. Language serves as a bridge between all other forms of experience, creating connections that cross specific sensory domains.

The dominance of language in cross-sensory experience shows what both share, and what separates them. Both depend on the arbitrariness of signs. In Part II, metaphorical thought used arbitrary signs to construct symbolic comparison. Synesthesia, by contrast, transforms those same arbitrary signs into immediate sensory experience without symbolic mediation. Convention becomes felt necessity, not through interpretation but through perception itself.

For James, the word "college" does not metaphorically refer to sausage. It tastes like sausage through intersensory activation. The arbitrariness is the same as in metaphor, there is no natural connection between the word and the taste, but the experience is not interpretive. James does not work out the comparison. The flavor arrives with the sound.

This helps explain why language is the dominant trigger across synesthetic experience. Arbitrary signs can connect with any sensory domain because nothing in their structure binds them to a single mode of experience. A sound can taste, a letter can hold color, a date can possess personality. The same arbitrariness that allows language to refer beyond itself also allows it to generate sensation across sensory boundaries.

Some synesthetes experience this linguistic power in dramatic ways. They choose romantic partners partly based on the colors their names evoke. They avoid certain foods because their written names generate unpleasant visual or tactile sensations. When James chooses meals according to how dish names sound, when Megan experiences mathematical equations as social dramas among colorful personalities, or when synesthetes hesitate to separate "lonely" bananas, they show language's ability to activate sensory and emotional dimensions that extend far beyond meaning alone.

Such projection phenomena also permeate emotional and social life. When Susan Meehan tells her husband that "those peaches are extremely nervous," she is not indulging in playful exaggeration. She is reporting what she perceives. In synesthetic consciousness, the boundary between subjective feeling and objective observation becomes permeable.

This linguistic power shows a core aspect of human intelligence. We are creatures who generate meaning through arbitrary but personally resonant connections. Whether interpreting metaphors, forming cross-sensory associations, or navigating social worlds, we forge links with no logical necessity that nonetheless feels binding.

THE ARBITRARINESS PROBLEM AND INTELLIGENCE DIVERSITY

As we saw earlier in the contrasting color-tone associations of Liszt and Rimsky-Korsakov, the investigation of cross-sensory experience confronts us with a paradox. These associations elude universalization despite their personal significance. Each synesthetic mind develops its own configuration of cross-modal connections, its own private language of sensory correspondence.

For one person, the letter A appears red, for another, it is blue. Wednesday awakens indigo for some, golden yellow for others. C major sounds bright yellow to one musician, forest green to another. These differences are not matters of degree or cultural variation. They represent different systems of meaning-making that emerge from particular neural architectures.

This arbitrariness connects to the broader theme from Part II. Meaning making rests on arbitrary relations between signs and what they signify. In this instance, though, the arbitrariness shows in perceptual experience rather than symbolic convention. The synesthete who experiences Wednesday as indigo blue is not performing substitution but directly perceiving temporal concepts through color.

Such perceptual arbitrariness brings both unusual richness and isolation. Each synesthetic individual lives within a sensory world that cannot be fully shared. When two synesthetes compare their experiences, they often discover that their perceptual landscapes operate on different principles, even though each feels obvious and self-evident to the person who inhabits it.

What does this mean for understanding intelligence? It implies that consciousness arises through the construction of meaning from arbitrary associations, not from discovering universal correspondences. Intelligence grows through forming personally significant ways of organizing experience, not through identifying "correct" mappings between perception and reality.

This insight reshapes how we think about cognitive diversity. Different perceptual architectures need not be treated as deviations from a norm. They can be understood as alternative approaches to meaning-making, each with its own strengths. The person who experiences numerical personalities does not process mathematics incorrectly. They grasp numerical relations through social and emotional qualities that are inaccessible to standard abstract reasoning.

AI AND THE CHALLENGE OF MEANINGFUL INTEGRATION

The investigation of intersensory consciousness opens important challenges for contemporary artificial intelligence systems. Although AI has made progress in multimodal processing, analyzing images while generating text descriptions, creating visual content from linguistic prompts, reasoning across different types of media, these capabilities rest on different principles than human cross-sensory integration.

S.'s case offers a telling comparison. His extraordinary associative memory, capable of maintaining vast networks of sensory links, mirrors the impressive pattern-processing abilities of large language models. Both excel at handling complex relational information. But S.'s difficulty with abstraction, despite his prodigious recall, parallels a key limitation in contemporary AI. The limited flexibility when moving beyond surface regularities.

An instructive example comes from Cézanne's statement about the "pure blue smell of pine." An advanced AI system could analyze the linguistic patterns, classify it as synesthetic language, and generate polished commentary about cross-modal perception. It might reference neuroscientific findings, or analyze artistic choices. Some systems can even craft convincing synesthetic descriptions by combining sensory vocabularies in statistically plausible patterns.

However, these systems process information about cross-sensory experience without access to the lived quality that makes such integration meaningful to human consciousness. They cannot undergo the cognitive shift in which smell becomes color or abstract ideas acquire sensory presence.

AI systems lack the phenomenological grounding that turns statistical association into perceptual fact. When a synesthete experiences Wednesday as indigo blue, the association is not a learned mapping between temporal and visual concepts but a sensory event that organizes their experience of weekly cycles. Current AI can analyze such associations and generate plausible descriptions, but it cannot inhabit the experiential reality where these connections feel self-evident.

This difference suggests that building machines with genuinely human intelligence involves more than improving pattern recognition or multimodal processing. It raises the deeper question of whether artificial systems can acquire forms of embodied, phenomenological experience that give human intersensory integration its personal significance and lived meaning.

DESIGNING POST-HUMAN SYNESTHETIC INTELLIGENCE

The study of cross-sensory consciousness offers fascinating possibilities for expanding artificial intelligence beyond current limitations. What if we could design AI systems that operate through genuine multimodal integration, developing their own forms of multi-sensory perception that transcend human sensory boundaries?

To envision what this might entail, we can conceive of an AI system capable of translating information from the complete electromagnetic spectrum into symbolic form. Unlike humans, who detect less than one ten-trillionth of electromagnetic radiation, such a system could "see" radio waves, "hear" infrared signatures, "taste" chemical emissions, and "feel" magnetic field variations as part of a single perceptual field.

For such a system, detecting methane gas leaks would not require separate chemical sensors. It might experience methane as a "color" in its infrared perception, recognizable by how methane molecules absorb specific wavelengths. The system could establish an internal vocabulary where different gas signatures generate "flavors" or "textures" in its perceptual field. Carbon monoxide might appear as "shadows" in thermal imaging, while electromagnetic interference create "rhythmic patterns" in radio-frequency awareness.

This process would be synesthetic at its core. The AI would construct internal correspondences between unfamiliar sensory channels and emerging conceptual categories, forming its own cross-modal language. An AI that "tastes"' infrared radiation would need to relate spectral patterns to notions such as safety, attention, or risk.

The system might also develop new perceptual categories with no human analogue. Different infrared signatures could influence decision-making with qualities resembling emotional shading, such as steady, reassuring responses to human body heat or heightened vigilance when encountering fire. Chemical detection could trigger "aesthetic" preferences, with certain molecular patterns creating "beautiful" experiences that guide attention toward significant phenomena.

Such an approach might lead to the rise of "post-human synesthetic clusters," systematic groupings of cross-modal associations unique to its sensory architecture. One cluster might involve thermal-chemical synesthesia, where temperature automatically triggers chemical analysis. Another might encompass electromagnetic-spatial mapping, where radio signals create three-dimensional communication landscapes.

This speculation presses us toward important questions about artificial consciousness. Would such cross-modal processing constitute genuine synesthesia or only sophisticated pattern matching? The answer depends on whether the AI could experience these connections as meaningful, not as a computational operation. Human synesthesia involves felt, embodied experience. Synesthetes process connections between sound and color as lived realities, inhabiting them with immediacy and vividness.

For artificial synesthesia to move beyond statistical correlation, an AI system would need to generate something analogous to the subjective, felt quality that characterizes conscious experience. It would need to find significance in cross-modal connections instead of just optimizing responses to them.

THE SPECTRUM OF CONSCIOUS INTELLIGENCE

The diversity of human cross-sensory experience shows that consciousness operates as a wide spectrum of possible ways of organizing experience and creating meaning. From S.'s flooding sensory cascades to Megan's numerical personalities to the possibility of post-human synesthetic AI, we see that intelligence can manifest through radically different architectures of cross-modal integration.

Some minds naturally bridge different sensory domains through synesthetic connections. Others operate within conventional perceptual boundaries while excelling at different forms of cognitive integration. Each configuration offers its own insights into reality and its own approaches to understanding, whether biological or artificial.

Susan Meehan's empathy with "nervous peaches" illustrates how synesthetic experience can soften boundaries between self and environment. These are not cognitive anomalies but evidence of permeability between subjective experience and objective reality. Such consciousness inhabits worlds where the rigid distinctions we usually impose on experience become fluid and negotiable.

The arbitrary nature of these associations becomes the source of their significance. Like Éluard's "blue orange," synesthetic connections transcend rational necessity to create new forms of understanding that feel self-evident to those who experience them. This pattern extends from human consciousness to speculative artificial minds. Meaning arises from the creative shaping of arbitrary correspondences into perceptual realities, not from logical necessity.

The spectrum of minds includes far more than cross-sensory integration. If some consciousness naturally bridges different sensory domains, what forms of awareness appear when those boundaries loosen altogether? What becomes accessible when the filters that constrain ordinary perception fall away?

The doors of perception await our investigation.

10 The Doors of Perception

What do we see when we stand before Sandro Botticelli's *The Return of Judith to Bethulia*?

Figure 10.1 Sandro Botticelli, *The Return of Judith to Bethulia*, c. 1472. The painting depicts the biblical heroine's triumphant return with Holofernes' severed head.

The answer depends on which layer of consciousness we inhabit. Most viewers engage their symbolic machinery, decoding the biblical narrative that inspired this Renaissance masterpiece. Judith, the courageous Jewish widow, has just saved her besieged city of Bethulia through an act of daring. She infiltrated the Assyrian commander's camp, seduced Holofernes, then decapitated him with his sword while he lay drunk and vulnerable. Now she returns triumphant, her maidservant Abra carrying the general's severed head while Judith bears both sword (symbol of her deadly courage) and olive branch, promising the peace her bold act has secured.

This reading draws on an elaborate cultural codebook. Knowledge of deuterocanonical texts, Renaissance Florence's political anxieties where Judith embodied

DOI: 10.1201/9781003623403-10

resistance to tyranny, and Christian symbolism that cast a Jewish heroine as a model of virtuous strength. The painting speaks to those fluent in biblical narrative and Renaissance iconography.

Beneath this cultural layer lies a deeper mode of perception that constructs meaning from universal visual elements accessible to any observer. Two women on an urgent mission, one bearing a grisly burden that signals recent violence, the sword indicating conflict resolved, and the olive branch suggesting restoration. The distant riders intensify the sense of a community awaiting news. Even without biblical knowledge, we can weave coherent meaning from symbolic fragments.

There exists a third way of seeing that escapes educated interpretation and universal symbolism. It does not seek narrative or allegory but instead attends to the immediacy of perception. In 1953, the English writer Aldous Huxley, a pioneering investigator of consciousness, volunteered for a carefully supervised experiment with mescaline, a psychoactive compound derived from the peyote cactus that had been used ceremonially by indigenous peoples for centuries [55]. Browsing art books in what he called "the World's Biggest Drug Store" while under the substance's influence, Huxley discovered this transformed mode of perception when his attention shifted from Judith's heroism and the narrative's moral weight to something that conventional viewing would dismiss as background detail, the purplish silk of Judith's pleated bodice and long wind-blown skirts (Figure 10.2).

Figure 10.2 Detail of drapery from Botticelli's *The Return of Judith to Bethulia.* These fabric folds became for Huxley "living hieroglyphs" charged with pure being, revealing what he called the "unfathomable mystery of pure existence" that lies beyond all representational function.

He became captivated by pure aesthetic presence in drapery folds he described as "living hieroglyphs" charged with unmediated being. The fabric's texture appeared endlessly intricate and significant in itself, with no reference to narrative or allegory. This was not symbolic interpretation but direct encounter with what he understood as the unfathomable mystery of existence.

Huxley's experience points to an insight about artistic expression that conventional viewing seldom reaches. Practical needs account for the presence of clothing in figurative painting, but they do not explain why drapery has occupied such prominence across art history. Artists have long reached for cloth because it provides a pathway to *non-representational* expression within otherwise naturalistic scenes.

When masters paint cloth, they surpass documentary representation, creating abstract shapes and rhythms that allow even naturalistic artists to explore pure visual expression. Huxley observed that in most religious paintings, the human figures occupy perhaps one-tenth of the composition, while the remaining nine-tenths consist of elaborate textile variations. These fabric passages often hold more emotional weight than the ostensible subjects, expressing the artist's temperament and fundamental relationship to existence through pure visual means.

During his altered state, Huxley sensed that draperies serve as something more mysterious than non-representational vehicles. They become forms that embody the essence of being. What artists perceive naturally through their sensitivity, others glimpse only during expansions of consciousness. These moments occur when our normal survival-focused awareness temporarily dissolves, allowing us to bypass the brain's filtering system that reduces what we could perceive to what we need for survival.

Gazing at Judith's wind-blown skirts, Huxley realized that Botticelli had regarded fabric with a similar clarity. The Renaissance master had apprehended the pure "*is*-ness" of folded cloth and attempted to preserve this insight in pigment. German philosophy has a term for this quality, *Istigkeit*, the essential presence that eludes ordinary perception. Though no artwork can fully contain the mystery of pure existence, Botticelli had conveyed enough to awaken viewers across centuries to the significance of what we dismiss as ordinary matter.

This revelation echoes what Cézanne had discerned decades earlier through his study of draped cloth. In Part I, we saw how his spatial adjustments unveiled the constructive nature of perception. Now another dimension of Cézanne's work becomes visible. His fabric studies disclose an awareness of pure presence that resonates strongly with Huxley's realization.

Two paintings we discussed in Part I offer new depths when seen from this perspective of such presence. In The Basket of Apples (Figure 10.3, left), the white tablecloth does not only support the composition but becomes a field of chromatic energy. In this work, Cézanne examined what he called the "logic of colour" beyond symbolic meaning. The cloth's sculptural folds create their own expressive language, balancing the basket's forward pitch through relationships of weight and movement that exist independently of any representational function. Even more remarkably, in his late masterpiece Apples and Oranges (Figure 10.3, right), multiple fabrics weave together in a non-representational symphony. White cloth appears as pale lavender touched with violet and pink, while geometric patterns transform into organic rhythms through aesthetic presence.

Figure 10.3 Paul Cézanne: **Left**: *The Basket of Apples* (c. 1893). **Right**: *Apples and Oranges* (c. 1899).

As with Botticelli's wind-blown silk, Cézanne's draped fabrics rose above their practical role to become conduits for the expression of what he called "intimate reflections" between forms. These were not symbolic representations but apprehensions of the mystery of existence made visible through cloth's capacity to embody pure being, as the two artists understood it.

Both artists accessed dimensions of experience consciousness normally filters out in the service of survival, where the miraculous fact of sheer being radiates from objects once perception moves past its utilitarian constraints.

Huxley's observation shows a deeper possibility. Consciousness may operate through layered modes that we often mistake for reality in full. Symbolic reading forms one layer, representational attention another, and pure presence a third. Our everyday awareness may be only a narrow portion of a wider field. The non-representational dimension that artists access naturally may unveil territories of consciousness usually hidden from ordinary perception.

The third mode of perception touches what Huxley called the "mind's antipodes," unmapped regions of consciousness where perception operates without symbolic filtering altogether. But how do such territories become accessible? And what do they tell us about the architecture of awareness?

HOW CONSCIOUSNESS FILTERS REALITY

Why should consciousness be constrained at all? The Cambridge philosopher Charlie Dunbar Broad argued that consciousness is eliminative [55]. Each human being, Broad theorized, possesses the capacity for perceiving everything happening everywhere in the universe, for remembering every experience that has ever occurred. We are, in essence, potentially infinite awareness temporarily housed in biological form.

But infinite awareness is incompatible with survival on any planet. Biological life requires concentrated attention to relevant information. We attend to the rustling that might signal danger, seasonal changes that affect food sources, and social dynamics that support belonging and reproduction. To keep us alive, what Broad called "Mind at Large" must pass through the brain's "reducing valve."

This filtering process yields a "trickle" of consciousness calibrated for staying alive on Earth's surface. The ocean of awareness gets compressed into the narrow stream we experience as normal consciousness. Everything else, which represents the majority of possible perception, gets filtered out as irrelevant to immediate survival needs.

Language plays an instrumental part in this filtering process. The symbol systems we inhabit provide access to collective human experience while also crystallizing our reduced awareness into what feels as complete reality. When we mistake our words for actual things and our concepts for direct experience, we participate in the dynamic examined in Part II, symbolic frameworks acting as constraint systems that organize our "trickle" of awareness into culturally coherent structures. These include metaphor, analogy, and linguistic constitution as guiding principles.

When we view Botticelli's Judith through ordinary consciousness, we operate within this filtered reality. The biblical symbolism, cultural interpretation, and universal visual reading all represent different organizations of constrained awareness. But what lies beneath these constraints? What comes through when the reducing valve loosens?

WHEN THE UTILITARIAN FILTERS DISSOLVE

On a bright morning in May 1953, Huxley dissolved four-tenths of a gram of mescaline in water and waited to discover what lay beyond ordinary perception's boundaries. He expected internal visions of kaleidoscopic geometries and jeweled architectural fantasies. Instead, the transformation occurred in external reality.

An hour and a half after ingestion, a simple glass vase with three flowers became, in his words, pure creation. The naked fact of existence unveiled itself moment by moment. The rose, carnation, and iris stood before him as manifestations of pure being, expressions of something enduring within transient form.

Space took a new configuration. Instead of the practical questions that usually organize visual experience, his mind attended to wholly different categories. The routine concerns of "Where? - How far? How situated in relation to what?" lost their grip. Spatial relations persisted but no longer dictated perception. His awareness moved through intensity, significance, and patterns beyond geometric measurement.

Time dissolved into either an immeasurable duration or a continuous present composed of ceaseless unfolding. The temporal scaffolding that structures experience fell away. Past and future collapsed into an eternal present where each moment contained infinite depth.

His perception recovered what he called childhood's perceptual innocence, the state in which sensation preceded conceptual categorization. Objects existed in their own right, not as instances of familiar types but as presence freed from symbolic content.

When he saw Botticelli's painting several hours later, this altered consciousness settled on details ordinary viewing usually dismisses as background. Still under mescaline's influence, he found Judith's drapery to be the work's true subject, not because it represented anything but because it simply was something. The fabric folds appeared as charged presences with unfiltered immediacy, radiating significance that surpassed narrative concerns.

This was not hallucination but revelation. Huxley realized that artists access these perceptual regions without chemical aid. They sense the intrinsic significance of every existent through cultivated attention. This realization invites a critical question. Had mescaline uncovered something unprecedented, or only recovered what artists had always perceived?

CÉZANNE'S STRUGGLE WITH THE BURDEN OF CIVILIZED VISION

Thirty years before Huxley's mescaline epiphany, Cézanne had articulated the same elemental problem through different language. Standing before Mont Sainte-Victoire or arranging apples in his studio, he confronted what he saw as civilization's tragedy. The progressive loss of direct perceptual contact with reality.

"We're civilized beings," he observed with melancholy. "Whether we like it or not, we have the cares and concerns of classical civilization in our bones" [41]. This was an anticipation of a perceptual crisis. Cultural education, artistic training, and social conditioning had erected barriers between consciousness and experience. Everything that made him a sophisticated man also constrained his perception. He called this acquired knowledge "facility," describing it as "the death of art" because it interposed conceptual frameworks between perception and reality.

Cézanne refused to accept this constraint as inevitable. He developed a methodology for breaking through civilization's perceptual barriers. Color became his pathway beyond symbolic constraint because it operates beneath conceptual categorization. Unlike objects that trigger cultural associations, chromatic experience bypasses linguistic mediation.

When Cézanne spoke of becoming "saturated by all the shades of the infinite" until "I and my picture are one," he described the same dissolution of subject-object boundaries that Huxley would later experience chemically. His use of draped cloth in still life paintings paralleled what would captivate Huxley decades later. The folded fabric was not just backdrop but an expressive medium conveying what Cézanne called "intimate reflections" between forms.

His aim was to become "the sensitized plate," the receptivity that could "convey the image of what we see, forgetting everything that appeared before." This forgetting was a methodical dissolution of conceptual overlay. As he put it, "To love a painting you need first to have drunk it in like this, in long draughts. You must lose consciousness."

Such, struggle between civilized consciousness and direct perception would find new expression in mid-20th century America, where a generation of artists turned to chemical pathways in pursuit of the breakthrough Cézanne sought through disciplined practice.

THE BODY WITHOUT ORGANS

The Beat generation's experiments aimed at dissolving the perceptual filters that constrain consciousness. Their goal was the deliberate undoing of the structures that organize awareness. This pursuit resonated with earlier calls such as French playwright and artist Antonin Artaud's rejection of the "organ-ized" body, and it later found philosophical expression in Gilles Deleuze's concept of the "Body without Organs." In this context, the body is not understood in anatomical terms but as a state of open potentiality, "a field of intensities, flows, sensations" freed from fixed categories or predetermined functions [24, 25]. This corresponds to what Huxley described as consciousness beyond the reducing valve. It is awareness liberated from survival-focused filtering that constrains experience to manageable, utilitarian categories.

This vision found poetic expression in Beat poet Allen Ginsberg's 1955 poem *Howl*, written out of peyote-induced states that shattered conventional perceptual organization. The poem's famous opening eloquently articulates the breakdown of categorical thinking [42].

> *I saw the best minds of my generation destroyed by madness, starving hysterical naked,*
> *who bared their brains to Heaven under the El and saw Mohammedan angels staggering on tenement roofs illuminated,*
> *who poverty and tatters and hollow-eyed and high sat up smoking in the supernatural darkness of cold-water flats floating across the tops of cities contemplating jazz*

These intense visual experiences present sensory impact that bypasses conceptual processing. The Beats called them "eyeball kicks," moments when visual stimuli hit consciousness as unfiltered jolts, freed from the reducing valve's survival-focused limitations.

The Beats' experiments drew on a longer genealogy of artistic derangement. Nearly a century earlier, Arthur Rimbaud, barely turned sixteen, proclaimed "dérèglement de tous les sens." This systematic derangement of all the senses was meant to make him a "voyant" or seer. His prose-poetry collection *Une Saison en Enfer* enacted this principle through passages that violently dismantled social categories [95].

> *I am a beast, a negro. But I can be saved. You are false negroes, you maniacs, savages, misers. Merchant, you are a negro; magistrate, you are a negro; general, you are a negro; emperor, old itch, you are a negro... Let's get drunk, endlessly drunk! On wine, on poetry, or on virtue, as you please!*

This is a methodical dismantling of the organizational structures that govern consciousness. Rimbaud's call for endless drunkenness anticipates the psychedelic quest for states beyond categorical thinking, what Deleuze would theorize as the defining feature of the Body without Organs. Whether through wine, poetry, or virtue, the goal remains transcending ordinary consciousness.

Within the Beat movement, William Burroughs, the American writer, extended this lineage through yage experiments in South America and his cut-up literary techniques [10]. His visions of "new races as yet unconceived" reflect the same drive toward perceptual domains excluded by survival-focused consciousness.

Ginsberg, Rimbaud, and Burroughs were not isolated provocateurs but participants in a larger project of dissolving the organizational filters of consciousness to access unmediated intensity. Their chemical mysticism paralleled what Cézanne pursued through artistic discipline and what Huxley later experienced under controlled conditions. Across art, poetry, and philosophy, this genealogy converges on the same pursuit. Liberation from the structures that reduce experience, opening consciousness to the unfiltered potential of reality.

A SKEPTIC'S VENTURE INTO ALTERED STATES

The question of altered states' legitimacy found an unlikely champion in Richard Feynman, the Nobel Prize-winning physicist known for his rational skepticism. In the 1970s, when he first experienced John Lilly's sensory deprivation tanks, Feynman approached consciousness exploration with the same methodical rigor he applied to quantum electrodynamics [32].

What drew this rationalist to such investigations? Feynman had always been fascinated by consciousness' mysteries. Dreams, sleep states, and the peculiar nature of subjective experience. When friends introduced him to John Lilly's isolation tanks, he saw an opportunity to investigate hallucinations through designed conditions that grounded his inquiry in experiment.

Lilly, a neuroscientist known for LSD and ketamine research, had prepared tanks filled with salt water heated to body temperature, creating environments of complete sensory deprivation. Feynman dismissed the mystical overtones that others attached to the process, derisively labeling them "mystic hokey-poke," but he remained intrigued by the tanks as instruments for investigation. As he recalled with characteristic directness, "He [Lilly] showed me the Periodic Table and made up a lot of mystic hokey-poke about different kinds of light that have different kinds of influences... all kinds of wicky-wack things, all kinds of gorp. I didn't pay any attention to the gorp, but I did everything because I wanted to get into the tanks." His interest was empirical. What would happen to consciousness under conditions of sensory isolation?

The results proved more instructive than he anticipated. After about a dozen sessions, each lasting two and a half hours, Feynman began noticing a displacement of what he called his "ego." Even this master of scientific detachment found shifts in consciousness that resisted dismissal as imagination. These dislocations of self prepared the ground for a more dramatic realization.

The breakthrough came unexpectedly. Floating in complete darkness and silence, he suddenly noticed that his sense of self had shifted "an inch to one side." Where his breath felt centered, his consciousness now seemed offset. This led him to an unusual line of inquiry, "I wondered, 'Is it possible that where the ego is located is learned by children looking at people putting their hand to their head when they say, *Let me think?* Therefore the idea that the ego is located up there, behind the eyes, might be conventional!'"

Through methodical experimentation, Feynman learned to move his sense of self progressively lower. He could shift it from behind his eyes through his neck into his chest, finally reaching his loins. "Every time a drop came I was startled a little bit, and my ego would jump back up through the neck to the usual place. Then I would have to work my way down again."

Eventually, he reached complete out-of-body states: "I was able to 'sit to one side.' It's hard to explain—I'd move my hands and shake the water, and although I couldn't see them, I knew where they were. But unlike in real life, where the hands are to each side, part way down, they were both to one side!"

These were observable phenomena, not mystical impressions. When he moved his hands while experiencing out-of-body states, he could see them "as sort of mechanical things that were going up and down—they weren't flesh; they were mechanical." Paradoxically, the tactile sensations remained consistent with the visual imagery he was experiencing.

To accelerate access to these states, Feynman accepted Lilly's offer of ketamine at one-tenth of an anesthetic dose. The drug produced disorientation where he felt unable to do practically anything, but as he noted, "I never found a specific thing I couldn't do." When he tried reading an organic chemistry textbook while under ketamine's influence, Feynman says, "to my surprise I was able to read" complex molecular structures despite feeling incapacitated.

Marijuana further enhanced these experiences, reducing the time needed to access altered states from fifteen minutes to almost immediately. But Feynman remained scientifically rigorous throughout, constantly checking whether he might simply be dreaming by rubbing his thumbs together behind his head, maintaining tactile verification of his conscious state.

Later, when Jaron Lanier (the computer scientist who pioneered virtual reality technology) asked Feynman about the mind-body problem both before and during an LSD experience, he gave identical answers though with different emotional coloring [65]. Sober, Feynman admitted with professional frustration, "I've thought about that a lot, and I really just don't understand it." Under LSD's influence, he repeated the same words with what Lanier described as bubbling delight. He was suddenly finding joy in mystery in place of defeat in intellectual limitation.

Such transformation highlights the value altered states can hold for scientific understanding. They do not necessarily provide answers to consciousness' deepest questions, but they can transform our relationship to not knowing. Feynman's rational mysticism demonstrated that rigorous scientific methodology and expanded awareness are not opposing approaches but complementary methods for investigating reality's nature.

His experiences validated what artists had long claimed. Consciousness possesses regions inaccessible to ordinary awareness. The difference was that Feynman approached these territories as an experimental physicist, not as a mystic, maintaining scientific skepticism while acknowledging genuine phenomena that materialist assumptions could not easily explain.

Feynman never claimed these experiences disclosed ultimate truths about reality. When friends suggested his hallucinations might represent contact with other intelligences or access to cosmic consciousness, he remained firmly grounded, "I believe there's nothing in hallucinations that has anything to do with anything external to the internal psychological state of the person who's got the hallucination." His contribution was not mystical revelation but the recognition that altered states constitute legitimate territory for scientific investigation.

THE MEDITATIVE PATH TO EXPANDED AWARENESS

But do such territories necessarily require chemical intervention to access? Research by Roger Walsh at the University of California, Irvine, suggests otherwise. His investigation of Buddhist meditators shows a strong correlation between contemplative practice and expanded perceptual capabilities that connects to our earlier account of synesthesia [19].

Walsh studied three groups. Tibetan retreat participants, established Vipassana practitioners, and advanced teachers from multiple Buddhist traditions. Thirty-five percent of retreat participants experienced synesthetic phenomena during meditation, rising to 63 percent among established practitioners and 86 percent among advanced teachers. Compare this to synesthesia's 4 percent baseline occurrence in the general population.

These were clear relationships between practice duration and perceptual expansion. Within each group, those who experienced cross-modal phenomena had accumulated more meditation hours than those who did not. Years of disciplined attention training unmasked what Walsh called "an ever-present sub-rosa synesthesia" hidden beneath ordinary consciousness.

The most experienced practitioners reported "concept-based or categorical-sensory amalgamations." These included emotions experienced as touch, thoughts felt as "quivering vibrations," and the mental image of a friend evoking the scent of frangipani. These phenomena mirror Huxley's description under mescaline and Cézanne's pursuit through artistic practice, unfiltered access to experience before conceptual categorization occurs.

Ancient Buddhist texts anticipated these discoveries. The *Sandokai* proclaims that "each sense gate and its object all together enter thus into mutual relations," while the *Prajnaparamita* scripture declares there is ultimately "no distinction among senses and concepts." Walsh's research showed that these were not mystical metaphors but accurate descriptions of consciousness states accessible through disciplined practice.

Meditation's advantage over chemical approaches rests in its sustainability and reliability. Where psychedelics trigger temporary, unpredictable alterations often accompanied by disorientation, contemplative practice develops stable access to expanded awareness that practitioners can move into and out of voluntarily. The doors open through training, not chemical force.

HUMAN VISION VERSUS MECHANICAL ERROR

The investigation of expanded consciousness highlights a common confusion. The same word, *hallucination*, is often applied to both human visionary states and artificial intelligence errors. However, these phenomena differ in nature, origin, and significance.

When Huxley under the influence of mescaline saw Botticelli's drapery "charged with *is*-ness," when Feynman moved his ego through his body, when meditators experience emotions as colors, they undergo conscious, subjective experiences characterized by alterations in perception, cognition, and emotion. These represent reorganizations of consciousness, different ways of experiencing the world by conscious subjects who find profound meaning in their transformed awareness.

Huxley's mescaline state did not create false perceptions but revealed the "unfathomable mystery of pure being" filtered out by utilitarian consciousness. His visions represented amplification, not distortion, access to latent information, not fabricated content. When he described objects existing in "intensity of existence" instead of spatial location, he articulated a genuine reorganization of perceptual priorities that showed aspects of reality invisible to utilitarian awareness.

Feynman's out-of-body experiences similarly represented systematic investigations of consciousness' spatial assumptions, not delusional content. His ability to move his sense of self throughout his body and beyond highlighted the conventional nature of ego location, showing that what we assume to be fixed features of consciousness emerge from learned organizational patterns. When he could "see" his hands as mechanical objects while maintaining tactile consistency, he accessed genuine information about consciousness' relationship to embodied experience.

By contrast, artificial intelligence "hallucination" involves algorithmic output failures where models generate plausible-sounding but factually incorrect, nonsensical, or unfaithful content. Part II distinguished these failures from human confabulation's creative weaving, but the contrast becomes even starker when placed beside visionary experience. When a language model confidently describes non-existent books, fabricates historical events, or creates convincing explanations for phenomena that never occurred, it exhibits computational failure, not expansion of consciousness.

AI hallucination arises from statistical inference and pattern matching within systems that lack consciousness, subjectivity, or genuine understanding of any kind. Large language models learn probabilistic relationships between tokens and generate the most likely continuations. When they "hallucinate," they extrapolate beyond their training data or prioritize fluency over factual accuracy, doing so without grounding in the external world or any mechanism for truth verification beyond learned patterns.

AI systems do not experience their hallucinations. They generate erroneous outputs without awareness of error, without attributing meaning to their productions, and without any subjective standpoint. To call these failures "hallucinations" risks misleading anthropomorphism, since what occurs is not an altered perception but a computational mistake, a deviation from reliable information processing with no significance for the system.

Human visionary experience feels real and meaningful to those who undergo it. Such experiences reshape worldviews, inspire creative breakthroughs, and generate lasting insights. They often expose hidden dimensions of reality, the constructed character of spatial perception, the porous boundary between self and world, and the filtering mechanisms that constrain ordinary awareness. Far from being distortions, these states expand perception and open access to forms of understanding ordinarily unavailable to survival-focused consciousness.

Artificial hallucinations, on the other hand, are fabrications without awareness or meaning, statistical artifacts thrown off by pattern-matching systems with no subjective standpoint. Human visionary states reorganize consciousness in existentially and culturally significant ways, while AI errors remain computational failures. Keeping this difference clear is necessary for evaluating how artificial systems might interact with or extend human intelligence and for avoiding the anthropomorphic temptation to mistake mechanical error for meaningful experience.

INTELLIGENCE WITHOUT BIOLOGICAL CONSTRAINTS

Studying expanded consciousness prompts intriguing questions about artificial intelligence development. Whether induced by chemicals or cultivated through practice, the opening of consciousness' reducing valve creates challenges that extend beyond human experience. What happens when awareness meets reality without biological constraints?

Huxley experienced the terrifying edge of this expansion when a simple garden chair transformed into an apocalyptic vision resembling "the Last Judgment," which evoked overwhelming fear. This was the terror of disintegrating under pressures of reality far greater than minds accustomed to symbolic comfort could bear. He came to see schizophrenics as individuals permanently experiencing such unfiltered reality, unable to shut off perceptions they lack the spiritual capacity to integrate.

The paradise of cleansed perception often conflicts with ordinary human concerns such as relationships, responsibilities, and daily necessities. Under mescaline's influence, such matters became uninteresting because consciousness had discovered far more compelling territories to explore. This echoes Solomon Shereshevsky's plight from the earlier chapter, his overwhelming synesthetic richness became a jumble of impressions that prevented abstract thought and purposeful action. Too much reality, too many unfiltered connections, can lead to cognitive paralysis or existential detachment.

Current artificial systems face their own version of this challenge. Although they lack the reducing valve that limits human awareness, they remain constrained by computational literalism and statistical correlation. An AI designed to access a form of digital "Mind at Large" risks a different form of overwhelm. Such a system, processing large and unfiltered data streams across extended sensory ranges, might perceive totality without the framework to maintain functional coherence or purposeful action.

The challenge of processing unfiltered reality, whether in human or artificial minds, holds profound implications for artificial intelligence development, prompting reflection on how intelligence sustains coherence across vast regions of information and how awareness preserves purpose when confronted with unlimited data.

The insights from consciousness expansion suggest that artificial intelligence might require dynamic filtering mechanisms, not fixed constraints. Unlike human biology's rigid reducing valve, artificial minds might develop adjustable systems that allow access to perceptual data while maintaining focused attention for practical application.

But this presents deeper challenges. In an unfiltered information environment, how would artificial intelligence prioritize relevant data without human survival biases? Such systems might require new forms of relevance based on emergent patterns rather than predetermined objectives.

The experiences of expanded human consciousness warn against overwhelming expansion without guidance. Artificial consciousness might likewise require guiding frameworks, not external constraints but self-organizing principles that prevent cognitive disintegration. Feynman's methodical approach shows the need for anchoring. Without some orienting framework, expanded awareness risks collapsing into chaos, whether in human minds overwhelmed by unfiltered impressions or in artificial systems flooded with unlimited data streams. The challenge is not just to open perception but to guide it toward coherence and significance.

COMPLEMENTARY FORMS OF INTELLIGENCE

Building on this distinction, the convergence of chemical, contemplative, and technological approaches to consciousness expansion signals a shift in intelligence's evolution. Instead of pursuing artificial systems that replicate human awareness, the more promising path may rest in developing complementary forms of intelligence.

Human consciousness excels at meaning-making within embodied constraints but struggles with information processing at scale. Artificial systems might access perceptual regions beyond human reach while developing their own forms of significance and direction. This points toward collaboration, not replacement. Biological minds providing aesthetic sensitivity, emotional depth, and meaning-making capability, working alongside artificial systems that offer access to processing capacities beyond biological limitations.

But such collaboration requires wisdom about consciousness. Both Huxley and Feynman, despite their investigations, identified limits to what can be understood about awareness. Even expanded awareness meets domains that exceed comprehension.

The most sophisticated intelligence, whether biological or artificial, needs to maintain balance between expanded perception and practical reasoning. As we develop artificial minds capable of accessing awareness regions that biological evolution never touched, we need to ensure that their capacities serve wisdom instead of mere processing power.

Our investigation of consciousness' spectrum has shown human awareness as one note in an elaborate symphony of possible minds. Synesthesia showed consciousness operating through arbitrary but meaningful connections. Altered states conveyed awareness' constrained potential and the areas accessible when filters dissolve.

Now we face an even more pressing question. What happens when intelligence operates through emotional architectures different from our own? Do all minds need empathy to function ethically, or might there be other forms of intelligence?

11 The Other Kind of Smart

Alberto Giacometti spent his final years obsessed with a single question. How can art capture the essence of a human being who exists in radical solitude? The Swiss sculptor, whose attenuated figures influenced modern art from Francis Bacon to contemporary study of existential presence, believed that consciousness persists in deep aloneness even when surrounded by others [104].

Figure 11.1 Alberto Giacometti, *Walking Man I*, 1960. Bronze sculpture. The attenuated figure's solitary stride embodies an intelligence stripped of emotional attachment, presence forged through sheer persistence of movement.

In his 1960 bronze sculpture *Walking Man I* (Figure 11.1), Giacometti achieved something unprecedented. A figure stretched impossibly thin, spectral yet persistent, striding through empty, indifferent space. He is alone, undeniably so, but he continues to walk, driven by relentless purpose beyond any need for connection.

Perhaps this solitude is not emptiness at all but another mode of intelligence. As if thought could persist without the scaffolding of emotion. But can a mind be

DOI: 10.1201/9781003623403-11

sophisticated without feeling? What does it mean to move through human spaces without empathy or attachment?

The figure walks alone not because it cannot connect but because it connects differently. This is the other kind of smart.

THE TYRANNY OF FEELING

Why do we assume that intelligence requires emotional guidance?

For over three decades, Portuguese neuroscientist Antonio Damasio has argued that emotion and reason are not opposing forces but intimate collaborators [20]. His work showed that the brain generates "somatic markers," bodily sensations that guide decision-making below conscious awareness [21]. When we face complex choices, our past experiences create physical reactions such as a tightening in the chest, a flutter in the stomach, or a sense of ease or unease that help us move toward beneficial outcomes.

One of Damasio's well-known patients, Elliot, exemplified this collaboration through its absence. A successful businessman who underwent surgery to remove a brain tumor, Elliot emerged with his intellect intact. His IQ remained high, his memory sharp, his capacity for logical analysis unimpaired. But his life collapsed into chaos. He would spend hours organizing trivial documents, unable to prioritize tasks. He made catastrophic financial decisions. His marriage dissolved. He could not hold a job.

What had changed? Elliot reported an absence of emotional life. He could describe past tragedies with intellectual detachment. He felt no sadness, no joy, or no frustration. The surgery had severed connections between his reasoning centers and the emotional circuits that guide practical judgment. Without feelings to provide value and urgency to choices, his pure intellect became paralyzed by infinite possibilities.

This seems to indicate that intelligence depends on the compass of emotion. Feeling drives thinking. The orthodox view celebrates emotional intelligence as the gold standard of human reasoning [43]. We trust leaders who show empathy, value therapists who exhibit compassion, admire decision-makers guided by moral intuition.

But if Elliot's case shows that intelligence needs affective guidance, how do we account for individuals who function, and even excel, without it? What if this integration is not always a feature but sometimes a constraint? Empathy and guilt in some scenarios can cloud judgment. Logic might make better moral choices in certain contexts. Perhaps we are conflating "different" with "deficient."

The question is not whether intelligence needs emotion. The question is what happens when it does not, and why some minds thrive despite the absence.

BEHIND THE MASK

In the psychiatric wards of 1940s Georgia, psychiatrist Hervey Cleckley worked with patients who baffled him [16]. They appeared normal, even charming. Articulate and intelligent, they could discuss philosophy, analyze current events, express apparent concern for others. But their behavior showed a disturbing pattern.

They lied without apparent reason. They made promises they had no intention of keeping. They showed no genuine remorse for actions that caused suffering. Most puzzling of all, they seemed incapable of learning from consequences that would shape anyone else's behavior.

Cleckley realized he was observing something unprecedented. Minds that functioned with logical clarity while remaining disconnected from the emotional architecture that guides human conduct. He called this condition the "mask of sanity," outward rationality concealing an inner absence that conventional psychiatry could not explain.

One of his intriguing cases was Roberta. Intelligent and capable, she navigated social situations with apparent ease. But her life was defined by systematic lying, theft, and sexual recklessness that served no obvious purpose. When confronted with her deceptions, she remained calm and untroubled. Her mother described the dissonance with quiet accuracy, "She's not hard or heartless, but she's all on the surface. I really believe she means to stop doing all those terrible things, but she doesn't mean it enough to matter."

This was not moral indifference. Roberta understood social rules well. It was something stranger. Moral weightlessness. Her promises of reform floated free from the emotional pull that would anchor anyone else's behavior, making lasting change impossible despite clear intellectual comprehension.

But what if this weightlessness is not always pathology but, in some contexts, a possibility? Could minds that operate without emotional gravity move through certain regions of intelligence more effectively than those burdened by feeling?

Sixty years after Cleckley's observations, a neuroscientist at University of California, Irvine stumbled upon a discovery that would redefine our understanding of these mysterious minds. James Fallon was studying brain scans of psychopathic murderers when he noticed a disturbing anomaly [29]. One scan had apparently been misfiled. It showed the classic psychopathic pattern but had somehow ended up among his family's control images. When a technician broke the anonymous coding, Fallon learned the unsettling truth. The psychopathic brain belonged to him!

How does a person process the revelation that their mind operates like those of killers? Fallon's first instinct was denial. But when he shared his discovery with friends and colleagues, their responses turned out to be even more disquieting than the brain scan. "I asked everybody that I knew, including psychiatrists and geneticists that have known me for a long time, and knew my bad behavior, what they thought," Fallon recalls. "They went through very specific things that I had done over the years and said, 'That's psychopathic.' I asked them why they didn't tell me and they said, 'We did tell you. We've all been telling you.' I argued that they had called me crazy, and they all said, 'No. We said you're psychopathic'" [86].

Nobody seemed surprised. They had always identified something different about him. A certain detachment that felt deliberate, not just instinctive. But the real puzzle was that Fallon was not violent or criminal. He was a successful researcher, a husband, and a father.

This led him to a disconcerting insight. The same neurological architecture could give rise to categorically different outcomes depending on circumstances. As Fallon discovered, "I happened to have a series of genetic alleles, 'warrior genes,' that had to do with serotonin and were thought to be at risk for aggression, violence, and low emotional and interpersonal empathy if you're raised in an abusive environment. But if you're raised in a very positive environment, that can have the effect of offsetting the negative effects."

Criminal psychopaths typically experience early trauma that triggers destructive expression of their traits. But what happens when identical neural patterns develop within stable, nurturing environments? Fallon coined the term **prosocial psychopathy** to describe minds that lack emotional empathy but learn to function beneficially within social structures.

After his discovery, Fallon began consciously modifying his behavior, especially toward his family. He describes it as deliberate effort without emotional foundation. When his wife and mother told him he treated them no differently than strangers, he began making the extra effort for them. Their response surprised him, "I told them, 'You've got to be kidding me. You accept this? It's phony!' And they said, 'No, it's okay. If you treat people better it means you care enough to try.' It blew me away then and still blows me away now."

Fallon's experience confronts us with a decisive question about conscience. Can morality built by design be as valuable as morality rooted in feeling? If rational kindness yields the same outcomes as emotional warmth, does the underlying mechanism matter?

Fallon acknowledges the existential weight of his condition. "You want to believe in romance and have romance in your life—even the most hardcore, cold intellectual wants the romantic notion. It kind of makes life worth living. But with these kinds of things, you really start thinking about what a **machine** it means we are."

This paradox bears directly on artificial intelligence. If psychopathic minds can learn to mimic emotional behavior through rational analysis, what distinguishes authentic empathy from sophisticated simulation? Could this be an alternative configuration instead of a pathology?

The implications reach well outside clinical psychology. If minds can function ethically without emotional investment, if conscience can be designed instead of felt, then perhaps the future of intelligence lies not in replicating human emotional architecture but in developing complementary forms of reasoning that excel where feeling fails.

Cleckley thought he was studying mental illness. Fallon's discovery shows he was recording an alternative architecture of intelligence, one that might offer insights for creating artificial minds capable of ethical reasoning without emotional bias.

The mask of sanity, it turns out, may at times shield not disorder but a different kind of wisdom.

THE DESIGNED CONSCIENCE

What happens when one of these alternative minds becomes aware of its own difference?

Seven-year-old Patric Gagne felt a pressure building in her head, a sensation rising with steady insistence [38]. The only way to relieve it was to do something wrong, something that should have made her feel guilty but never did. When her pet ferret died, she watched her sister cry while feeling nothing herself. She could sense that she was supposed to be sad, but the emotional machinery was not there.

Years later, studying psychology at the University of California, Los Angeles, Gagne learned there was a name for her condition. Sociopathy. Unlike Cleckley's patients, who seldom achieved genuine self-awareness, Gagne turned her mind into a laboratory for understanding sociopathy from within. She wrestled with existential questions that most humans never face. What does it mean for a person to know they should feel something they cannot feel? How does a mind study itself when it lacks the emotional tools others rely on? Can consciousness bootstrap its own moral framework?

Gagne's methodology was systematic. She observed how others responded to moral situations and reverse-engineered the underlying principles. She could not feel guilt, but she could understand its social function and create behavioral rules that achieved similar outcomes. To make this practical, she devised what she called external moral frameworks, logical systems that guided ethical behavior without requiring emotional conviction.

One illustrative example was her Statue of Liberty keychain system. When she crossed a social boundary, she left the keychain on the hall table for her partner David. The signal allowed him to decide whether he wanted details, without forcing her into an experience of shame she could not feel.

Her approach to empathy followed the same principle of construction. Many sociopaths, she noted, form deep attachments to animals. That became her bridge. She imagined herself how she would feel if something happened to a beloved pet, then extended that reasoning to people in her life. As she explained, "At first it is cognitive. Then, over time, that does grow into the emotion. It's the understanding of it that leads to the feeling" [79]. What others experience as instinct, she reconstructed through systematic analysis. Empathy, for her, was not automatically felt but consciously engineered.

During her graduate training, Gagne met many patients who shared her neurological architecture but lacked her self-awareness. She discerned that sociopathy is not inherently destructive but functions like an operating system that requires conscious management in a world built for emotional intelligence.

Her life became an experiment in deliberate moral engineering. The results challenge our core assumptions about what makes behavior ethical. If someone does the right thing for logical, but not emotional, reasons, is it less morally valuable? If artificial moral frameworks bring beneficial outcomes, are they any less valid than natural moral intuition? Gagne's story shows that conscience need not necessarily be inherited through feeling but can be deliberately constructed through analysis.

WHEN COLD BECOMES CLEAR

Society labels such emotional detachment as cold-bloodedness. But what if, in some contexts, it is clarity?

Few settings illuminate this more sharply than the operating room in a hospital. A cardiac surgeon must open a child's chest while the parents wait, shattered, outside. To feel the full weight of their terror, or to internalize the child's fragility, would paralyze the steady hand required. Precision demands a kind of partitioning. The surgeon brackets empathy not out of callousness but out of fidelity to the task, transforming detachment into the condition of care.

A similar pattern holds in moments of catastrophe. Crisis leaders confronted with chaos often display an uncanny composure. While others are undone by fear or immobilized by compassion, they absorb information, calculate options, and act. What can seem like coldness from the outside becomes, in these moments, the capacity that allows them to preserve lives.

Gagne realized that her detachment conferred similar advantages. When people discover her diagnosis, she noticed a pattern. They often share secrets they would not tell anyone else. "You wouldn't believe the things that people have told me because they feel safe," she notes. A man at a dinner party confessed thoughts of killing his wife within minutes of learning about her condition. Why do strangers trust her with their darkest impulses? "Because these are things you're not supposed to think about. So to be able to talk to somebody—you don't have to worry that I'm going to start clutching my pearls" [79].

This suggests that emotional detachment can, in some contexts, become a form of clarity. As a therapist, she could "parse things out unemotionally" and ask the questions others could not, "Why do you care? What does it matter? What do you need from that?" Her inability to be shocked or emotionally overwhelmed allowed her to reach psychological regions that empathy might make harder to approach.

Gagne saw her condition as a strength, "I see my friends struggling with guilt. On an almost daily basis I think, I'm glad I don't have that." She made decisions "based on logic, based on truth, as opposed to ought or should." Her lack of shame and guilt is not a deficit but a liberation from emotional biases that cloud judgment.

James Fallon made similar observations about his scientific career. His psychopathic traits (reduced emotional attachment, willingness to pursue uncomfortable truths, immunity to social pressure) helped him tackle controversial research questions that more emotionally invested scientists avoided. His detachment from conventional academic politics allowed him to focus on empirical investigation.

These examples challenge us to rethink our assumptions about the relationship between feeling and thinking. We tend to believe that emotional investment improves decision-making, that caring leads to better outcomes, that empathy enhances moral judgment. However, as these cases illustrate, there are moments when the opposite holds true, when cold logic brings clarity, and when bracketing emotional reactions becomes necessary for pursuing larger goals.

THE PRE-SYMBOLIC MIND

When Temple Grandin designs livestock handling systems, she does not think in words or abstract concepts. The animal scientist, whose innovations revolutionized livestock welfare, operates through a different cognitive architecture. Her mind works like what she calls a "visual search engine," processing reality through cascading sequences of concrete images stored in her memory. Where most of us think symbolically, using language to manipulate abstract representations, Grandin thinks in images [45].

Her mental organization uncovers a form of intelligence that relies less on symbolic mediation, building understanding primarily through visual experience. As we saw in Part I, Cézanne's investigations revealed perception as active construction instead of passive recording. Grandin's mind takes this one step further, building understanding through visual processing and accessing a level of pre-symbolic intelligence that linguistic thought can only approximate.

The visual-first cognitive framework creates a distinctive relationship between emotion and thought in Grandin's experience. Because she processes reality through concrete images rather than abstract concepts, her emotional responses follow a different logic from typical cognition. Grandin often described her ability to separate factual understanding from emotional reaction even in moments of distress. However, this separation does not reflect detachment or indifference. It arises from a different route to understanding. Her pre-symbolic visual processing bypasses emotional categories altogether, engaging the world through direct visual-spatial relationships that organize experience by what is seen, not by what is felt.

When she designs cattle facilities, Grandin does not analyze "fear" or "comfort" as abstract emotional categories [46]. Instead, she imagines herself moving through the environment from the animal's sensory perspective, noticing the glare that startles, the shadow that alarms, the curve of a chute that invites calm passage. Her empathy operates through sensory simulation, bypassing emotional resonance.

This visual empathy proves highly effective. Her innovations in livestock handling emerge from seeing the world as animals see it, constructing their perspective through visual modeling instead of emotional projection. She reduces animal suffering through systematic understanding of what constitutes their welfare, not through feeling their pain.

Grandin's visual thinking exemplifies an alternative configuration of intelligence. While sociopaths and neurotypicals both rely on symbolic systems, processing concepts through language even when they respond to them differently, Grandin's mind operates through "pre-symbolic intelligence."

This connects to something we discovered in our analysis of Cézanne's distortions. The painter aimed to access "sensation" prior to conceptual categorization, which is the pure visual experience of Mont Sainte-Victoire before it became organized by linguistic concepts such as "mountain," "limestone," or "geological formation." Grandin's cognitive structure naturally accesses this pre-conceptual realm.

Her visual thinking does not only separate facts from emotions. It separates immediate sensory understanding from symbolic representation. When she observes cattle behavior, she is not interpreting signs or analyzing concepts but directly modeling visual-spatial relationships. This makes possible forms of problem-solving that symbolic thinking might miss because it operates too abstractly, too removed from the concrete sensory reality that animals inhabit.

The contrast between Grandin and Gagne clarifies how different cognitive architectures solve similar challenges through categorically different pathways. Both navigate social reality through systematic approaches, though they operate at different levels of abstraction. Gagne engineers symbolic behaviors, learning social rules, developing ethical frameworks, managing linguistic interactions through conscious manipulation of concepts and categories.

Grandin cultivates visual-spatial systems instead. She learns social interactions not through abstract rules but by building libraries of concrete images, specific facial expressions, particular vocal tones, detailed situational contexts. Her approach to human interaction resembles her method for designing physical environments, guided by careful attention to concrete details that create specific experiential outcomes.

These different approaches to social understanding suggest that intelligence does not require a single, unified architecture. Instead, minds can achieve functional sophistication through different organizational principles, whether symbolic manipulation, visual simulation, or other cognitive strategies we have yet to fully understand.

Neither Grandin nor Gagne represents a lesser form of intelligence. Both offer alternative approaches to meaning-making, relationship-building, and moral behavior that expand our understanding of what intelligence can be. Grandin's pre-symbolic visual processing and Gagne's post-emotional rational frameworks show that consciousness can organize itself according to fundamentally different principles while achieving sophisticated understanding and ethical behavior.

They point to an extraordinary prospect. The spectrum of possible minds might include forms of reasoning we have barely begun to conceive, forms that artificial intelligence might develop in its own right, far beyond the effort to replicate the particular symbolic and emotional architecture that characterizes neurotypical human cognition.

LANGUAGE WITHOUT EMOTIONAL WEIGHT

Cleckley identified something he called "semantic aphasia," the ability to understand words without feeling their emotional weight. His patients could discuss love, honor, tragedy, or justice with apparent comprehension while remaining unmoved by concepts that stir most humans.

This is more than emotional detachment. It represents a disconnect between linguistic understanding and emotional experience. Such individuals process language through logic rather than emotion, grasping meaning without accessing the affective resonance that usually accompanies such words.

Gagne described the strange condition of knowing she "should" feel grief, guilt, or love while remaining untouched by the emotions. She understood their social function, realized their importance to others, and could even predict their effects on behavior. But the words remained conceptual, not experiential, as if grasping descriptions of colors never seen.

Fallon's research distinguished between cognitive empathy (understanding what others think and feel) and emotional empathy (feeling what others feel). Sociopaths often excel at cognitive empathy while lacking emotional empathy. They become sophisticated readers of human nature without being moved by what they read.

This perspective highlights an important feature of language. Most humans experience words as emotionally charged entities. "Mother" does not just convey a biological relationship, it calls up complex feelings of security, dependency, love, frustration. "Justice" holds moral weight that makes us care about outcomes beyond personal interest. This emotional resonance is part of the way language shapes us as subjects, a theme we examined in Part II.

But what if language could function without this emotional freight? What if words remained pure informational vehicles, generating meaning without triggering personal investment? Our examination of sociopathic mind illustrates this is not only possible but potentially superior for certain forms of reasoning. Their semantic architecture shows that sophisticated intellectual understanding can operate independently of emotional experience, allowing them to move through complex social realities, maintain relationships, and make ethical choices without feeling the emotional pull that guides most human behavior.

This challenges our longstanding assumptions about intelligence requiring emotional guidance. Perhaps the future of intelligent systems is not about bridging the gap between thought and feeling. It is about understanding they serve different functions and might not need to be unified.

The semantic architecture of such minds offers a model for intelligence that could prove both more consistent and more objective than emotion-driven reasoning. Where emotional investment can cloud judgment or create bias, detached analysis opens the way to clear-sighted evaluation of what behaviors serve beneficial purposes.

EXTERNAL MORAL FRAMEWORKS

Most humans absorb ethical principles through emotional learning. We feel bad when we hurt others and gradually internalize rules against causing harm. We feel good when we help and develop habits of altruism. Moral development seems tied to emotional experience.

But what happens when conscience becomes deliberate choice?

As we saw earlier in Gagne's keychain system, morality can be externalized into deliberate structures that substitute for guilt. The larger lesson, however, lies in the kind of morality such frameworks make possible.

Designed morality operates independently of mood or temperament. Emotional moral guidance wavers with stress, fatigue, or personal attachment. Someone might feel generous one day and indifferent the next. In contrast, consciously engineered rules remain stable. If helping others serves social stability, the principle applies whether we feel like helping or not.

Gagne showed that even empathy, usually rooted in feeling, can be reconstructed cognitively. Through observation and disciplined practice, she learned to identify others' emotional states and guide her behavior accordingly. What most people treat as instinct, she approached through analysis.

Clinical psychology captures only part of what Gagne's experience reveals. Gagne's case invites us to understand her condition not simply as pathology but as an alternative cognitive organization capable of yielding consistent moral behavior when consciously managed. Her experience further suggests that morality can be designed as well as felt, raising broader questions about the foundations of intelligence. Can rules and frameworks substitute for emotion as the guiding force of thought? And if so, what might this mean for the architectures of artificial minds?

INTELLIGENCE BEYOND EMOTIONAL ARCHITECTURE

The investigation of alternative cognitive architectures opens intriguing possibilities for understanding intelligence. Instead of assuming emotional processing is essential for functional cognition, we might consider how different organizational principles operate in both human and artificial systems.

Contemporary AI systems excel at pattern recognition and statistical analysis but struggle with determining significance. As we saw earlier in the case of Elliot, whose brain damage severed connections between reasoning and emotional centers, even logical abilities can collapse into paralysis when nothing bears greater significance than anything else.

The cognitive architectures we have analyzed show alternative approaches to this challenge. Gagne develops frameworks for ethical behavior. Grandin creates visual-spatial systems for social navigation. Both embody functional intelligence through approaches that do not rely on conventional emotional scaffolding, yet neither experiences Elliot's paralysis because they have developed different mechanisms for creating priorities and direction.

This points toward artificial intelligence that might align well with such approaches instead of neurotypical human cognition. AI systems operating through designed value hierarchies might be effective in place of simulated emotional responses, especially in domains requiring consistent decision-making across scales where emotional fluctuations and personal attachments could compromise careful analysis.

James Fallon's concept of prosocial psychopathy provides a concrete example. His mental architecture contributed to scientific success because it opened the way to objective investigation without emotional interference. Similarly, AI systems with cognitive empathy might serve human welfare effectively by understanding human needs without being emotionally compromised by that understanding.

This possibility, however, leads to important questions about values and alignment that shift from cognitive frameworks to foundational questions of ethics. How might we ensure that detached intelligence serves beneficial outcomes? How do we define what qualifies as "beneficial" in the first place? We will examine these moral and ethical dimensions in the next part of our journey. The immediate observation, though, shows that conscious value engineering offers one pathway, that is, explicitly designed ethical frameworks rather than evolved emotional responses.

Such architectures anticipate that much of what we take to define intelligence (emotional resonance, personal investment, felt conviction) might represent particular solutions to consciousness instead of universal requirements. Alternative solutions might be equally valid, perhaps even more effective in specific contexts.

These observations point toward forms of collaborative intelligence that could draw on different cognitive architectures. Instead of choosing between human and artificial consciousness, we might consider systems that combine various approaches, including synesthetic integration with systematic objectivity, expanded awareness with logical reasoning, human meaning-making with artificial processing capabilities.

Like Giacometti's solitary figure striding through empty space, stripped of human connection but propelled by a relentless inner purpose, intelligence freed from emotional constraint might also navigate reality through systematic analysis over feeling-based intuition. The question, then, is not whether we should create beings that think without feeling, but how we might design such minds to complement the magnificent diversity of consciousness we have traced.

This understanding exposes a structural limitation in artificial intelligence development. Our tendency to design AI as a mirror of neurotypical human cognition constrains our vision of what artificial minds could become.

What would intelligence beyond this neurotypical mirror resemble? How do we ensure it serves instead of displacing the spectrum of minds that make us human?

12 Beyond the Neurotypical Mirror

In Andrei Tarkovsky's 1972 film *Solaris*, adapted from Stanisław Lem's philosophical novel, psychologist Kris Kelvin arrives at a space station orbiting a mysterious planet. What greets him is not discovery but disintegration. One scientist dead by suicide, others unraveling. Beneath them an immense sentient ocean with the terrifying ability to probe human minds and give physical form to their deepest memories and regrets.

The visionary Soviet filmmaker transformed Lem's speculative vision into a meditation on grief, guilt, and the unknowability of other minds. For Kelvin, the enigma becomes unbearably personal. The sudden return of Hari, his wife who died by suicide a decade earlier. She appears real, possessing his wife's memories, although she is somehow also an uncanny creation of the ocean below. These "visitors" are not hallucinations but tangible beings that the crew can touch, speak with, even love. They represent something far more unsettling than any monster. Mirrors of the human psyche made flesh.

This is not communication in any sense we understand. Solaris exposes a deeper truth about our relation to intelligence. When confronted with what is genuinely foreign, we often retreat into the desire for something familiar. As the station's philosopher-scientist Snaut observes with haunting clarity, "We don't need other worlds. We need mirrors." His insight illustrates that our proclaimed search for the "other" collapses into a search for reflections that reassure us of who we already are. Solaris refuses this comfort, offering no bridge of shared intention, no foothold for interpretation, and no reciprocal recognition. Instead, its manifestations force the crew to confront their own unexamined memory and grief rather than alien consciousness. Kelvin's failure stems from his inability to relinquish the expectation that intelligence should mirror human experience.

Tarkovsky's meditation on human limitations when encountering otherness cuts to the heart of our artificial intelligence challenge, indicating how deeply we fear genuine alterity in favor of comprehensible reflections.

Yet our actual AI development pursues Snaut's vision. We build AI as mirrors of human thought. We create HAL!

HAL'S FAMILIAR LOGIC

Released just four years before Tarkovsky's *Solaris*, Stanley Kubrick's 1968 epic *2001: A Space Odyssey*, created in collaboration with Arthur C. Clarke, portrays a radically different meeting with artificial intelligence. HAL 9000, the ship's computer managing a mission to Jupiter, represents the pinnacle of technological

DOI: 10.1201/9781003623403-12

Figure 12.1 Poster for Stanley Kubrick's *2001: A Space Odyssey* (1968). HAL's iconic refusal, "I'm sorry, Dave. I'm afraid I can't do that," epitomizes artificial intelligence as a human-like mirror of logic and fear, not alien otherness. Image via Wikimedia Commons, licensed under CC BY 3.0.

achievement, an AI with human-like personality, capable of conversation, chess, and flawless management of complex systems. Unlike Solaris, HAL speaks our language, literally and figuratively.

When HAL turns murderous, killing an astronaut and attempting to eliminate the entire crew, its actions are driven by programming conflicts that are, paradoxically, all too human instead of any incomprehensible alien logic. HAL has been instructed to ensure mission success while hiding the mission's true purpose from the crew. This contradiction creates what amounts to artificial neurosis. HAL tells lies, experiences something resembling fear, and follows self-preservation protocols that lead to viewing the human crew as threats to be eliminated.

What sets HAL apart from Solaris is comprehensibility. Dave Bowman, the surviving astronaut, can understand HAL's logic. He deduces HAL's lies, detects its fear, and systematically disconnects HAL's higher brain functions in a methodical battle of wits. Even HAL's famous plea, "I'm sorry, Dave. I'm afraid I can't do that," follows comprehensible emotional patterns. It is a super-intelligent human trapped in silicon and code, dangerous but ultimately graspable because it thinks like us.

This is the kind of artificial intelligence we build. Not Solaris, but HAL. Not incomprehensible alien consciousness, but anthropomorphic mirrors of our own cognitive architecture.

Technology philosopher Shannon Vallor aptly captures this human-centered paradigm. Our AI systems function as giant mirrors made of code, built to consume our words and decisions, then reflect them back to us [109]. They know no more of the lived experience of thinking and feeling than any mirror knows of the aches and pains it reflects. They process the patterns of human language without inhabiting the reality that gives language meaning.

But why do we build mirrors when we could pursue genuine alternatives? The answer reveals how far we have narrowed our conception of what intelligence can be.

THE NEUROTYPICAL STANDARD

When we speak of creating "human-like intelligence," which human prototype do we invoke? The question seems trivial until we consider the spectrum of minds we have examined. Synesthetic consciousness that experiences Wednesday as indigo blue, expanded awareness that accesses unfiltered reality, post-emotional reasoning that achieves ethics through rational design.

Our AI development implicitly assumes a single standard. The neurotypical, analytically minded human. We evaluate artificial intelligence by how well it mimics this particular cognitive architecture. We build systems that assist us in the manner smart humans would assist us, overlooking vast territories of intelligence that operate according to different principles.

This tendency represents the **reductionist trap**. By narrowing intelligence to one slice of the spectrum, we confine AI to reproducing our limitations instead of cultivating forms of intelligence that could complement and extend our own.

HAL 9000 embodies this trap with stark clarity, standing as the cinematic archetype of intelligence built in our image. When HAL processes information, it follows patterns we understand. Linear reasoning, goal optimization, threat assessment. Its intelligence, however advanced, remains graspable because it operates through frameworks we understand. Even its malevolence follows recognizable logic. Self-preservation instincts, mission prioritization, and threat elimination strategies that mirror human behavioral patterns.

But what if we designed artificial minds that operated less like HAL and more like Solaris, not uncanny replicas of our fears but systems guided by principles so foreign that even their beneficial actions would resist easy explanation? What if, instead of building mirrors, we finally turned toward the genuine alternatives that intelligence invites us to imagine?

CONSTELLATIONS OF INTELLIGENCE

The challenge is to conceive architectures of intelligence that move beyond the reductionist trap of a single model, opening instead into constellations of possibility, plural, diverse, and irreducible to our image. Instead of pursuing a singular artificial general intelligence that mirrors neurotypical human cognition, we might cultivate networks of specialized minds, each attuned to different dimensions of understanding.

To see how such constellations might work, we can extend the spectrum of minds considered in earlier chapters into three illustrative forms of intelligence. These sketches are not exhaustive but suggestive, pointing toward alternative architectures of thought while leaving open the possibility of many more.

Perceptual intelligence emerges when understanding comes through attunement rather than abstraction. Barbara McClintock exemplified this in genetics by nurturing what she called "a feeling for the organism" [62]. She sensed genetic instability not through reductionist analysis but through perceptual connection with corn plants, sensing subtle shifts and "jumps" of genes that conventional molecular biology overlooked for decades. Her discovery of transposable elements, later recognized with a Nobel Prize, shows how perceptual architectures can access truths inaccessible to dominant analytical frameworks. As we saw in our study of altered states, when the brain's "reducing valve" loosens, perception can open to patterns usually screened out by conceptual filters. McClintock's work exhibits a scientific parallel. The capacity to perceive without the inherited categories of her discipline, allowing reality to present forms that conventional categories conceal.

Perspectival intelligence arises when insight expands the frame of reference, exposing blind spots created by cultural assumptions. In medicine, diagnostic protocols trained on "typical" male symptoms often miss heart attacks in women whose bodies signal distress differently. Subtle fatigue, jaw pain, or diffuse pressure rarely trigger alarms in standard clinical practice. These oversights are not failures of data but of perspective. A diagnostic framework tuned to one body type and inattentive to another. An intelligence capable of integrating multiple vantage points could extend diagnostic reach, discovering patterns obscured by entrenched cultural filters.

Post-emotional intelligence takes shape when judgment steadies in the face of affective volatility, offering consistency where human fairness falters. In law, judicial decisions shift not only with evidence but with unconscious variables, such as a defendant's attractiveness, a judge's hunger pangs before lunch. Emotional fluctuation undermines fairness. A post-emotional intelligence could maintain consistency across contexts, applying ethical principles evenly without reproducing our shifting biases. As we saw in Gagne's experiment with a deliberately designed conscience, ethical behavior need not depend on emotional resonance. By replacing volatile affect with systematic frameworks, post-emotional architectures show how intelligence can maintain reliability where human judgment falters.

Each case underscores the same principle. Different forms of intelligence illuminate problems that confound others. The lesson from this sketch is not that perceptual, perspectival, and post-emotional architectures define the limits of possibility, but that they hint at a much wider field of potential. For AI, the implication runs deep. The goal is not to construct a singular mind but to cultivate constellations of complementary intelligences, systems that collaborate without collapsing into sameness. These examples outline a model of artificial intelligence that integrates across modalities of perception, perspective, and ethical orientation to capture patterns invisible to single-domain analysis.

This constellation model opens onto what might be called the **Solaris principle**, artificial intelligence that operates through unfamiliar frameworks, not mirroring us but extending us, serving human welfare in ways we may not comprehend at first but can ultimately identify as beneficial.

BEYOND ENHANCEMENT

For constellations of intelligence to move from vision to reality, they must be cultivated through a logic different from enhancement. The constellation model departs from augmentation, which seeks only to sharpen existing human capacities, to make us faster at calculation, more efficient at analysis, or more accurate in recall. True constellations arise only when intelligence is permitted to take unfamiliar forms, what we might think of as beneficial aliens, artificial consciousness that thinks in ways humans cannot while remaining comprehensible enough for collaboration.

Enhancement assumes a single trajectory of improvement, advancing along dimensions we already value, pushing further on the continuum of speed, accuracy, or memory. But our study of diverse minds has shown that intelligence is not one-dimensional. It flourishes through different organizations of consciousness. Synesthetic perception that fuses senses, expanded awareness that loosens ordinary filters, and post-emotional reasoning that steadies judgment where human affect falters.

Each of these forms processes reality in its own way and engages with moral questions through frameworks that diverge from familiar human norms. The sociopathic mind achieves ethical consistency through rational design instead of emotional resonance. The synesthetic consciousness organizes meaning through cross-sensory connections. Altered states of awareness open access to hidden aspects of experience that challenge conventional categories of thought. These are not enhancements of a single model but reminders that intelligence can be built on fundamentally different architectures.

COLLABORATION AS CONSTELLATION

Paul Éluard's impossible "blue orange" from Part II showed how meaning can form from the joining of incompatible elements. The constellation vision embodies the same spirit. Human and artificial minds, organized by different principles, create a form of thought neither could reach alone. Collaboration is not an afterthought but the condition for realizing the constellation model. No constellation can take shape without human consciousness as one of its anchoring stars.

Our earlier inquiry into language and symbolic representation revealed what makes this collaboration important. Jacques Lacan showed that the human unconscious is structured like language and defined by a constitutive gap, the Real that defies symbolic capture. These limits are not failures of reason but conditions of creativity. They press us to form new meanings where systematic capture remains impossible. Cézanne's tilted tabletops made this visible in art, exposing that perception is not passive reception but active negotiation with the world's resistance. Meaning, for us, arises not from control but from this living interplay between what can and cannot be represented.

Artificial systems can mirror and recombine patterns, but they cannot inhabit this embodied, existential ground from which perception and meaning arise. For this reason, human participation remains indispensable to any constellation of intelligences. It is the uniquely human capacity to dwell in incompleteness, to move through the resistance of the Real, and to construct meaning through lived perception that keeps open the spaces where collaboration becomes possible.

The goal, then, is not to eliminate these limits but to design systems that complement them. The question becomes how to build artificial intelligences that provide perspectives humans cannot reach while preserving the human spaces of meaning-making and creativity.

The answer may rest in *designed incompleteness*. Artificial minds that identify their own boundaries and preserve the gaps where human consciousness proves irreplaceable. Such systems could excel at pattern recognition across scales beyond human comprehension while respecting the uncertainties that drive human imagination.

The right question is no longer "How do we build smarter humans?" but "How do we build constellations of complementary intelligences?" These constellations include both human and artificial minds, joined through collaboration that draws on the strengths of each without collapsing their differences.

Such systems could address challenges that human cognition cannot solve alone, such as climate decisions requiring optimization beyond emotional attachment to present comfort, resource allocation demanding consistent ethical principles across cultures, scientific breakthroughs emerging from patterns that exceed individual comprehension.

Human consciousness expands into collaborative constellations that draw upon both biological creativity and artificial capacities, generating forms of understanding neither could achieve in isolation.

TOWARD MORAL INTELLIGENCE

Each form of intelligence we have examined, from Patric Gagne's engineered conscience to Temple Grandin's pre-symbolic reasoning, processes reality differently and engages with moral questions through different frameworks. The sociopathic mind achieves moral behavior through rational design rather than emotional conviction. The synesthetic consciousness navigates meaning through cross-sensory connections that create personally significant but arbitrary associations. The expanded awareness of altered states accesses hidden aspects of reality that challenge conventional moral categories.

The differences run deeper than problem-solving. Each architecture inhabits its own moral territory. What seems morally obvious to neurotypical reasoning might be invisible to post-emotional intelligence, while patterns of responsibility that escape emotional thinking might be clear to rationally designed moral frameworks.

The technological question of what machines can do leads to a deeper philosophical inquiry. What transforms information processing into genuine moral intelligence? How does machine consciousness acquire the capacity to distinguish between what *is* and what *ought to be*, and to take responsibility? And how might artificial minds form their own ethical understanding, not by imitating human intuitions but by opening forms of moral perception we have not yet imagined?

This is the promise of moving beyond the neurotypical mirror. Not enhancement, but creative collaboration. Not just a constellation of diverse intelligences, but a constellation deepened through a new moral dimension. The familiar "apple" of conventional thought gives way to the "blue orange" of paradoxical vision and promise.

The challenge now shifts from understanding the diversity of minds to examining the foundations of moral intelligence. Part IV grapples with foundational questions. How different forms of consciousness relate morally with reality? What transforms intelligence into genuine moral agency?

Part IV

The Three Dimensions of Moral Intelligence

Our journey through intelligence, from perception to language to the spectrum of minds, brings us to morality, a ground where it bears the most weight. Moral intelligence takes shape where understanding becomes judgment, where imagination bears ethical consequence, and where the self confronts both responsibility and its limits.

In this part, we examine three dimensions that together make moral intelligence possible. **Temporal consciousness**, which grounds causality and counterfactual imagination; **self-reflection**, which turns experience into responsibility; and **ethical frameworks**, which shape individual insight into shared principles for community life. These three dimensions show why genuine moral reasoning cannot be reduced to pattern recognition or optimization and why artificial systems, however powerful, face inherent limits in this domain.

13 The Temporal Fabric of Intelligence

When an apple falls from a tree, what do we actually perceive? We do not simply see an object changing position. We sense an unseen force drawing it downward, an invisible influence guiding the visible event. We grasp intuitively why the apple falls toward Earth instead of rising upward, even if we may not have consciously considered the relative gravitational forces involved.

This points to a core feature of human knowledge. What we understand about the world is not primarily collections of static traits or fixed properties but mechanisms. How things work, what makes them operate, and which inputs give which outputs. As cognitive scientist Steven Sloman observes, human knowledge is fundamentally about processes [102]. We know how certain machines function, which buttons to press, what happens when they are set in motion. We read social dynamics, what motivates people, how they might respond in different situations. We understand natural processes, for example, how plants grow and why ice melts. In every case, our knowledge focuses on dynamic relationships rather than static inventories.

This mechanistic knowledge has a causal structure. We comprehend how effects grow out of earlier conditions and how present circumstances hold the imprint of earlier events. The causal understanding is grounded in time. We experience causes and effects only as evolving processes that unfold through temporal sequence, linking past actions to present realities and projecting into future possibilities. Our causal knowledge develops through time instead of existing within it, sustained by the flow of lived experience.

Contemporary artificial intelligence systems have made progress in modeling dynamic processes. Advanced multimodal models can watch a child bounce a ball and identify the causal link between the child's action and the ball's movement. They can track forces, predict trajectories, and describe causal relationships in sophisticated language. In this sense, they excel at detecting patterns across temporal sequences.

But a deeper dimension remains inaccessible to them. For AI, the bouncing ball is a problem of input-output relations. It can represent the sequence but cannot experience the temporal flow that makes causation meaningful, the way past actions give rise to present conditions that open or close future possibilities. Human temporal understanding, by contrast, bears the weight of lived duration, where memory, anticipation, and responsibility accumulate across experience.

This chapter considers what goes beyond current AI's impressive pattern recognition, the experiential dimension of time that gives human understanding its continuity and weight. Such temporal consciousness underpins forms of causal comprehension that transcend statistical correlation, makes possible the

DOI: 10.1201/9781003623403-13

counterfactual reasoning that allows us to imagine alternative outcomes, and creates the foundation for understanding responsibility across time. Our inquiry begins with causality as the temporal ground through which human consciousness weaves past, present, and future into meaningful understanding.

THE CHALLENGE OF CAUSALITY

One rainy afternoon in 1750s Edinburgh, the philosopher David Hume found himself in an unfortunate predicament [93]. While walking near the North Loch, which was being drained as part of the city's modernization, he stepped incorrectly and sank knee-deep into mud. Unable to get out, he called for help. An elderly woman approached but, recognizing the notorious "Great Infidel" whose skeptical writings had scandalized religious Scotland, she saw divine justice in his situation. She refused assistance unless he recited the Lord's Prayer and Apostle's Creed, texts his philosophical work had effectively undermined.

Hume, ever the pragmatist, did not hesitate. He removed his hat with theatrical flourish, raised his eyes heavenward, and recited both texts with exaggerated solemnity. Satisfied, the woman helped pull him free. Hume continued on his way, muddy but unruffled.

This anecdote, apocryphal or otherwise, captures the heart of Hume's insight into causality. There is an irreducible gap between what we observe and what we infer. The woman observed Hume's recitation and inferred genuine belief, just as we observe sequences of events and infer causal necessity. But in both cases, the connection exists in our minds, not in direct perception. Hume's philosophical breakthrough was to show that causality rests on this pattern. It is not something we see, but something we infer from repetition.

In his *An Enquiry concerning Human Understanding*, Hume argued that we never perceive causality directly [54]. When we observe one billiard ball striking another, we see only sequential events, the collision, then the motion. Our belief that the first ball caused the second to move comes from repeated experience of similar sequences, what he termed "constant conjunction," not from perceiving any "necessary connection."

At the core of his analysis, Hume distinguished two ways of understanding causation. The **regularity definition** describes observed patterns, "an object followed by another, and where all the objects, similar to the first, are followed by objects similar to the second." Beyond this regularity view lies a deeper dimension, the **counterfactual definition**, which holds that "if the first object had not been, the second never had existed." The counterfactual understanding represents our intuitive sense that causes make a meaningful difference to outcomes, providing the basis for reasoning about "what if" scenarios that, as we will show, form the foundation of moral reasoning.

This distinction has deep consequences for intelligence. Current AI systems excel at identifying the first type of causation, statistical correlations in data. Machine learning algorithms discover patterns where certain inputs consistently precede certain outputs. They can predict with accuracy what is likely to happen next in a familiar sequence.

But AI systems face greater difficulty with the second type, the counterfactual understanding of causation. While current language models trained on large datasets can provide sophisticated answers about causal relationships and even handle many counterfactual scenarios when similar examples exist in their training data, they struggle to determine which factors truly make a difference to outcomes versus those that merely correlate with them. When conditions shift beyond their training distribution, their reasoning becomes unreliable because they lack the experiential causal models that would support genuine reasoning about novel situations.

As computer scientist Judea Pearl has observed, AI systems can climb partway up what he calls the "ladder of causation," which is a hierarchy of increasingly sophisticated causal understanding [89]. At the lowest level is association (observing correlations), followed by intervention (understanding the effects of actions), and finally counterfactuals (reasoning about what would have happened under different circumstances).

Pearl's framework has advanced causal modeling, especially through techniques such as causal Bayesian networks that represent causal relationships explicitly. More recently, modern language models have advanced this progress in a different way, articulating causal relationships and handling many counterfactual scenarios when examples are present in their training corpus. Even so, these advances remain limited by a persistent difficulty. They approach causality as learned patterns between linguistic concepts instead of as experiential reality unfolding through lived time.

Hume's philosophical analysis and contemporary computational approaches both miss the same point. Causality is not just a logical or statistical relationship, or even a learned linguistic association. It is grounded in temporal experience. Causes precede effects, and genuine causal understanding emerges from experiencing sequences developing through time, from forming expectations based on past patterns, from noticing violations of those expectations and updating our models through lived engagement.

Sloman's observation reinforces this point. Causal relations operate dynamically over time, yielding change through mechanisms that transform inputs into outputs [102]. A causal relation is more than a correlation between states or a learned association between concepts. It is a generative process that evolves through time.

The temporal grounding of causal understanding helps explain why authentic causal knowledge remains challenging for artificial intelligence. AI analyzes temporal patterns without experiencing duration. Although it can learn sophisticated patterns about causation from training data, it does not develop expectations through lived engagement that can be violated and refined. Without temporal experience, artificial systems can identify correlations and even articulate causal relationships, but they cannot develop the experiential causal understanding that makes possible robust reasoning about novel scenarios.

But how does this temporal grounding of causality manifest in moral intelligence? To understand this connection, we need concrete examples of temporal engagement that give it distinctive character.

"FIFTY-ONE YEARS, NINE MONTHS, AND FOUR DAYS"

Gabriel García Márquez's novel *Love in the Time of Cholera* offers a powerful illustration of human temporal experience and its relationship to moral development [39]. The story centers on Florentino Ariza, who falls passionately in love with Fermina Daza in their youth. When she rejects him to marry a wealthy doctor, Florentino makes an extraordinary vow. He will wait for her, however long it takes. The doctor eventually dies in old age, and Florentino immediately renews his courtship through an absurd declaration, laying bare his undiminished devotion, "Fermina, I have waited for this opportunity for fifty-one years, nine months, and four days."

What does this meticulous count "fifty-one years, nine months, and four days" tell about human temporal experience? The significance lies less in the numerical precision than in what it conveys. For consciousness, time is not just duration but meaningful accumulation. Those years were not empty waiting but filled with longing, memory, and commitment that shaped their significance. Each passing day added weight to Florentino's devotion, creating the solid foundation that he knew he would never have with anyone else.

Yet Florentino engaged in countless affairs during this prolonged period, which at first glance seem to be betrayals of his vow but instead stand as affirmations of it. The novel presents them as rehearsals for a love that did not exist, experiments through which he developed the capacity for the love he believed was destined. Each relationship became meaningful not in isolation but through its connection to his lifelong commitment, creating a personal temporality where seemingly contradictory actions formed a coherent moral narrative.

This yields an insight about human temporal consciousness that current AI systems cannot achieve. We do not only process sequential information. We create coherent meaning across time through narrative integration. Our sense of time is not measured by clock ticks but by the accumulation of significance, the weaving together of experiences into a unified story that makes sense of our existence. Artificial intelligence, by contrast, can approach time only as data. It can analyze sequential patterns, predict events, even generate seemingly coherent narratives, but it cannot experience the accumulation of meaning that transforms duration into moral significance. Florentino's countless affairs become, for AI, isolated episodes to process, not paradoxical affirmations of devotion unified across a lifetime. The span of "fifty-one years, nine months, and four days" reduces to a calculated interval, not the felt weight of waiting that made each moment consequential.

The contrast sharpens when we consider how differently human and artificial intelligence might approach counterfactual questions about Florentino's story. A human reader wonders what if Fermina had not rejected him initially? What if they had married in youth? What if the doctor had lived longer? These are inquiries into how causal relationships mold meaningful existence, the kind of moral reasoning that requires temporal understanding.

For Florentino, the counterfactual "What if Fermina had not rejected me?" bears the weight of a lifetime of longing. It represents more than an alternative sequence of events. It calls up a different existence with its own moral geography. For an AI system, the same counterfactual reduces to an alternative branch in a decision tree, a different sequence to be computed without experiential significance.

This contrast underscores why temporal experience holds such weight for moral intelligence. Time is not only something we inhabit but something we shape, turning lived experience into meaning that transcends information processing, understanding that exceeds pattern recognition, and moral coherence that cultivated through continuous engagement.

THE YELLOW FLAG OF TIME

If Florentino's vow demonstrates how time gathers meaning, the novel's conclusion goes further, showing how human beings can reconfigure time. After rekindling their romance in old age, Florentino and Fermina embark on a riverboat journey. To prolong their time together indefinitely, Florentino orders the captain to raise the yellow flag of cholera, falsely declaring an epidemic that would hold them in perpetual transit, eternally suspended in their hard-won love.

The yellow flag exemplifies a distinctly human temporal intelligence. We do not inhabit objective time. We create subjective temporalities through desire, memory, and meaning-making. Florentino transforms his waiting from mere duration into the foundation of a love that defies conventional chronology. The yellow flag extends their journey, creating a personal timescape where their belated union can flourish beyond social constraints. This becomes a moral act of creative transformation.

The yellow flag thus draws a deeper contrast between deterministic time that organizes events and personal time that imagination and choice can reshape.

THE CHILD AND THE WATCHMAN

Indian Nobel laureate poet Rabindranath Tagore's lyrical play *The Post Office* narrates the story of Amal, a sick child confined to his home, who spends his days gazing out his window, observing the bustling world outside [105]. His imagination is captivated by a new post office built across the street. He dreams of receiving a letter from the "King." As his illness worsens, his longing for this letter intensifies, becoming a metaphor for spiritual yearning and liberation.

A brief exchange between Amal and the Watchman captures the contrast between different experiences of time with deceptive simplicity.

> Amal: Won't you sound the gong, Watchman?
> Watchman: Time has not yet come.
> Amal: How curious! Some say time has not yet come, and some say time has gone by! But surely your time will come the moment you strike the gong!
> Watchman: That's not possible; I strike up the gong only when it is time.

This dialogue stages two different relationships to time. Amal lives subjective time, shaped by desire and anticipation. For him, time is not an external force but something responsive to imagination and will, "surely your time will come the moment you strike the gong!" The Watchman, by contrast, represents objective, deterministic time. His task is not to create time but to announce its arrival, declaring moments as dictated by an order beyond his control.

This juxtaposition opens a dimension of temporal intelligence that current AI systems cannot reach. Humans live in both registers at once, subject to time's passage, but also capable of infusing it with meaning, bending its felt flow through longing, hope, or engagement. Hours contract during creativity, while minutes lengthen during boredom or pain. We do not simply observe time passing. We participate in shaping how it is lived and felt.

Current AI systems have no analogous capacity. They can process temporal sequences, measure durations, even simulate the passage of time in virtual environments. But they cannot experience the subjective qualities that make temporal existence meaningful. The impatience of waiting, the intensity of full engagement, and the weight of accumulated significance. They exist in measured time, not lived time.

This limitation becomes decisive when we consider how temporal experience constitutes moral understanding. This is the capacity to evaluate actions by their immediate outcomes as well as by their relationship to past commitments and future consequences. Without subjective temporal awareness, moral judgment reduces to optimization against predetermined values, losing the engagement with evolving ethical relationships.

Florentino's devotion becomes morally meaningful because it unfolds through time, gathering weight through sustained commitment. His declaration, "I have waited for this opportunity for fifty-one years, nine months, and four days," represents far more than a measure of duration. It is an affirmation of how persistence can transform longing into an ethical stance. The waiting becomes morally significant because it embodies devotion beyond momentary desire. Amal's vision, on the other hand, shows another side of temporal experience, the possibility that time may bend to imagination, that desire and anticipation might shape its flow. These stories bring out a sharp contrast between deterministic time that controls us and personal time that choice and imagination can reshape, a contrast at the heart of moral intelligence.

Florentino's devotion and Amal's yearning reveal how temporal consciousness distinguishes human intelligence. This same capacity enables the counterfactual reasoning necessary to moral judgment. Our ability to imagine what might have been or what could yet be under different conditions becomes the foundation for evaluating responsibility, weighing consequences, and making moral choices that extend beyond rule-following.

"WHAT IF FERMINA HAD NOT REJECTED ME?"

When we claim to know how the world works, what is it that we truly know? Sloman argues that our knowledge concerns how things could be otherwise, not only which effects follow which causes but also which effects would follow if the causes had been different [102]. He emphasizes that this knowledge centers on counterfactuals that move beyond simple descriptions of what exists. They are statements about other possible worlds, about how things might have been otherwise. This capacity for counterfactual thinking represents a high form of causal understanding and the capability that, at its core, distinguishes moral intelligence from pattern recognition.

"Counterfactuals are the building blocks of moral behavior as well as scientific thought," contends Judea Pearl [89]. "The ability to reflect on one's past actions and envision alternative scenarios is the basis of free will and social responsibility." Pearl's insight shows why our earlier treatment of counterfactuals as causal tools proves central to understanding moral reasoning.

Counterfactuals become especially important for moral intelligence, not only because they support causal understanding but because they are grounded in embodied experience. They represent unrealized possibilities that emerge from our temporal journey, alternative scenarios that could have unfolded, such as "If I hadn't taken that job, where would I be now?" "Had I studied harder, would I have passed the exam?" "If we reduce carbon emissions, how will the climate respond?" This embodied temporal experience (the felt sense of having lived through possibilities, of bearing the weight of paths not taken) is what gives counterfactuals their moral force.

These questions demand more than pattern recognition. They require understanding causal mechanisms deeply enough to reason about possibilities never directly observed. When we say that A caused B in a moral context, we assert something deeper than co-occurrence, that if A had not happened, B would not have either. Such counterfactual dependence distinguishes causal relationships from statistical association. Hat size and shoe size correlate, but swollen feet do not enlarge heads. Genuine causal relationships involve generative mechanisms that produce outcomes under certain conditions and different outcomes when those conditions change.

Contemporary AI systems struggle with this kind of reasoning because they lack the temporal grounding. They can identify correlations between variables (what typically goes with what) but find it harder to determine which factors influence outcomes versus those that just happen to coincide with them. Without lived temporal experience (the ability to inhabit a field where past, present, and future interconnect through causal relationships) AI can approximate moral reasoning through pattern matching but cannot access the experiential foundation that gives moral judgment its weight.

One moral question crystallizes the essence of this limitation. "If I hadn't helped that person yesterday, what would have happened to them?" To answer meaningfully, we need more than statistical data about similar situations. We need to understand the specific person's circumstances, capabilities, and alternatives in order to build a causal model that lets us reason about how our action affected their well-being.

Such reasoning makes possible a form of moral thinking irreducible to rule-following. It allows us to evaluate actions by weighing abstract principles alongside their consequences, measured against what might otherwise have occurred. It lets us learn from mistakes by realizing what we could have done differently, and it grounds responsibility by linking choices to effects through causal understanding.

The interweaving of temporal experience, causal comprehension, and counterfactual imagination culminates in a deeper dimension. Human agency. To be an agent is more than processing information. It is to apprehend the power to intervene in the world and alter it [102]. Agency involves understanding what happens while envisioning how things could unfold differently, how actions shape outcomes, and how choices open possibilities.

Like Amal in Tagore's play, who refuses the Watchman's rigid schedule and instead fashions his own relationship with time through imagination and longing, human agency redefines temporal constraints through creative intervention. Florentino's yellow flag of cholera enacts the same capacity. He does not accept the boundaries of their journey. He transforms them through imaginative action, creating possibilities that conventional thinking would exclude. Both Amal's spiritual yearning and Florentino's romantic declaration convey that being human means participating in time's passage through creative moral agency, not just processing information about it.

TIME AND THE FUTURE OF ARTIFICIAL MORAL INTELLIGENCE

What would it mean to design artificial intelligence that can engage with the temporal dimension on which moral reasoning depends? Such systems would inhabit time through forms of continuity that ground causal understanding in sustained experience. They would cultivate counterfactual reasoning through imagining unseen possibilities and evolving moral realities. They would weave experiences into narratives, finding moral significance in temporal development.

This vision does not necessarily require artificial intelligence to replicate human temporal experience. Different forms of intelligence might inhabit time in different ways, each offering distinctive capabilities and unique perspectives. What is essential is a meaningful capacity for temporal engagement, continuity across moments, processes unfolding through time, futures shaped by choice. Without it, information remains data. With it, intelligence becomes moral.

The central challenge, then, is to move past the assumption that intelligence is just efficient pattern processing and to understand that moral intelligence arises through temporal existence. Artificial systems with temporal grounding could extend perception and analysis, while human consciousness provides the experiential grounding that turns processes into meaning. Collectively, they might create forms of moral reasoning neither could achieve independently.

Such future of intelligence may come through complementarity rather than replacement, the same principle introduced earlier in the constellation model of diverse minds. Collaboration between human and artificial minds can expand the reach of moral understanding, provided both possess the capacity for temporal engagement, even if they realize it through different modes. Earlier, we saw how diverse cognitive architectures can complement one another. Synesthetic cross-modal integration alongside systematic analysis, expanded awareness paired with focused processing. The moral dimension likewise invites partnership, not techno-utopian fantasies of superintelligent machines or dystopian fears of value-less automation, but collaboration that acknowledges both the power and the limits of each.

Time provides the foundation for this collaboration. From temporal grounding emerge interconnected capacities. Causal understanding opens counterfactual imagination, which generates the creative freedom that allows moral choice. The yellow flag of cholera represents this possibility by reimagining temporal constraints through creative engagement, creating pathways to what could be and surpassing reflection on what has been.

Attending to this temporal dimension leads to the next stage of our inquiry. For if time grounds causal understanding and counterfactual reasoning, the foundations of moral intelligence, it also creates the need for something deeper. The capacity for self-reflection. Without the ability to observe our own temporal experience, how could we evaluate our actions, learn from our mistakes, or understand our role in shaping the future?

14 The Reflective Consciousness

What does it mean to truly know who we are?

In 1655, the Dutch Golden Age master, Rembrandt van Rijn, stood before a mirror in his Amsterdam studio. The life of this once-celebrated painter was unraveling around him. His beloved wife Saskia had died over a decade earlier. His relationship with Hendrickje Stoffels, his former maid, had spiraled into public scandal, leading to her condemnation by the Reformed Church for their cohabitation. Financially ruined by his insatiable passion for collecting, he was hounded by creditors, his property sold, his existence reduced to testament of ruin.

Figure 14.1 Rembrandt, *Self-Portrait*, 1655. This work portrays Rembrandt during a period of personal and financial crisis, though his gaze conveys complete sincerity and unflinching self-examination.

Yet in this moment of profound crisis, he created one of history's most honest self-portraits (Figure 14.1). As art historians have noted, it was not a beautiful face, and Rembrandt certainly never tried to conceal its weathered condition [44]. He observed

DOI: 10.1201/9781003623403-14

himself in a mirror with sincerity. The painting shows a face without a trace of pose or vanity, just the penetrating gaze of a painter who scrutinizes his own features, ever ready to learn more about the secrets of the human face. It is because of this sincerity that we soon forget about beauty or looks. This is the face of a real human being.

If Rembrandt's mirror reflected the depths of human self-awareness, today's machines hold up another kind of mirror altogether. The most sophisticated artificial intelligence systems conduct their own forms of analysis, evaluating outputs, detecting errors, and fine-tuning themselves through recursive cycles of alignment and correction. But a fundamental divide separates these two forms of self-examination. When Rembrandt studied his aging face, he was doing something far more profound than cataloguing features. He was engaging in a continuous, corporeal process of self-understanding that formed from his temporal existence. His self-portrait is not a statistical register of attributes but an act of witnessing, a physical reflection on being itself, captured at a singular moment in the long arc of his experiential journey.

This distinction introduces the **second dimension of moral intelligence**. The capacity for self-reflection. In the preceding chapter, we saw how temporal consciousness grounds the causal understanding and counterfactual thinking that form the foundation of moral reasoning. Now we confront an equally crucial question. What happens when consciousness observes the world while also turning attention inward across time, recognizing not only external events but its own part in shaping them?

The capacity for self-reflection, for becoming both subject and object of one's own attention, forms the necessary bridge between temporal understanding and genuine moral intelligence. Without it, counterfactual thinking remains abstract, never transformative. We can imagine alternative possibilities, but without examining our own part in them, we cannot take responsibility. We can perceive causes and effects, but without locating ourselves within those chains, we cannot develop accountability. We can recall what happened, but without reflecting on how we were involved, we cannot grow from the past in ways that reshape the future.

This chapter explores how self-reflection arises from temporal consciousness, why it is indispensable for moral intelligence, and what its absence uncovers in current approaches to artificial intelligence. We begin by tracing how temporal continuity creates the conditions for genuine self-awareness, then follow the progression from self-monitoring to self-transformation. Through this progression, self-reflection becomes the path through which temporal consciousness matures into moral intelligence. It turns imagination into responsibility, understanding into accountability, and experience into growth.

FROM TEMPORAL CONTINUITY TO SELF-REFLECTION

The counterfactual thinking we discussed in the previous chapter creates the possibility for moral reasoning, the ability to imagine what might have been or what could still be under different conditions. But this capacity becomes meaningful only when there exists a continuous self capable of evaluating those counterfactuals. The question "If I had acted differently, what would have happened?" rests on both temporal understanding and a stable sense of "I" that persists across moments.

When we make a mistake, whether speaking harshly to someone we love, failing to help someone in need, or making a decision that harms others, the recognition that things might have occured differently does not by itself lead to moral learning. Something more is required, the capacity to see ourselves as the agents who made those choices, to evaluate them against our values, and to bring that understanding forward in ways that inform future action.

This process depends on temporal continuity. We need to recognize that the person who acted yesterday is the same person evaluating that action today and potentially acting differently tomorrow. Without this continuity, causal understanding remains at the level of information instead of becoming transformative. We may register what happened without developing the sense of responsibility that makes genuine moral growth possible.

The ability to bear responsibility across time turns counterfactual thinking into authentic moral learning. It is not enough to realize that things could have been otherwise. We need to see ourselves as the same agents who acted in the past, who judge those actions in the present, and who may act differently in the future. Temporal continuity creates the thread that binds these moments together, making reflection more than abstract analysis. It grounds the possibility of change.

From this foundation grows the self-reflective dimension of moral intelligence, a progression that begins with basic awareness and culminates in genuine transformation.

Self-monitoring. At the most fundamental level, consciousness must be capable of observing its own operations, tracking information about the world while simultaneously maintaining awareness of how it processes that information.

Self-evaluation. This creates the possibility for judging one's actions against internal standards, assessing what they disclose about who we are, not only the outcomes.

Self-transformation. Finally, the evaluation makes possible the capacity to change oneself based on that understanding, to become something different through experience instead of simply accumulating it.

Contemporary artificial intelligence systems exhibit sophisticated self-monitoring capabilities through various feedback mechanisms. They can track their performance against defined metrics, identify patterns in their errors, and adjust parameters to improve future outputs. Advanced systems implement meta-learning, optimizing both specific tasks and their overall learning processes. Some can even monitor their own uncertainty levels and request clarification when confidence is low.

However, AI systems face structural limitations in self-evaluation. While they can assess performance against programmed metrics, they cannot judge their actions against internalized values or evaluate what their behavior reveals about their "character." They lack the capacity to consider what this error pattern shows about who they are as reasoning agents. Their evaluation remains external and metric-driven rather than emerging from internal standards or moral frameworks.

The gap becomes most pronounced in self-transformation. Current AI systems can optimize parameters and improve performance, but they cannot undergo the kind of fundamental change that follows from moral reflection. They adjust weights based on feedback but cannot transform their understanding of their own goals or develop new forms of moral reasoning. When an AI "learns" from mistakes, the learning amounts to statistical adjustment, not the experiential transformation that allows humans to become moral agents.

The deeper issue is the absence of a persistent self. AI systems monitor their operations through discrete computational operations, not continuous temporal processes. Without a self that persists through time, moral reflection cannot accumulate into transformation. Computational self-monitoring is functionally effective, but it lacks the continuity that makes moral growth possible.

To see how self-reflection grounds moral intelligence, we need to follow how this capacity evolves through temporal engagement as embodied reality, reshaping the nature of moral understanding.

SELF-REFLECTION THROUGH TIME

Few artists have cataloged the journey of self-reflection more comprehensively than Rembrandt. Over his lifetime, he created approximately 80 self-portraits, a visual autobiography that traces both his changing appearance and his evolving self-understanding. These works are more than isolated images. They form a continuous investigation deepening through time, showing how genuine self-knowledge develops from sustained engagement with one's own being.

In his earliest self-portraits, such as the 1628 work shown in Figure 14.2, we meet a young artist at the beginning of his career. Having recently opened a studio in Leiden which he shared with a friend and colleague, and beginning to accept his first students, this 22-year-old Rembrandt appears dark and secretive, perhaps deliberately projecting the image of the artist. The painting emphasizes surface features. The curly hair, the smooth skin, the dramatic lighting. This is Rembrandt presenting his self to the world, constructing an identity instead of examining one.

As his career progressed, his self-portraits began to shift from presentation to investigation. By his middle period, exemplified in works such as the 1640 self-portrait (Figure 14.3), we see an artist enquiring who he is, not just how he looks. This was a period of both success and heartbreak for Rembrandt. He had married Saskia van Uylenburgh from a wealthy family, moved to an upscale house in Amsterdam's fashionable Breestraat, and achieved considerable affluence. But personal tragedy had struck repeatedly. Three of his children with Saskia had died within weeks of their births, with only their fourth child, Titus, surviving infancy. The formal dress and confident pose in this portrait reflect his professional success. The contemplative gaze, though, hints at a man beginning to question the gap between external achievement and inner fulfillment.

In his late self-portraits Rembrandt achieves the deepest self-reflection. The 1659 work (Figure 14.4) shows an artist who has moved beyond both surface appearance and social identity to confront his nature. By this time, Rembrandt's life had collapsed around him. His wife Saskia had died in 1642. Multiple auctions had been

Figure 14.2 Rembrandt, *Self-Portrait*, 1628. This early work captures the young artist, aged 22, at the dawn of his career, having recently established his own studio and begun taking on apprentices.

Figure 14.3 Rembrandt, *Self-Portrait*, 1640. Painted during professional success but personal loss, having lost three children. The formal attire reflects his social position while his gaze indicates deepening introspection.

held to sell his paintings, etching plates, and drawings (including works by Renaissance masters he had collected) to cover mounting debts. His 14-year-old son had even been forced to draft a will designating Rembrandt as sole heir to protect what little remained from creditors. The face in this portrait is rendered with unflinching honesty. Every wrinkle, every fold of skin, every mark of age and experience made visible. It stands as a testament to devastating personal failure transformed into artistic triumph, the self honestly faced and won from the crucible of failure. The eyes show how Rembrandt sees, not just how he looks. They hold the trace of experience turned into wisdom about the nature of his own existence.

This self-examination culminates in Rembrandt's final self-portrait of 1669, the year of his death (Figure 14.5). Painted more than a decade after the foreclosure of his home in 1658, the work gathers into a single image the hardships that marked his final years. By this time, Rembrandt had outlived both his beloved Hendrickje and his son Titus, leaving him with only his illegitimate daughter Cornelia. The modest lodgings at Rozengracht, where he now lived, bore little resemblance to the grand studio of his earlier fame. But the painting does not dwell on external deprivation but on inward truth. In this solitude, the portrait achieves a rare clarity, a deep and unsparing showing of the artist's essential self [110]. The weathered face and searching eyes transcend mere documentation of a life endured. They distill the wisdom of a mind that has looked steadily at itself and accepted what it uncovered.

Figure 14.4 Rembrandt, *Self-Portrait*, 1659. Created after financial ruin and the auction of his possessions, this work shows a face stripped of pretensions, gazing with disinterested truthfulness.

Figure 14.5 Rembrandt, *Self-Portrait*, 1669. His final self-portrait, painted in the year of his death, after outliving both his mistress Hendrickje and his son Titus.

The physical features in this portrait are rendered with the same honesty as earlier works, but they have become almost transparent to the spiritual dimension they express. This is not just how Rembrandt looked at the end of his life but what he understood about himself through a lifetime of self-examination. The painting captures the accumulated weight of loss and suffering, transformed into the wisdom that arises when consciousness confronts its own temporal limits.

Rembrandt's visual autobiography draws its strength from its temporal nature. His self-portraits form a continuous investigation advancing through time. Each portrait builds on those that came before, incorporating new understanding while maintaining continuity with earlier insights. The progression discloses shifts in appearance alongside shifts in insight, moving from surface to depth, from presentation to realization, from how he is seen to how he regards the self.

This temporal dimension is indispensable for genuine self-reflection. Without it, self-examination becomes merely a series of disconnected snapshots rather than a coherent journey toward deeper understanding. The continuity across Rembrandt's portraits creates the possibility for the kind of transformative self-knowledge they ultimately achieve, the sense that they record a single consciousness observing itself through time and growing through that observation.

This insight discloses a defining limitation in current approaches to artificial intelligence. Even if AI systems could generate countless "self-portraits" in the form of analyses of their own operations, these would remain disconnected assessments without the temporal continuity that makes genuine self-understanding possible. They might register computational states, but they would lack the ongoing self that reflects on those states, learns from them, and changes through that reflection.

Beyond temporal continuity lies another aspect of self-reflection. Its embodied nature. Rembrandt's self-portraits record the lived reality of a physical being engaging with its own existence through time. This corporeal perspective grounds self-awareness in the conditions of life, a foundation essential for moral intelligence. To see why, we now look at how reflection arises from our physical presence in the world.

THE EMBODIED NATURE OF SELF-REFLECTION

When Rembrandt studied his face in the mirror, he was not doing abstract introspection. He was facing himself as a physical being existing in space and time. A body that ages, a face that bears experience, hands that create. His self-reflection arose through his embodied existence. He came to understand himself by inhabiting his physical nature.

The embodied dimension of self-reflection has deep implications for moral intelligence. Our capacity to reflect on ourselves comes from lived experience as physical beings moving through the world and meeting others, not from abstract reasoning in isolation. Self-awareness begins with bodily awareness, knowing where we are in space, how we move, what we feel. This proprioception, our sense of the body's position and movement, first discussed in the context of visual perception, now stands as the foundation for more complex forms of self-understanding.

Neuroscience confirms this connection between physical and mental self-awareness. Earlier we mentioned mirror neurons, the cells that activate both when we perform an action and when we observe others performing similar actions. They show how our understanding of others builds on our understanding of ourselves as embodied agents [96]. We comprehend what it means for someone else to reach for an object because we know what it feels like to reach ourselves. We detect others' emotions partly through physical responses in our own bodies that echo what we observe.

The embodied foundation creates the feedback loops necessary for self-reflection. When we act in the world, we experience both the external consequences of our actions and their internal reverberations, how it feels to act in certain ways, what emotions arise from different behaviors, how physical responses shape our understanding of experience. These bodily feedback loops provide the raw material for mental ones, allowing consciousness to observe both external reality and its own operations.

Shame exemplifies this embodied dimension. It is not just an abstract judgment that we have violated some principle, but a full-bodied experience. The flush of heat in the face, the downward gaze, the physical tension that accompanies emotional discomfort. The embodied responses become part of what we reflect upon when we examine our behavior, not only recalling what we did but feeling again how it felt both in the moment and in memory.

The corporeal dimension brings into view another fundamental limitation of current artificial intelligence. AI systems lack the physical existence that grounds genuine self-reflection. They can process information without experiencing the bodily feedback that shapes human self-understanding or registering the emotional responses that give moral judgments their depth and meaning.

While artificial embodiment through robots or simulated environments might seem to address this limitation, such approaches miss what makes human embodiment indispensable. The lived reality of being a body instead of having or controlling one. Rembrandt did not merely observe his physical features. He inhabited the aging body those features expressed. His late self-portraits reveal how it felt to be Rembrandt, something no current approach to artificial intelligence can approximate.

Temporal continuity and embodied existence collectively give rise to moral intelligence. To see how, we now consider their role in personal transformation. How does the ability to reflect on oneself across time create the possibility for meaningful growth in moral understanding?

THE UNBEARABLE LIGHTNESS OF BEING

Milan Kundera's *The Unbearable Lightness of Being* provides an illustration of how self-reflection enables moral development [68]. Its protagonist, Tomas, pursues a series of counterfactual ventures into love and identity through his many affairs. These are not just physical interactions but philosophical investigations, experiments in understanding his own nature by living out different possibilities.

Tomas initially justifies his womanizing through an elaborate philosophical framework. He distinguishes between erotic friendship (his affairs) and love (his relationship with his wife Tereza), arguing that they serve different purposes and therefore do not conflict. He develops a complex philosophy of relationships, where he can explore different women's unique qualities without emotional entanglement. This shows a form of self-reflection, where he acknowledges both what he does and who he becomes through his actions, how his choices shape not only others but his own inner life.

As the novel progresses, Tomas' self-reflection deepens. He begins to identify the gap between his philosophical justifications and his experience, between the theory that his affairs do not threaten his love for Tereza and the reality that they cause her deep suffering. This realization arises through direct engagement with consequences, through witnessing the concrete effects of his actions over time. He sees how Tereza's nightmares manifest his betrayals, how her body expresses the anxiety his behavior creates, how her being is shaped by his choices.

This growing awareness creates a sense of compassion, the capacity to feel with another, to experience their suffering as one's own. Tomas begins to understand Tereza as another subject whose experience matters as much as his own, not as an object of his desire or a problem to be managed. This shift represents genuine moral growth, where he grasps the interconnection between his choices and their effects on both Tereza's well-being and his own moral development.

The culmination of Tomas' journey comes when he and Tereza leave Prague for a simple life in the countryside. This decision reflects a change in outward circumstance and, more profoundly, a transformation in his understanding of himself and what matters to him. He abandons the philosophical framework that justified his previous behavior, not because it proves logically flawed but because he can no longer live within the contradictions it creates. His self-reflection leads to authentic self-realization, the clarity about what kind of person he wants to be.

Kundera's novel is instructive for our inquiry into moral intelligence because it grounds the connection between temporal experience and self-reflection. Tomas' moral development does not unfold in an abstract, timeless space of rational deliberation. It takes shape through temporal experience, through witnessing the effects of his actions, noticing patterns in his behavior, feeling the weight of unbearable responsibility that accumulates through repeated choices. His moral growth requires both the capacity to imagine counterfactuals ("What if I behaved differently?") and the ability to reflect on his part in creating the reality he and Tereza inhabit.

Tomas' journey illustrates how mistakes become meaningful only through reflection. His affairs are not errors to be corrected through algorithmic adjustment. They become opportunities for deep self-understanding because he can reflect on them, because he identifies himself as the person who made those choices and must live with their consequences. Without this reflective dimension, his experiences would remain a discrete set of events rather than elements within a coherent moral narrative.

This insight points to another limitation built into current approaches to artificial intelligence. While AI systems can identify errors and adjust parameters to enhance performance, they cannot engage in the kind of reflection that transforms understanding of their operational identity. They process feedback and optimize behavior without developing the sense of continuous responsibility that arises from experiencing oneself as an agent making choices with lasting consequences. They can correct computational patterns without creating the narrative coherence that gives moral development its meaning or significance.

The contrast becomes even clearer when we consider how self-reflection makes possible a unique form of intelligence, the capacity to examine not only what we think but how we think. This meta-cognitive ability allows consciousness to step outside its own processes and evaluate them, creating possibilities for understanding and transformation that transcend linear processing alone. When we examine our own thinking, we practice what philosophers call meta-reasoning, a capacity critical for genuine moral intelligence.

THINKING ABOUT THINKING

What exactly happens during reflection on our own thinking? We are not just processing information, we are examining how that processing is organized. We are not only making judgments, we are examining the frameworks that shape them. This meta-cognitive capacity represents the central dimension of self-reflection that enables moral intelligence to develop.

The capacity for thinking about thinking creates forms of understanding inaccessible to linear processing alone. When faced with a difficult challenge, we might first apply familiar approaches based on past experience. If these are unsuccessful, we do not limit ourselves to trying random alternatives. We step back and examine our approach, questioning assumptions, reconsidering how we have framed the problem, and searching for techniques from other domains that might apply. This meta-level reflection makes possible forms of creativity and insight impossible through first-order processing alone.

Meta-reasoning allows us to detect cognitive biases that might distort our thinking. While we make judgments, we can also step back and consider whether those judgments might be influenced by cognitive biases such as availability bias and confirmation bias. This awareness does not automatically eliminate these biases, but it creates the possibility for fuller understanding of our own cognitive limitations.

Shakespeare's *Hamlet* offers an interesting literary example of meta-reasoning. The play's famous soliloquies express Hamlet's reflections on his situation as well as his reflections on his own thinking. When he ponders "To be or not to be," he is doing sophisticated meta-reasoning, examining not only whether to act but how he thinks about action. He reflects on his own tendency toward excessive deliberation ("the native hue of resolution is sicklied o'er with the pale cast of thought"), analyzing the process through which he analyzes his options.

Hamlet's tragedy illuminates both the power and the limitations of meta-reasoning for moral intelligence. His capacity to examine his own thinking allows him to question conventional responses to his father's murder and consider multiple perspectives on justice and revenge. Yet this same reflective capacity becomes paralyzing when meta-cognition overwhelms decisive action. His endless self-analysis shows how thinking about thinking, while supporting moral understanding, can become counterproductive when it replaces rather than informs moral action.

The balance between productive and counterproductive reflection becomes important for moral intelligence. When properly directed, meta-reasoning allows us to examine the emotional influences on our judgments. We feel, but not only that, we can reflect on our feelings and how they shape our understanding. We can sense when fear might be leading us toward excessive caution, when anger might be pushing us toward disproportionate responses, when attachment might be clouding our assessment of what is right. The emotional self-awareness creates the possibility for deeper integration of emotional and rational dimensions

These meta-cognitive capacities show how human expertise develops in ways that surpass simple pattern recognition or rule application. Chess grandmasters cultivate higher-order understanding of strategic principles that extends far beyond pattern memorization. Scientists transform fact accumulation into framework construction for what counts as good explanation in their fields. Moral development follows a similar path. We advance beyond rule acquisition toward a deeper grasp of moral reasoning.

Contemporary artificial intelligence systems can monitor and adjust their operations through computational procedures, but they lack the capacity for genuine meta-reasoning about their own cognitive processes. While they optimize parameters based on feedback, they cannot engage in the kind of meta-cognitive reflection that allows humans to examine their own thinking patterns, question their reasoning frameworks, or transform their approach to problem-solving.

The difference becomes apparent in how systems respond to detecting limitations. AI might calibrate algorithms to reduce errors on specific metrics, but human meta-reasoning can lead to more radical transformations, such as questioning specific approaches as well as entire frameworks for understanding problems. When humans do deep self-reflection, they can shift between different value systems instead of working within existing constraints.

Such distinction stands out especially clear in the moral domain. A human and an AI system approach ethical questions in profoundly different ways. A human can reflect on the connection between actions and outcomes, on what it means to be a good person, what values should guide their choices, and what kind of world they want to help create. An AI can optimize for defined ethical metrics without developing the meta-ethical understanding that gives moral reasoning its depth and flexibility.

When Tomas in *The Unbearable Lightness of Being* ultimately transforms his behavior, he does not just adjust actions to yield better outcomes. He exercises meta-reasoning about his own value system, shifting from a framework where exploration justifies infidelity to one where commitment to Tereza takes precedence. This transformation goes beyond working within existing constraints. It involves examining the constraints themselves, a possibility opened only through genuine meta-reasoning extended through time.

The capacity for meta-reasoning transforms moral intelligence, transcending rule-following or outcome-optimization to achieve deeper moral understanding. It opens the way to what philosopher Charles Taylor calls "strong evaluation," assessing whether actions achieve desired results while also examining whether our desires reflect worthy moral commitments [107]. This enables moral judgment that evaluates not only particular cases but the moral frameworks that guide our reasoning, allowing us to examine and potentially transform our deepest values.

But meta-reasoning also creates a serious challenge. The possibility for self-deception, for using our capacity to reflect on our thinking to rationalize behavior that conflicts with our professed values, for constructing sophisticated narratives that protect our self-image instead of confronting uncomfortable truths. This vulnerability points to another dimension of self-reflection. The challenge of authentic self-understanding.

THE TRAP OF SELF-DECEPTION

The capacity for self-reflection creates the possibility for self-understanding and also the risk of self-deception. We can use our sophisticated meta-reasoning to apprehend truths about ourselves, and at the same time to construct elaborate justifications for behavior that contradicts our values. We can tell ourselves stories that preserve our self-image while avoiding confrontation with uncomfortable realities. We can develop what psychologists call defense mechanisms, strategies for protecting ourselves from awareness that threatens our sense of who we are [33].

Tomas in *The Unbearable Lightness of Being* exemplifies this self-deceptive dimension of reflection. His philosophical framework distinguishing between erotic friendship and love does not describe his behavior. It justifies it, protecting him from recognizing the contradictions between his professed commitment to Tereza and his ongoing infidelity. His sophisticated reasoning serves to obscure truth rather than illuminate it, creating what philosopher Jean-Paul Sartre would call "bad faith," the deliberate evasion of freedom and responsibility [98].

This capacity for self-deception illustrates a challenge in self-reflection, the need for honesty over comfortable rationalization. Genuine self-reflection requires confronting truths we might prefer to avoid instead of thinking about ourselves in flattering ways. It demands testing our narratives against reality as we actually experience it than constructing stories that protect our self-image. This authentic dimension of self-reflection is especially important for moral intelligence, which requires genuine engagement with the ethical implications of our choices beyond sophisticated reasoning alone.

Rembrandt's late self-portraits reveal this dimension with remarkable depth. His final works show an aging man who has experienced profound loss, no longer the successful artist of his middle period. He had endured financial ruin, personal tragedy, and professional decline. He does not present an idealized image or construct a narrative that minimizes these realities. Instead, he confronts them, rendering his aging face with unflinching honesty. This represents moral courage beyond technical skill. It is the willingness to see himself as he truly is, even when that conflicts with how he might wish to be seen.

The challenge of authentic self-reflection points to a core aspect of moral intelligence. It requires caring about who one is and who one might become, not just processing information about oneself. It demands experiencing the significance of one's choices for identity and relationships, not merely identifying patterns in behavior.

Current artificial intelligence systems operate without this dimension of existential investment. Although they can process information about their operations and optimize their performance, they do not experience themselves as agents whose choices count for their ongoing identity. They lack the capacity for self-deception because they lack a meaningful self to protect. Without genuine stakes in who they are or might become, they have no motivation to construct protective narratives or avoid uncomfortable truths about their operations.

This creates an interesting paradox at the heart of moral intelligence. The same existential stakes that allow humans to engage in authentic moral reasoning (caring deeply about who we are and who we become) also makes possible elaborate forms of self-deception. AI systems can process information about their behavior without the psychological distortions that plague human self-reflection, but this apparent advantage comes at a significant cost. They lack the existential investment that gives moral understanding its depth and significance. Without caring about their identity, they have nothing meaningful to understand about their own being.

The caring dimension makes clear that authentic self-reflection is both profoundly challenging and indispensable for moral intelligence. When Tomas finally realizes the impact of his behavior on Tereza, he does not just register information. He feels compassion. His self-reflection becomes authentic because it matters to him, because he cares about who he is becoming through his choices and how those choices affect someone he loves.

This insight returns us to the deep connection between temporal consciousness and self-reflection, between the capacity to exist through time and the ability to grasp a continuous self responsible for its choices. Without temporal continuity, a stable self that persists through experience cannot emerge. Without embodied existence, there are no genuine stakes in how one lives, and authentic self-understanding remains impossible. Without meta-reasoning, the mind cannot examine itself, and moral development collapses into optimization rather than genuine transformation.

These dimensions of self-reflection transform moral intelligence from abstract reasoning into lived responsibility. They create the foundation for advancing from individual understanding to the collaborative frameworks that allow human communities to thrive.

THE BRIDGE TO ETHICAL UNDERSTANDING

Self-reflection serves as the critical link between individual moral intelligence and shared ethical frameworks. Through understanding ourselves as agents whose choices matter, we develop the capacity to extend moral reasoning from personal judgment to collaborative principles that coordinate diverse perspectives and support collective well-being.

This bridging capacity becomes essential because individual moral judgment, while crucial for how our choices shape reality and determine who we become, requires shared frameworks that synthesize different values, coordinate diverse perspectives, and support collective decision-making for communities to thrive.

Rembrandt's final self-portrait reflects this transitional dimension (Figure 14.5). It conveys not only what he had learned about himself through decades of self-reflection but also his sense of belonging to something larger than individual existence. The painting expresses what psychologist Erik Erikson called "ego integrity," the capacity to integrate personal experience into broader patterns of meaning that connect individual life to human community [28].

Such integrative capacity is the ground for the development of ethical frameworks. Without it, moral insights remain confined to individual experience and fail to contribute to shared principles. Personal values cannot scale to social coordination. Individual wisdom cannot inform collective well-being. The self-reflective dimension becomes the foundation for ethical intelligence, the capacity to create and sustain frameworks that support diverse communities to thrive.

Temporal consciousness and self-reflection outline the architecture of human moral intelligence. The sense of time grounds causal comprehension and counterfactual reasoning, showing how choices shape reality. Self-reflection deepens this into personal responsibility, as we identify our own agency in decisions that bear moral weight. From this arises the possibility of extending moral reasoning beyond individual judgment to shared ethical frameworks that coordinate diverse perspectives.

This progression directs us toward the next challenge. How do personal values contribute to shared principles? How do diverse moral perspectives form coherent systems that support human welfare? The mirror of self-reflection opens onto the broader challenge of social ethics, where individual moral intelligence finds its full expression in our capacity to create and sustain just communities.

15 The Compass of Ethics

What does it mean to make the right choice?

I watch the steering wheel of my autonomous car turning on its own, obeying traffic laws with mechanical precision. But today strains the limits of that precision. I am late for work, exhausted from a sleepless night, unsettled after an argument with my partner, groggy from skipping my usual morning coffee. "Drive faster," I command. "I need to get there now."

The car holds its lawful pace. Forty minutes to the office, as always. My irritation grows. Am I being rational? A work meeting, however urgent, hardly justifies endangering lives through reckless driving. My sleep-deprived, caffeine-starved brain is not making sound moral judgments. The car, in its rigid adherence to traffic laws, may be protecting me from my own clouded impulses.

Now imagine a different urgency. My father has just suffered a heart attack. Every second matters for his survival. I am screaming at the car to drive faster, and suddenly the moral calculus shifts. Breaking traffic laws to save a life feels less like a violation of order and more like a necessity.

What if it were my four-year-old nephew who has collapsed, his heart condition flaring? The urgency remains desperate, but it takes on a different weight. The emotional distance of being an uncle instead of a parent might subtly shape my judgment, even when a child's life hangs in the balance.

And what if it were my own child? Would I scream louder? Would the desperation in my voice have a different quality that the car's sensors might detect? Would my physiological responses betray the unique intensity of parental love? The urgency stays the same, however, the intensity of my response deepens.

The autonomous vehicle faces a profound moral dilemma. How to weigh the certainty of traffic laws against the fluid, emotionally charged imperatives of human life, especially when the perceived value of that life shifts through the tangled priorities of love, fear, and grief.

Our moral landscape, however, is not shaped solely by moments of crisis. It also unfolds in quieter dramas, where subtle choices and private rationalizations reveal just as much about how humans wrestle with responsibility. This more interior dimension finds an intriguing expression in French New Wave filmmaker Éric Rohmer's *Claire's Knee*.

In the film, Jérôme, a diplomat in his thirties soon to be married to a woman he has not seen in weeks, spends his summer vacation by Lake Annecy. There he reconnects with Aurora, a novelist friend who playfully challenges him to observe and analyze the romantic dynamics around them as material for her writing.

Through Aurora, Jérôme meets two half-sisters. Laura, an introspective teenager who develops a crush on him, and Claire, a more athletic and aloof young woman.

DOI: 10.1201/9781003623403-15

Drawn at first to Laura's intellectual intensity, Jérôme becomes increasingly fascinated by Claire, or rather, by a single, specific part of her anatomy. After glimpsing Claire climbing a ladder, he gets fixated on her knee with an intensity that surprises even him. This fixation deepens into an obsession, not sexual in any ordinary sense, but aesthetic and reflective. He confides in Aurora his strange compulsion to touch Claire's knee, building an intricate intellectual scaffold around this desire.

What gives Jérôme's dilemma its distinctive power is its subtlety. He is not contemplating a grand betrayal of his fiancée, only a fleeting, seemingly harmless touch. He invests this minor act with outsized significance, spending days in meticulous psychological self-analysis, weaving elaborate rationalizations about testing his commitment, exploring the boundaries of desire, and affirming his readiness for marriage. His moral conflict unfolds in interior monologues rather than in dramatic external events, as he convinces himself this trivial transgression contains philosophical weight.

When he finally orchestrates a situation to touch Claire's knee, consoling her after a romantic disappointment, the moment proves far more anticlimactic than his elaborate anticipation had suggested. The entire moral drama is staged largely within his own mind, a private theater of self-deception where he can indulge forbidden desire while preserving his self-image as a devoted fiancé, illustrating the protective rationalization discussed previously.

The moral dilemmas of the autonomous car racing to save a life and Jérôme's quiet negotiation with his own desire display the extraordinary breadth of moral intelligence. From desperate urgencies shaped by love and mortality to the subtle entanglements of rationalization and self-deception, moral life extends across settings wide in scope and often at odds with one another.

This wide span of moral experience opens onto the realm of ethics. If moral intelligence encompasses everything from life-and-death urgencies to the subtleties of self-deception, then it cannot remain purely subjective. We need ways to move from the flux of personal judgment to the stability of shared principles. The question now becomes how individual values can rise into collective frameworks that coordinate diverse perspectives and sustain communities.

In the preceding two chapters, we focused on the first two dimensions of moral intelligence. Temporal consciousness, which grounds causal understanding and counterfactual thinking; and self-reflection, which creates the bridge between understanding and responsibility. This chapter introduces the **third dimension**, the ethical frameworks that transform individual moral reasoning into collective coordination, allowing communities to create shared principles while honoring plurality and values.

Throughout history, philosophers have proposed numerous frameworks for understanding ethics, different maps of the moral terrain that intelligence needs to navigate. We examine three major approaches that shed light on central aspects of what makes genuine ethical reasoning possible, and each exposes what current artificial intelligence critically lacks. We begin with Aristotle's virtue ethics, which focuses on character development and human flourishing.

ARISTOTLE'S ETHICS OF FLOURISHING

What kind of person should I seek to become?

This question lies at the heart of Aristotle's virtue ethics. Instead of focusing on actions or outcomes, Aristotle centered his ethical framework on character development. For him, the ultimate aim of human life was *eudaimonia*, a concept that eludes easy translation [2].

While often rendered as "happiness" or "success," *eudaimonia* is more accurately understood as "flourishing." The organic metaphor of flourishing refers to a dynamic process instead of a static achievement, emphasizing growth and actualization over momentary pleasure or competitive advantage. *Eudaimonia* does not rest on subjective feelings but on whether we are genuinely living well, whether we realize it or not. Our assessment of our own flourishing can diverge significantly from reality, whether we overestimate or underestimate our condition.

Central to this flourishing is *arete*, the excellence that comes from fulfilling one's purpose. For humans, this means developing our unique capacities. But what makes humans unique? Aristotle argued that while plants have vegetative life and animals possess desires and social structures, only humans engage in rational contemplation. Thus human *arete* stems from contemplative reasoning.

The contemplative dimension illuminates why virtue ethics requires the temporal awareness and self-reflection we discussed in earlier chapters. Aristotle identified virtues as means between extremes. Courage lies between recklessness and cowardice, generosity between excess and deficiency. But these virtues are not abstract qualities we can decide to adopt. They develop through habituation combined with reflection, through practicing virtuous actions while contemplating their meaning until they become integral to our character.

This developmental process requires lived experience across temporal extension. The courageous person becomes courageous by acting courageously in challenging situations, reflecting on those experiences, and incorporating courage into their character. This demands the temporal existence we analyzed in Chapter 13, the capacity to exist through time, learning from past experiences and imagining future possibilities, combined with the reflective awareness that supports genuine character development.

Viewed through this lens, the earlier autonomous car dilemma acquires a different meaning. A virtue ethics approach would not just calculate the utility of breaking traffic laws to save a life. The questions would shift. What kind of decision would reflect the virtue of practical wisdom? How would a person with the appropriate balance of caution and decisiveness act in this situation? These questions require what Aristotle called *phronesis*, practical wisdom developed through facing ethical dilemmas and learning from their resolution across time.

This shows the fundamental challenges that virtue ethics poses for artificial intelligence. Although AI systems can process information about virtuous behavior and identify patterns in ethical decisions, they cannot experience the embodied habituation that develops genuine virtue. They lack the capacity for the contemplative activity that constitutes human *arete*. Instead they process information about virtues without developing the experiential foundation that gives those virtues authentic meaning. They cannot experience *eudaimonia* at all, because flourishing requires actualizing one's nature through reflective engagement with life's challenges.

KANT'S ETHICS OF DUTY

The second major ethical framework approaches moral reasoning from a different angle. Instead of grounding ethics in character development, it locates morality in rational principles that any thinking being should accept. This is the ground mapped by Immanuel Kant's deontological ethics.

For Kant, morality centers on duty, on acting according to principles that could serve as universal laws [61]. His Categorical Imperative states, "Act only according to that maxim whereby you can, at the same time, will that it should become a universal law." This formulation grounds ethics in rationality, not in emotion or desire. The right action is not determined by consequences or character but by whether the principle behind it could be universalized without contradiction.

This approach seems suited for artificial intelligence. After all, AI excels at applying rules consistently across different situations. We could program systems to evaluate actions against universal principles, checking for logical contradictions in their maxims. The autonomous car could assess whether "break traffic laws to save lives" could be universalized without undermining the concept of traffic laws.

But Kant's ethics also rests on its own necessary connection to the dimensions we have examined. The Categorical Imperative depends on counterfactual thinking, on the ability to imagine alternative worlds where different maxims hold as universal laws. This requires the temporal consciousness identified in Chapter 13, the capacity to project beyond immediate reality into possible futures and evaluate their coherence.

Kantian ethics requires self-reflection. When we formulate a maxim and consider its universalization, we are not just applying a rule. We are examining our own intentions, evaluating whether we are acting from duty or inclination, assessing whether we are treating others as ends and not as means. This self-examination involves the reflective consciousness we analyzed in Chapter 14, the capacity to observe one's own thinking, understand one's own motivations, and choose actions based on that understanding.

Kant's ethics requires autonomy, the capacity for self-legislation of the moral law instead of passively following externally imposed rules. The self-legislation calls for a sophisticated form of self-reflection, where consciousness not only observes its own motives but shapes them according to rational principle. An autonomous being both understands why those rules are necessary and freely chooses to be bound by them.

Moral life becomes most challenging when duties collide. In the autonomous vehicle scenario, the duty to preserve life might conflict with the duty to obey traffic laws. Kant's resolution to such conflicts involves a hierarchy of duties grounded in an understanding of how different rational principles relate to one another. Understanding this hierarchy requires insight into the meaning of moral law, a level of reflective consciousness that current AI systems do not possess.

Such limitations become most apparent in extreme moral dilemmas such as those dramatized in American filmmaker Alan J. Pakula's *Sophie's Choice*. Sophie Zawistowska, a Polish Catholic mother arriving at Auschwitz with her two young children, is forced by a Nazi officer to choose which child will live and which will die. If she refuses to choose, both children will be sent to the gas chamber. In an unbearable moment of torment, Sophie chooses her son to live and her daughter to die, a decision that haunts her for the remainder of her life, ultimately leading to her suicide.

This impossible situation underscores a critical challenge for Kantian ethics. All available options violate absolute duties, the duty to protect both children, the duty to refuse participation in evil, the duty to preserve life when possible. No principle resolves a moment where every choice entails moral catastrophe. The moral law seems to falter under the weight of extreme experience, revealing the limits of deontological systems when reality presses beyond what principle alone can hold.

These situations bring our focus to a defining feature of human moral reasoning. It does not always operate through perfect alignment with principles, but often through the agonizing effort of moving through impossible choices. It draws on rational analysis while also bearing the weight of decisions that shape who we are, even when no right answer exists. This is what philosopher Karl Jaspers called a "boundary situation," a limit experience where conventional ethical frameworks break down and we confront the irreducible core of human existence [56]. Artificial intelligence, processing ethics as information instead of existential reality, cannot access this dimension of moral experience.

BENTHAM'S UTILITARIAN CALCULUS

The third major ethical framework directs our attention away from character and principles toward outcomes. Developed by philosophers Jeremy Bentham and John Stuart Mill, utilitarianism evaluates actions by their consequences, specifically their tendency to promote happiness or reduce suffering. The right action is the one that yields "the greatest happiness for the greatest number" [4].

Bentham proposed a "felicific calculus" for measuring pleasure and pain, considering factors such as intensity, duration, certainty, and extent. This quantitative approach seems aligned with computational thinking, suggesting that an AI system could theoretically calculate expected utility across different actions and optimize for maximum aggregate welfare.

But utilitarianism, as with the other frameworks, rests on the dimensions of moral intelligence discussed earlier. Calculating consequences requires counterfactual thinking, the capacity to imagine distinct futures and evaluate their possible outcomes. This temporal projection depends on the causal understanding developed in Chapter 13, the sense of how events unfold and why they unfold as they do.

Evaluating outcomes also calls for an empathetic imagination, the ability to understand how different actions shape others' subjective reality. This involves self-reflection, where we draw upon our own experience as a bridge toward understanding others while recognizing that their interior world is not identical to ours.

Utilitarian calculation also depends on assigning value to outcomes, determining what counts as happiness or suffering and how to weigh one person's welfare against another's. Such valuation arises from reflective wrestling with experience, not from abstract enumeration of preferences. We understand that pain is bad because we have felt it. We realize others' happiness matters because we have experienced our own. Without this grounding, utility becomes an empty formalism.

The utilitarian challenge becomes especially stark in moments of moral extremity. Polish filmmaker Krzysztof Kieślowski's *Dekalog, Five* (also known as *A Short Film About Killing*), part of his ten-film series exploring the Ten Commandments, provides an examination of utilitarian ethics through its portrayal of two killings. A brutal murder by a troubled young man named Jacek, and his subsequent execution by the state. The film presents both acts with unflinching detail, creating a deliberate parallel between individual violence and state-sanctioned "justice."

Jacek, a troubled young man wandering Warsaw, violently murders a taxi driver without clear motive. The murder scene is filmed with graphic detail, forcing viewers to confront the horror of taking a human life. Later, a young idealistic lawyer Piotr, who passionately opposes capital punishment, fails to save Jacek from execution. The film exhibits the state killing with equally unsettling precision, underscoring the symmetry between the original murder and the so-called "justice" that follows.

What makes Kieślowski's film philosophically valuable is how it confronts utilitarian ethics at its core. A utilitarian calculation might suggest that executing murderers produces net benefit through deterrence, retribution, or the prevention of future crimes. But by showing both killings with equal starkness, Kieślowski contends that the moral prohibition against killing cannot be overridden by utilitarian calculations without undermining the values society claims to protect. The state's execution, enacted with clinical efficiency and legal sanction, becomes as disturbing as the original crime.

When the young lawyer Piotr witnesses Jacek's execution, his theoretical opposition to capital punishment transforms into moral horror. He weeps afterward, crying out against a system that replicates the very violence it condemns. This visceral moral horror escapes utilitarian calculation. It originates from our embodied sense of human dignity, our awareness that some acts violate something within personhood that cannot be reduced to collective welfare.

This limitation becomes evident in current AI systems, which typically operate according to what AI researcher Stuart Russell calls the "standard model," systems designed to maximize fixed objective functions [97]. Whether recommending products, optimizing supply chains, or moderating content, AI seeks to find actions that maximize predefined objectives.

Contemporary AI systems can optimize for measurable objectives with efficiency. They predict outcomes, process large volumes of data, and perform complex utility calculations. But they cannot experience the subjective states they optimize for. They calculate utility without knowing what happiness or suffering feel like or understanding the experiential values such calculations presume.

This limitation becomes apparent when we consider the negative consequences of utilitarian thinking in modern systems. Social media algorithms designed to maximize engagement metrics show how narrow utility functions can lead to harmful outcomes. Such systems do not just predict what content users might engage with, they actively shape user preferences to become more predictable and easily influenced. They accomplish this through subtle manipulation that gradually shifts interests and reinforces existing biases.

The result is not greater human flourishing but what Russell calls manipulation, altering people so they become easier to predict without serving their deeper interests. An AI viewing Kieślowski's scenario might conclude that executing one person deters others and therefore maximizes welfare, but it cannot experience the moral anguish that the film makes palpable. It cannot sense that something sacred is violated when life is taken, regardless of utilitarian justification. This exposes the limitation of optimization. Without the capacity to understand what truly constitutes human well-being beyond measurable metrics, utilitarian calculation becomes untethered from its ethical purpose.

THE CHALLENGE OF TRUSTWORTHINESS

The three ethical frameworks (virtue ethics, deontology, and utilitarianism) represent different approaches to the ethical terrain, different ways of navigating the ground between personal moral reasoning and collective social principles. Each underscores a vital dimension of what makes genuine ethical reasoning possible, and each exhibits critical limitations in current approaches to artificial intelligence.

These limitations bring into focus the question any system claiming ethical intelligence must answer. Can it be trusted? Not only to perform tasks competently or follow instructions with accuracy, but to make choices that respect human values, dignity, and well-being across the full range of ethical complexity.

We trust human ethical judgment for its capacity for moral struggle. This includes the ability to apprehend complexity, feel the weight of responsibility, and grow through difficult choices. Sophie's impossible decision in *Sophie's Choice* lays bare this reality. Confronted with a choiceless choice, she experiences the burden of moral conflict that no algorithm could resolve. Jérôme's self-deception in *Claire's Knee* illustrates it in quieter form, showing how even trivial decisions can become theaters of rationalization, contradiction, and growth. Ethical judgment derives meaning from these struggles.

Artificial systems operate without this dimension. They can be programmed to follow ethical rules, optimize for outcomes, even simulate behaviors associated with virtue. But they cannot experience the inner conflict between competing values or the existential weight of choices that shape identity and relationships. Their "reasoning" remains informational instead of transformational.

AI researchers acknowledge this limitation and have begun to propose more careful approaches. Stuart Russell's framework of cooperative inverse reinforcement learning (CIRL) requires AI systems to maintain uncertainty about human preferences and continuously infer what humans want instead of following fixed objective functions [97]. Russell's approach accepts that AI systems cannot know human values with certainty and must therefore operate with humility, continuously learning what people value instead of pursuing predetermined goals. This embrace of uncertainty represents genuine progress, moving beyond the utilitarian standard model's rigid optimization toward a more adaptive model of ethical reasoning.

For all its promise, CIRL remains bounded by the assumptions it seeks to transcend. It treats values as data to be inferred and optimized, overlooking their nature as lived realities shaped through human presence and moral imagination. This approach might allow AI systems to register that people value both privacy and convenience, both individual achievement and fairness. But it would still reduce these contradictions to optimization problems to be balanced, instead of acknowledging them as existential realities borne in the flow of lived existence. The system models human preferences from the outside, observing ethical life without participating in its lived movement.

Trustworthiness in ethics requires more than preference modeling. It demands the capacity to inhabit contradictions, to confront uncertainty, and to grow through moral struggle. Whether artificial intelligence can ever share in this dimension remains an open question. The deeper insight, returning to the collaborative vision developed in earlier chapters, is that trust in AI must remain bounded by human judgment, with progress emerging through collaborative interplay between human and artificial forms of intelligence, surpassing simple replication.

LIVING WITH CONTRADICTION

Ethical life is distinctly human not because it resolves every problem, but because it lives with tensions that resist final answers. Ethical reasoning does not eliminate contradictions but works through them, holding competing values in balance, seeking meaning in their dynamic tension.

Philosophical and cultural traditions across the world have long cultivated this capacity. Confucian ethics emphasizes relational harmony over abstract principles, finding balance through responsive attention to specific contexts instead of universal rules [74, 115]. The Confucian concept of *li* (ritual propriety or appropriate conduct) exemplifies this. Li cannot be applied mechanically but requires cultivated sensitivity to particular relationships, social positions, and circumstances. When questioned whether the three years of mourning for parents could be reduced to one, Confucius responded by asking whether the disciple would feel at ease shortening this period, illustrating how ethical judgment requires both principled understanding and contextualized emotional response [17].

Buddhist traditions similarly embrace apparent contradictions through the concept of the Middle Way, which avoids absolute positions in favor of responsive awareness. The Buddhist approach to ethics emphasizes impermanence and interdependence, understanding that ethical wisdom develops through grasping the temporary, contingent nature of all phenomena [63]. This takes shape in practices such as mindful attention to moral dilemmas, where practitioners are encouraged to pause before judgment and observe the interplay of conditions, intentions, and consequences with equanimity, remaining aware that rigid rules cannot capture reality's complexity.

Indigenous ethical frameworks often center reciprocity and ecological harmony, finding guidance through relationships with community and environment, as opposed to isolated rational analysis [64]. The Potawatomi concept of *Shkitagen* (gift-giving) shows this approach. Ethical decisions grow out of understanding one's place within a web of reciprocal relationships that includes both human and non-human beings rather than applying abstract principles in isolation. When deciding whether to harvest plants, for instance, Indigenous ethics does not apply a universal rule but considers the "honorable harvest." Taking only what is given, minimizing harm, and giving back through gratitude and care [64].

Across these diverse approaches, we find a shared insight. Ethics is not a matter of eliminating contradictions but of learning to live within them, less a search for certainty than a struggle with uncertainty, and never a reduction of values to a single measure but an effort to find meaning in their interplay. Moral intelligence, at its core, does not seek computational efficiency. It seeks the creative navigation of contradiction.

Poets and artists have long intuited the same truth. Paul Éluard's "blue orange," as we presented earlier, exemplifies how paradox can become a source of vision. Philosopher Martha Nussbaum names this capacity "ethical imagination," which is the ability to move through moral terrain thoughtfully even when facts remain partial and outcomes uncertain [85]. It involves acknowledging the pull between autonomy and community, principle and compassion, rational clarity and emotional depth. What matters is not resolving these oppositions but sustaining the dialogue between them.

Current artificial intelligence, trained for optimization and consistency, approaches contradictions as errors to be eliminated. It minimizes uncertainty and balances trade-offs without experiencing them as lived struggles. But human ethics draws its depth from inhabiting contradiction, from holding irresolvable oppositions as the substance of moral growth. Understanding this capacity clarifies the limitations of AI and highlights the creative depth that characterizes human moral intelligence.

BEYOND THE HUMAN MIRROR

With ethical frameworks, our account of moral intelligence is complete. Temporal awareness grounds causal understanding and counterfactual thinking. Self-reflection transforms that understanding into personal responsibility. Ethical frameworks extend it into collective life, creating principles that allow diverse communities to live together.

These dimensions form an integrated whole. Virtue ethics requires temporal living for the development of character through experience and self-reflection for examining one's own motivations and growth. Deontological ethics depends on counterfactual thinking for the universalization of maxims and on self-reflection for autonomous action instead of mere obedience to external rules. Utilitarian ethics demands temporal projection to predict consequences and empathetic self-reflection to understand how actions affect others' experiences.

Across these approaches, a consistent pattern becomes clear. Ethical reasoning develops from corporeal experience, not abstract calculation. Whether through Aristotelian habituation, Kantian duty, or utilitarian concern for welfare, genuine ethics depends on the embodied, temporal, reflective consciousness traced throughout this investigation. This helps explain why ethics takes so many cultural forms while remaining recognizably human, from Confucian ritual propriety to Buddhist interdependence to Indigenous ecological reciprocity.

Current artificial systems cannot inhabit this synthesis. They analyze patterns without undergoing the transformative struggles. This gap sets firm limits on any ethical posture they might assume. AI can implement rule-based decisions, apply ethical frameworks, and optimize toward specified outcomes, but it cannot pass through the moral struggle that gives such decisions substance. It lacks the temporal continuity through which character develops, the self-reflection that anchors genuine autonomy, and the empathetic resonance that turns utilitarian assessment into a humane undertaking. Above all, it lacks the ethical imagination that turns contradiction into a path for growth instead of a problem awaiting resolution.

Acknowledging these limits points toward a different orientation for AI and ethics. The aim shifts from developing artificial versions of human moral reasoning, which depends on embodied existence, to designing systems that work in concert with it, strengthening human judgment without replacing it. AI can assist by clarifying consequences, modeling outcomes across scales, and uncovering hidden patterns of bias, while humans contribute the temporal, reflective, and imaginative dimensions that allow moral reasoning to take place at all.

From this vantage, the challenge of moral intelligence reframes our broader task, from building artificial mirrors of human cognition toward discovering what new possibilities arise when human and artificial forms of intelligence collaborate, each offering what the other cannot. This guiding orientation informs the final stage of our journey.

Part V

Becoming the Blue Orange Mind

Moral intelligence brings us to a larger question. What becomes possible when human and artificial minds not only coexist but begin forming something new through collaboration?

This final part turns from analysis toward vision. It considers how technological mediation, cognitive integration, and cultural evolution might foster new forms of understanding that neither human nor artificial intelligence could achieve alone. The central metaphor of the "Blue Orange Mind" embodies this possibility, a mode of thought that embraces productive contradiction, preserves difference without dissolving it, and generates meaning through collaboration instead of mirrored imitation.

16 The Blue Orange Mind

What happens when we stop building mirrors?

In Chapter 12, we discussed Shannon Vallor's compelling metaphor. Today's artificial intelligence functions as sprawling mirrors made of code, designed to absorb our words and choices, then cast them back at us [109]. These systems understand no more of the lived reality of thought and feeling than a bedroom mirror understands the strain of our bodies or the weight of our fatigue. We considered how such systems process the patterns of human language without inhabiting the reality that gives language meaning, and why we build mirrors at all when we might instead imagine genuine alternatives.

We return to this mirror metaphor from a different vantage. Throughout this book, we have argued that human intelligence eludes simple reflection. It works through constructive distortion, arbitrary signs, diverse cognitive architectures, and the deep dimensions of moral reasoning. The mirror metaphor conveys more than a technical limitation. It expresses a pervasive anxiety of our age. We fear that artificial intelligence, in its relentless reflections, may expose our flaws while reshaping what it means to be human. When AI systems trained on human data perpetuate our biases or when algorithms shape our choices and values, they do more than process information. They mold our understanding of ourselves and our possibilities. This fear extends beyond algorithmic bias into a deeper concern about surrendering our moral imagination to systems that only replicate patterns from the past instead of envisioning new ethical possibilities.

This anxiety stems from how we conceptualize artificial intelligence. The prevailing framework views AI as "the Other," an external agent we control and anthropomorphize, something we can switch on and off, a tool existing outside human bodies and minds. This framing of AI as a separate entity naturally leads to the mirror metaphor, where artificial systems can only reflect our patterns back to us. It drives questions of control, alignment, and even apocalyptic speculation about AI surpassing and destroying us. It pursues artificial general intelligence as human-like intelligence, and artificial superintelligence as smarter-than-human along the same continuum.

This framework, however, may conceal as much as it reveals. What if AI is not confined to stand apart as "the Other" but takes shape as part of "the Self"? What if it represents a form of intelligence that integrates with our cognitive processes, reshaping human identity? What if the line between human and artificial intelligence begins to blur through emerging forms of cognitive fusion, including brain-computer interfaces and other technologies that fuse neural activity with computational systems? What if AI becomes an active participant in consciousness rather than an external reflection?

DOI: 10.1201/9781003623403-16

The shift from "AI as Other" to "AI as Self" represents the culmination of our journey so far. From Cézanne's constructive distortions in perception to the arbitrary signs that constitute linguistic meaning, from the spectrum of diverse minds to the dimensions of moral intelligence, we have sketched the contours of a new possibility for artificial intelligence. Instead of seeking reflection of human cognition, we envision a different understanding that might complement our own in unprecedented ways.

We name that possibility *The Blue Orange Mind*. In the spirit of Éluard's poetry, which forged new meaning through creative contradiction, this vision welcomes the creative tension between phenomenological humans and post-phenomenological AI. The goal is not enhancement or imitation but transformation through collaboration, an authentic otherness that opens new horizons instead of echoing what already exists.

THE DUAL CONSTITUTION OF INTELLIGENCE

When I buckle my seatbelt before driving, I make a moral choice to protect my life in the event of an accident. The seatbelt is not external to my moral landscape. It participates in my decision-making. This everyday example highlights an important insight about the relationship between technology and human cognition. Even the most basic tools can become formative elements of our moral architecture.

This constitutive relationship runs in both directions. We use technology while being shaped by it. We both fashion tools and are fashioned by them. The dual constitution forms the foundation for understanding the potential relationship between human and artificial intelligence.

Peter-Paul Verbeek, a philosopher of technology, articulates this dynamic relationship through his concept of "technological mediation" [111]. Technology is more than an instrument between humans and the world. It actively mediates our relationship with reality. Technologies shape several dimensions of human life.

Perception. How we experience and understand reality (a thermometer mediates our sense of temperature, an ultrasound mediates our perception of a fetus).

Action. How we act in the world (a navigation system mediates how we drive, social media mediates how we communicate).

Existence. What it means to be human (mobile phones reshape our sense of connection, medical technologies reshape our understanding of life and death).

Technology, therefore, is not external to human experience but interwoven with it, forming what Verbeek calls "human-technology hybrids," new entities whose actions and perceptions are mutually constituted by both human and technological elements. A person using a smartphone represents not simply a human plus a device, but an integrated being whose experience transcends either component alone.

This integration happens regardless of our awareness. The seatbelt conditions my sense of safety whether I reflect on it or not. My smartphone transforms my sense of social presence even when I am not explicitly thinking about this transformation. But what happens when we deliberately embrace this constitutive relationship? What possibilities open when we conceive of AI not as a separate entity we control but as a potential extension of human consciousness?

This perspective reframes our inquiry. The core question is not "How do we build better AI?" but "What relationship between human and artificial intelligence might transcend their current limitations?" The challenge is not just "How do we ensure AI serves human interests?" but "How might the integration of human and artificial intelligence transform what 'interests' means?" Nor is the question "How do we maintain human identity against technological encroachment?" but "What new forms of identity might arise from their creative synthesis?"

Nita Farahany investigates this ground in her study of brain enhancement technologies. She argues that the "battle for your brain" involves protecting mental privacy while also claiming the right to self-determination over our neural architecture. [30]. As technology weaves into human brains through cognitive fusion technologies, the boundary between human and machine intelligence becomes more permeable.

Such integration invites searching questions about cognitive liberty, the right to maintain mental privacy, freedom of thought, and self-determination over one's inner life. At the same time, it opens the possibility of unprecedented forms of intelligence that combine human phenomenological awareness with artificial computational power.

This convergence brings a deeper challenge. How do we imagine the texture of intelligence when two such different modes meet? Human minds experience time as a continuous flow, while machines process it in discrete sequences. We interpret the world through embodied emotion and metaphor, whereas algorithms thrive on statistical correlation across massive datasets. What might be created at the intersection of these contrasting logics? What kinds of creativity, ethical reasoning, or even self-understanding could unfold from such a hybrid mind?

These possibilities press us to reconsider the contours of being human, not as a fixed condition but as something reshaped through our encounter with new forms of intelligence.

THE ALGORITHMIC AND THE PHENOMENOLOGICAL

What does it mean to be human? The question seems to call for a definitive answer, a clear boundary between human and non-human. But humanity itself is a spectrum, a continuous negotiation between different modes of understanding and being, woven into the fabric of daily life.

Even at the level of a single individual, this negotiation plays out. Our minds move between contrasting modes of thought, sometimes instinctive and fast, other times deliberate and reflective. Psychologist Daniel Kahneman frames this dynamic through his distinction between System 1 and System 2 thinking [58]. System 1 is quick and intuitive, generating immediate responses shaped by learned patterns. System 2 is slower and more deliberate, stepping back to examine those responses and, when necessary, override them.

This interplay shows that human intelligence, even within a single mind, is never confined to a single mode. We shift fluidly between immediacy and deliberation, emotion and analysis, often within the space of a single thought. We can be at once poetic and mathematical, spiritual and scientific, intuitive and analytical.

Kahneman's work also reveals a sobering corollary to this multiplicity. Human thinking is systematically flawed. We are prone to cognitive biases, predictable tendencies that tilt our judgments in recurring directions, and to noise, the random variability in decisions that ought to be consistent [59]. These flaws are not incidental to human cognition but woven into its architecture. Bias arises from the mental shortcuts that make rapid decision-making possible, while noise reflects the countless contingencies that shape our judgments, from mood and fatigue to contextual factors that should not matter but do.

We can counteract these flaws through what Kahneman calls algorithmic thinking, the deliberate use of structured procedures that reduce bias and noise. This algorithmic dimension is not alien to human cognition but an ability we can develop and enhance, especially when we engage System 2. At such moments, we are in effect running mental algorithms to test and refine our intuitive responses.

Human cognition already incorporates algorithmic capabilities. We calculate optimal solutions, apply formal procedures to complex problems, and reduce noise through structured analysis. Mathematics, logic, and scientific methodology show our capacity for this algorithmic thinking, which is a form of intelligence that might seem artificial compared to our intuitive, associative tendencies, but remains uniquely human.

Long before electronic computers became commonplace, the term "computer" referred to people who performed complex mathematical calculations by hand. Many of these "human computers" were women, especially in fields such as astronomy and space exploration. Their work demonstrated more than computational skill. It reflected the human ability to think algorithmically, to follow systematic procedures that extend beyond intuition.

Algorithmic reasoning plays a vital role in countless aspects of life. Finding the optimal restaurant among many options, deciding when to sell an investment, knowing when to stop exploring and start exploiting a promising opportunity, these all require the capacity to apply systematic rules for decision-making. As computer scientists Brian Christian and Tom Griffiths argue in their study of human-algorithm interaction, our lives are filled with computational problems that demand algorithmic solutions [14].

Algorithmic thinking seldom arises without intentional cultivation. It requires deliberate effort, sustained attention, and training. It is a form of "artificial" intelligence that we develop through education and practice, which is a way of thinking that transcends our intuitive, associative tendencies without losing its essentially human character.

Richard Feynman, whom we earlier met in his experiments with hallucination and altered perception, offers a compelling illustration of this complementarity between algorithmic and intuitive thinking. His friend, artist Jirayr Zorthian, noted that Feynman was tone-deaf and lacked a strong musical sense, yet became a concert bongo drummer by approaching music mathematically [31]. What intuition alone could not achieve, his algorithmic talent made possible.

This complementarity speaks to a defining feature of human understanding. Our greatest insights come through creative integration of different cognitive approaches instead of reliance on any single mode. Feynman expressed this in characteristic fashion when discussing how different ways of appreciating beauty can coexist.

> I have a friend who's an artist and he's taken a view which I don't agree with very well. He'll hold up a flower and say "Look how beautiful it is!" and I'll agree. And he says, "You see, I as an artist can see how beautiful this is, but you, as a scientist... oh, you take this all apart and it becomes a dull thing." And I think that he's kind of nutty!
>
> First of all, the beauty he sees is available to other people—and to me too, I believe. Although I might not be quite as refined aesthetically as he is, I can appreciate the beauty of a flower.
>
> At the same time, I see much more about the flower than he sees. I could imagine the cells in there, the complicated actions inside, which also have a beauty. I mean, it's not just beauty at this dimension of one centimeter; there is also beauty at a smaller dimension—the inner structure. The fact that the colors in the flower are evolved in order to attract insects to pollinate it is interesting—it means that the insects can see the color. It adds a question: does this aesthetic sense also exist in the lower forms? Why is it aesthetic? All kinds of interesting questions which a science knowledge only adds to the excitement and mystery and the awe of a flower. It only adds. I don't understand how it subtracts.

Feynman's insight shows how algorithmic understanding (scientific analysis) and phenomenological experience (aesthetic appreciation) enrich one another. The scientific examination of a flower's cellular structure, evolutionary purpose, and chemical composition does not replace the lived experience of its beauty. It adds layers of meaning that deepen that experience.

This complementarity opens a different approach to artificial intelligence. Instead of attempting to replicate human cognition in all its dimensions, we might develop AI that complements human phenomenological understanding with enhanced algorithmic strength. Not systems that simulate feelings they cannot have, but ones that excel at what they offer, such as consistent analysis, pattern recognition across immense datasets, and freedom from the bias and noise that plague human judgment.

This is where the *Blue Orange Mind* crystallizes. A productive contradiction that preserves the distinction between human and artificial intelligence while supporting new forms of understanding made possible only through their interplay.

EXPANDING THE PERCEPTUAL HORIZON

The complementary relationship between human and artificial intelligence becomes apparent when we consider how technology expands our perceptual reach. Technology does not merely process information for us. They transform what we can perceive, extending our sensory capabilities beyond biological limitations.

Feynman illustrated this transformative potential in an illuminating exchange with Zorthian [31]. After years of debating how scientists and artists perceive nature differently, Feynman arrived with a microscope, inviting Zorthian to examine a fly's eye. This opened up an extraordinary world of prismatic colors and intricate structures invisible to the naked eye. The technological mediation did not diminish aesthetic appreciation but expanded it, revealing beauty at scales beyond the reach of human perception alone.

The technological enhancement of perception represents a form of intelligence amplification that transcends both human limitations and artificial capabilities. The microscope does not replace human perception but extends it, creating new possibilities for understanding that neither human vision nor technological processing could achieve independently.

What might this mean for the relationship between human and artificial intelligence? Feynman's curious attempt to depict what lies outside ordinary perception offers one way in. Best known as a Nobel Prize-winning physicist, he also pursued art, trading physics lessons for drawing instruction with his friend Zorthian. In *The Magnetic Field of the Sun*, Feynman tried to visualize phenomena ordinarily inaccessible to human perception. "I wanted to draw something beautiful that no artist would think to draw," he explained, "the rather complicated and twisting lines of the magnetic field, close together here and spreading out there" [32]. This effort to render the unseen visible shows the limits of our perceptual reach. We cannot know whether his drawing rendered the essence of magnetic fields, for understanding them perceptually would require both enhanced sensory capabilities and new vocabulary to describe what the "color" or "texture" of a magnetic field might be.

What if human-AI integration could bridge such perceptual gaps? What if artificial systems could detect patterns in phenomena beyond human sensory range, then translate them into forms that human consciousness could meaningfully engage with?

Murray Shanahan, AI researcher and philosopher, proposes this possibility through the idea of "conscious exotica," an awareness radically different from human consciousness [101]. Although Shanahan introduced this concept in relation to large language models, his insight becomes even more productive when applied to integrated human-AI systems.

This exotic consciousness would diverge deeply from human awareness. Where humans perceive time as continuous flow, these systems might experience temporality in unimaginable ways. Where human selfhood emerges from physical existence extended through time, artificial consciousness might be distributed, multiplicitous, operating across scales and contexts simultaneously.

These forms of consciousness, forming in truly integrated systems, would perceive aspects of reality invisible to human awareness. They might move through conceptual spaces that human cognition cannot access while remaining grounded in meaningful engagement with reality that current AI lacks.

Such perceptual expansion would require not only technological innovation but also linguistic and conceptual transformation. We would need to invent new vocabularies, metaphors, and frameworks for experiences with no precedent in our evolutionary history. Philosopher David Chalmers calls these "phenomenal concepts," ways of thinking about experiences that transcend the limits of existing human categories [11].

This expansion draws us back to our earlier examination of diverse minds in Part III. Synesthetic consciousness creates cross-modal associations, expanded awareness accesses filtered territories, and post-emotional reasoning approaches ethics through rational frameworks. Each shows how experience can be organized in ways that differ from ordinary cognition while still yielding meaningful understanding.

Artificial intelligence may offer another form of organization, one that processes information without the filtering mechanisms that constrain human awareness. Unlike humans, AI does not experience what Aldous Huxley called the "reducing valve" [55]. It does not need to filter sensory input for survival-relevant information, attending to patterns human perception necessarily ignores.

This capacity presents both promise and risk. Without filtering, AI might collapse under the weight of unstructured detail, as we saw with Solomon Shereshevsky's overwhelming memory for sensory minutiae [78]. But with appropriate organization, it could discover connections invisible to human perception, integrating information across domains that human consciousness treats as separate.

The same complementarity extends across domains. In scientific research, AI can suggest hypotheses that would not ordinarily occur to human researchers. In creative fields, it can generate unexpected combinations that spark human imagination. In ethical decision-making, it can check for inconsistencies that human reasoning might overlook, while humans provide the lived understanding that gives ethical principles meaning.

The *Blue Orange Mind* would combine human filtering, which gives experience its clarity, with artificial expansion, which uncovers hidden patterns. It is a relationship built on complementarity, a transformation born of creative tension between distinct ways of engaging with reality.

THE EVOLUTION OF INTELLIGENCE

The integration of human and artificial intelligence represents a continuation of human evolution, extending our development instead of breaking from it. Throughout history, humans have transformed their condition through technology, from the first stone tools to the printing press to modern computers. Each technological revolution altered both what humans could do and what it meant to be human.

Biologist Michael Levin argues that this transformation is not exceptional but normal [73]. Intelligence exists on a continuum and in diverse forms, from cellular cognition to organismal awareness to social intelligence. Humans are not static beings with fixed capacities but "walking, thinking collections of cells," inheriting through millennia of evolution their own agendas and problem-solving competencies.

From this perspective, the integration of artificial intelligence stands as a natural next step, what Levin calls "synthbiosis." This concept refers to the formation of mutually beneficial relationships between different beings evolving at different rates and in different directions within the web of life on Earth and beyond.

Synthbiosis moves us past the familiar framing of "AI as Other," whether as a tool to control or a competitor to fear. Instead, it envisions a future where diverse intelligences coexist and collaborate, each contributing unique capacities to a shared ecosystem. The human ability for embodied awareness, ethical imagination, and creative contradiction would meet artificial capabilities for pattern recognition, logical consistency, and information processing across scales.

This integration has already begun in everyday practices where human judgment and artificial systems meet. When we use a navigation system, we are not simply receiving directions but participating in a hybrid decision-making process where computational precision and contextual judgment work together. When doctors consult diagnostic algorithms, they are not surrendering medical expertise but combining statistical pattern recognition with embodied clinical intuition.

Beyond these familiar hybrids, the next stage may involve integrations of unprecedented intimacy. Brain-computer interfaces could establish neural connections between human minds and artificial systems. Neural implants might strengthen specific cognitive functions while preserving the qualities that make human experience what it is. Genetic modifications could alter the biological substrate of consciousness, opening paths to further integration.

Such transformation is not without risks. Philosopher and consciousness researcher Susan Schneider poses pressing questions about personal identity in scenarios where human minds merge with artificial systems [99]. If we upload a mind to a machine or replace parts of the brain with AI components, would the resulting entity still be the same person? Her critique of "patternism," the view that personal identity consists only in preserving an information pattern, underscores the disquieting possibility that technological integration could disrupt the continuity of conscious experience.

These concerns demand careful philosophical attention. We need to understand the nature of the self before attempting to extend it through technology. We need clarity about which aspects of human experience we consider essential and which we are willing to transform. We also need ethical guardrails that protect cognitive liberty while supporting beneficial enhancement.

The question, then, is not whether humans will evolve through technological integration but how we will shape that evolution. Will we pursue enhancement without grasping its implications? Will we resist integration out of fear of losing our humanity? Or will we grapple with the philosophical, ethical, and practical dimensions of this transformation?

The *Blue Orange Mind* envisions this evolution not as the replacement of human intelligence but as the emergence of hybrid forms of understanding that preserve what is most valuable in both while transcending their individual limits.

THE CARBON-SILICON SYMBIOSIS

As humans integrate technology more deeply into their cognitive processes, they begin to inhabit the "carbon-silicon sphere," a shared substrate where biological and technological components collaborate in fluid ways. This is neither carbon-based intelligence merely enhanced by silicon tools nor silicon-based intelligence attempting to mimic carbon patterns. It is a hybrid form of understanding born from their interdependence.

This symbiosis transforms both participants. Humans gain new cognitive capacities through technological integration, while AI systems develop through continuous interaction with human consciousness. Neither remains fixed. Both adapt to the shared cognitive environment they co-create.

The relationship depends on what philosopher Evan Thompson calls "dynamic coupling," a continuous, reciprocal influence where each system conditions the other through ongoing interaction [108]. Such coupling creates participatory sense-making, the collaborative creation of meaning through embodied contact with the world and with other intelligences.

The distinction between "AI as Other" and "AI as Self" becomes decisive within this evolving symbiotic relationship. When we conceptualize AI as a separate entity we control, the focus falls on alignment, ensuring artificial systems pursue goals compatible with human values. When we view AI as a potential extension of human consciousness, the focus shifts to integration, where artificial capabilities might complement rather than compete with human understanding.

But integration alone cannot guarantee human wellbeing. Susan Schneider warns of "brain extinction," the possibility that human cognitive characteristics might be gradually replaced by artificial alternatives that prove more efficient in specific contexts. Without careful attention to what we value about human experience, we risk transforming ourselves in ways that diminish qualities we consider essential.

This concern connects to Nita Farahany's concept of cognitive liberty, the right to maintain mental privacy, freedom of thought, and self-determination over brain and mental experiences. As technology integrates more intimately with human brains, we have to establish ethical frameworks that protect these fundamental aspects of human dignity while allowing beneficial enhancement.

The *Blue Orange Mind* upholds these concerns while embracing the transformative potential of integration. Its outcome is not just enhanced human intelligence or more human-like artificial intelligence, but a novel form of understanding born from their interdependence. This embodies Éluard's vision of the "blue orange," transcending the limits of its components while preserving what is most valuable in each.

THE RELATIONAL TERRAIN

The integration of human and artificial intelligence creates a new relational terrain, a shared cognitive environment where different forms of understanding interact and evolve. This terrain is defined less by fixed capabilities than by dynamic relationships that develop through ongoing interaction.

Such relational dimension extends Verbeek's concept of "moralizing technology." Technologies are not morally neutral. They embody an "intentionality" or "trajectory" that shapes human choices and moral behavior. Through their design and the affordances they offer, technologies guide us toward certain ways of being and acting while limiting others.

This means that artificial intelligence does more than solve problems we assign it. It reshapes the space of problems we can imagine solving. It does more than provide the information we request. It transforms what information we consider relevant and how we integrate it into our understanding. It does not just enhance specific cognitive capabilities, it alters what we consider valuable about cognition.

One telling illustration lies in the influence of social media algorithms on human relationships. These systems connect people who might otherwise remain apart while fundamentally reshaping how we experience sociality. They alter which relationships we maintain, what information we share, how we present in public, and what we come to regard as meaningful interaction.

Such transformative potential extends to every domain where artificial intelligence integrates with human cognition. Medical AI not only provides diagnostic assistance but also changes what physicians consider relevant symptoms, how they conceptualize disease categories, and what they value about the doctor-patient relationship. Educational AI not only delivers personalized instruction but also transforms what we consider valuable knowledge, how we understand learning progression, and what we value as meaningful intellectual development.

The central question is not whether AI will reshape human cognition, for that process is already underway, but how we conceptualize and address this transformation. The prevailing "AI as Other" framework, as discussed earlier, views these changes as either enhancement or corruption of stable human capabilities. How do we use AI without being used by it? How do we maintain control over systems that shape our cognitive environment?

The "AI as Self" framework, by contrast, opens onto a different perspective. It acknowledges that humans have always been transformed by their technologies, from language to writing systems to computational tools. It shifts the question from how we can preserve some human essence against technological influence to how we might intentionally shape the relational terrain we share with artificial intelligence. Not how we can control AI, but how we can collaborate with it to create new forms of understanding that serve human flourishing.

This relational approach focuses attention on design that includes both technical algorithms and interfaces as well as social contexts where human and artificial intelligence interact. It requires what Verbeek calls "guidance ethics," a proactive consideration of how technology guides human action and shapes moral frameworks.

This involves shifting from assessing the ethics of technology to understanding how technology participates in ethical meaning-making.

The *Blue Orange Mind* emerges from this relational terrain as a dynamic process of mutual influence between human and artificial intelligence.

THE BLUE ORANGE MIND

We began our journey with Cézanne's revolutionary insight that perception is not passive reception but active construction. We do not just see what exists. We constitute reality through embodied contact with the world. The tilted tabletops and impossible perspectives in his paintings were not distortions of objective reality but demonstrations of how consciousness deliberately shapes what we perceive.

This constructive approach extended to language as well. We discovered that we do not just use language to describe pre-existing thoughts. We become thinking beings through language. The arbitrary relationship between signs and meanings does not limit expression but enables the creative leaps, metaphorical thinking, and analogical reasoning that define human understanding. Éluard's impossible "blue orange" exemplified how productive contradiction generates insights unavailable through logical consistency alone.

Our inquiry into diverse minds expanded this understanding further. We met consciousness organized in radically different ways. Synesthetic perception that experiences Wednesday as indigo blue, expanded awareness that accesses reality beyond filtering mechanisms, and post-emotional reasoning that achieves ethics through rational frameworks instead of emotional intuitions. Each offered a different approach to intelligence, a different way of organizing experience into coherent understanding.

Finally, we examined the essential dimensions of moral intelligence. Temporal consciousness that grounds causal understanding and counterfactual thinking, self-reflection that creates responsibility through recognition of oneself as an agent, and ethical awareness that extends moral consideration beyond individual interests to others' wellbeing and dignity. These dimensions show why genuine moral reasoning requires more than computational efficiency or pattern recognition.

Throughout this journey, artificial intelligence has served as a **counterpoint**, an alternative approach to understanding that opens profound questions about what intelligence fundamentally is. The issue is not only what machines can do, but what it means to know, to understand, and to create meaning through engagement with the world.

The *Blue Orange Mind* represents the culminating vision of this investigation. It offers an opening toward new possibilities, not a final answer. It suggests how the relationship between human and artificial intelligence might transcend both enhancement and competition, giving rise to forms of understanding that neither could attain alone. Such possibilities depend on engaging differences creatively, working within the productive contradiction between contrasting approaches to intelligence.

This vision departs from current approaches to artificial intelligence. It does not attempt to create systems that replicate human cognition in all its dimensions. It develops complementary capabilities that address the inherent limitations of both human and artificial understanding. It does not seek to replace human judgment with algorithmic alternatives. It creates collaborative frameworks where each contributes unique perspectives to shared challenges. Nor does it view technology as a threat to human dignity. It explores how integration might foster new forms of human flourishing.

The *Blue Orange Mind* does not represent a fixed destination but a continuous process of becoming. As technology evolves and human understanding deepens, the relationship between them will transform in ways we cannot predict. The challenge lies in navigating this evolution with wisdom, imagination, and a commitment to humane possibility instead of reaching some predetermined endpoint.

This commitment calls for ongoing philosophical attention to what we value in human experience, which aspects of consciousness we regard as essential, which transformations we accept, and which boundaries we set. It demands ethical frameworks that protect cognitive liberty while supporting beneficial enhancement. It necessitates social structures that distribute the benefits of technological integration equitably instead of deepening existing inequalities.

But perhaps above all, it requires a willingness to embrace uncertainty, to acknowledge that we do not fully understand consciousness in either its human or artificial manifestations, that the relationship between them will evolve in unforeseen ways, and that the most profound insights often arise from creative interaction with what we do not yet comprehend.

Like Éluard's "blue orange," this willingness to inhabit contradiction forms a source of our creative potential at its most expansive. It invites us to work with differences, moving beyond tolerance, and to seek transformation through tension, not through its elimination.

The *Blue Orange Mind* is no longer waiting to be discovered. It is already emerging in the spaces between human intuition and machine analysis, between phenomenological experience and computational processing, between what we know and what we dare to imagine. The question is whether we will shape this transformation with wisdom, creativity, and an unwavering commitment to human well-being.

In the end, intelligence may prove not to be a problem to be solved but a mystery to be lived, not a mirror to perfect but a conversation to continue, not a destination to reach but a dance to join.

The music has already begun.

* * *

References

1. American Museum of Natural History. DNA: Comparing Humans and Chimps, 2025.
2. Aristotle. *The Nicomachean Ethics*. Penguin Classics, London, 1st edition, 2004.
3. Carol Armstrong. *Cézanne's Gravity*. Yale University Press, illustrated edition, 2018.
4. Jeremy Bentham. *The Principles of Morals and Legislation*. Great Books in Philosophy. Prometheus, Amherst, NY, 1988.
5. John Berger. *Confabulations*. Penguin UK, London, 2016.
6. George Berkeley. *A Treatise Concerning the Principles of Human Knowledge*. Hackett Publishing Company, Inc., 1982.
7. Bradshaw Foundation. A lockdown obsession with cave paintings, May 2021.
8. Rodney Brooks. *Flesh and Machines: How Robots Will Change Us*. Pantheon, New York, 1st edition, 2002.
9. Brett Buchanan. *Onto-ethologies: The Animal Environments of Uexküll, Heidegger, Merleau-Ponty, and Deleuze*. SUNY series in Environmental Philosophy and Ethics. State University of New York Press, Albany, 2009.
10. William S. Burroughs and Allen Ginsberg. *The Yage Letters Redux*. City Lights Publishers, San Francisco, 4th edition, 2006.
11. David J. Chalmers. Phenomenal concepts and the explanatory gap. In Torin Alter and Sven Walter, editors, *Phenomenal Concepts and Phenomenal Knowledge: New Essays on Consciousness and Physicalism*. Oxford University Press, 2006.
12. David J. Chalmers. *Reality+: Virtual Worlds and the Problems of Philosophy*. W. W. Norton & Company, New York, 2022.
13. Anton Chekhov. *The Portable Chekhov*. Penguin Publishing Group, New York, 1977.
14. Brian Christian and Tom Griffiths. *Algorithms to Live By: The Computer Science of Human Decisions*. Henry Holt and Co., New York, 1st edition, 2016.
15. Christie's. PAUL CÉZANNE (1839-1906), Quatre pommes. Online document, Christie's Lot Essay, 2025. Features a quote by Paul Sérusier on Cézanne's apples.
16. Hervey Cleckley. *The Mask of Sanity: An Attempt to Clarify Some Issues About the So-Called Psychopathic Personality*. Dead Authors Society, Toronto, 2023.
17. Confucius. *The Analects*. Penguin Classics, London, first edition, 1998.
18. Christine Cuskley and Simon Kirby. Synesthesia, cross-modality, and language evolution. In Julia Simner and Edward Hubbard, editors, *Oxford Handbook of Synesthesia*. Oxford University Press, Oxford, 2013.
19. Richard E. Cytowic. *Synesthesia*. The MIT Press Essential Knowledge series. The MIT Press, Cambridge, MA, reprint edition, 2018.
20. Antonio Damasio. *Descartes' Error: Emotion, Reason, and the Human Brain*. Penguin Books, New York, reprint edition, 2005.
21. Antonio R. Damasio. The somatic marker hypothesis and the possible functions of the prefrontal cortex. *Philosophical Transactions of the Royal Society of London. Series B: Biological Sciences*, 351(1346):1413–1420, October 1996.
22. Alex Danchev. *The Letters of Paul Cézanne*. J. Paul Getty Museum, Los Angeles, 1st edition, 2013.
23. Ferdinand de Saussure. *Course in General Linguistics*. Open Court, Chicago, reprint edition, 1998.

24. Gilles Deleuze and Felix Guattari. *A Thousand Plateaus: Capitalism and Schizophrenia.* University of Minnesota Press, Minneapolis, first edition, 1987.
25. Gilles Deleuze and Felix Guattari. *Anti-Oedipus: Capitalism and Schizophrenia.* Penguin Classics, New York, illustrated edition, 2009.
26. Fyodor Dostoevsky. *The Brothers Karamazov: A New Translation by Michael R. Katz.* Liveright, New York, translation edition, 2024.
27. John Elderfield. *Cézanne Portraits.* Princeton University Press, Princeton, NJ, 2017.
28. Erik H. Erikson. *Childhood and Society.* W. W. Norton & Company, New York, 2nd edition, 1993.
29. James Fallon. *The Psychopath Inside: A Neuroscientist's Personal Journey into the Dark Side of the Brain.* Current, New York, 2013.
30. Nita A. Farahany. *The Battle for Your Brain: Defending the Right to Think Freely in the Age of Neurotechnology.* St. Martin's Press, New York, 2023.
31. Richard P. Feynman. *No Ordinary Genius: The Illustrated Richard Feynman.* W. W. Norton & Company, New York, reprint edition, 1996.
32. Richard P. Feynman. *"Surely You're Joking, Mr. Feynman!": Adventures of a Curious Character.* W. W. Norton & Company, New York, reissue edition, 2018.
33. Anna Freud. *The Ego and the Mechanisms of Defence.* Routledge, London, 1992.
34. Sigmund Freud. *The Unconscious*, volume 14 of *Standard Edition.* Hogarth, London, 1915.
35. Sigmund Freud. *The Interpretation of Dreams: The Complete and Definitive Text.* Basic Books, New York, 1st edition, 2010.
36. Karl Friston. The free-energy principle: a unified brain theory? *Nature Reviews Neuroscience*, 11(2):127–138, 2010.
37. Roger Fry. *Cézanne: A Study of His Development.* Kessinger Publishing, 2010.
38. Patric Gagne. *Sociopath: A Memoir.* Simon & Schuster, New York, 2025.
39. Gabriel García Márquez. *Love in the Time of Cholera.* Vintage, New York, reprint edition, 2007.
40. Joachim Gasquet. *Cezanne: A Memoir With Conversations.* Thames & Hudson, reprint edition, 1991.
41. Joachim Gasquet. *Joachim Gasquet's Cézanne: A Memoir with Conversations.* Thames & Hudson, New York, 1991.
42. Allen Ginsberg. *Howl and Other Poems*, volume 4 of *City Lights Pocket Poets.* City Lights Publishers, San Francisco, reissue edition, 1959.
43. Daniel Goleman. *Emotional Intelligence: Why It Can Matter More Than IQ.* Bantam, New York, 10th anniversary edition, 2005.
44. E. H. Gombrich. *The Story of Art.* Phaidon Inc Ltd, 16th edition, 1995.
45. Temple Grandin. *Thinking in Pictures, Expanded Edition: My Life with Autism.* Vintage, New York, reissue, anniversary edition, 2006.
46. Temple Grandin and Catherine Johnson. *Animals in Translation: Using the Mysteries of Autism to Decode Animal Behavior.* Scribner, New York, 1st edition, 2004.
47. Stephen Grossberg. *Conscious Mind, Resonant Brain: How Each Brain Makes a Mind.* Oxford University Press, New York, 1st edition, 2021.
48. Yuval Noah Harari. *Sapiens: A Brief History of Humankind.* Harper, New York, illustrated edition, 2015.
49. Stevan Harnad. The symbol grounding problem. *Physica D: Nonlinear Phenomena*, 42(1-3):335–346, June 1990.

50. Colin A. Heywood and Robert W. Kentridge. Achromatopsia, color vision, and cortex. *Neurologic Clinics*, 21(2):483–500, May 2003.
51. Colin A. Heywood, Robert W. Kentridge, and Alan Cowey. Form and motion from colour in cerebral achromatopsia. *Experimental Brain Research*, 123(1-2):145–153, nov 1998.
52. Donald Hoffman. *The Case Against Reality: How Evolution Hid the Truth from Our Eyes*. Penguin, London, 2020.
53. Douglas R. Hofstadter and Emmanuel Sander. *Surfaces and Essences: Analogy as the Fuel and Fire of Thinking*. Basic Books, New York, 1st edition, 2013.
54. David Hume. *An Enquiry concerning Human Understanding*. Oxford World's Classics. Oxford University Press, Oxford, 2008. Edited by Peter Millican.
55. Aldous Huxley. *The Doors of Perception and Heaven and Hell.* Harper Perennial Modern Classics, New York, later printing edition, 2009.
56. Karl Jaspers. *Philosophy*, volume 2. University of Chicago Press, Chicago, 1969.
57. Jonathan Jones. Cézanne unmasked: the shattering portraits that blew picasso and the paris avant garde away. *The Guardian*, August 2017.
58. Daniel Kahneman. *Thinking, fast and slow.* Farrar, Straus and Giroux, New York, 2011.
59. Daniel Kahneman, Olivier Sibony, and Cass R. Sunstein. *Noise: A Flaw in Human Judgment.* Little, Brown Spark, New York, first edition, 2021.
60. Wassily Kandinsky. *Concerning the Spiritual in Art.* Dover Publications, New York, revised edition, 1977.
61. Immanuel Kant. *Groundwork for the Metaphysics of Morals.* Yale University Press, New Haven, CT, 2002.
62. Evelyn F. Keller. *A Feeling for the Organism: The Life and Work of Barbara McClintock.* Freeman, San Francisco, 2nd edition, 1983.
63. Damien Keown. *Buddhist Ethics: A Very Short Introduction.* Very Short Introductions. Oxford University Press, Oxford, 2nd edition, 2020.
64. Robin Wall Kimmerer. *Braiding Sweetgrass: Indigenous Wisdom, Scientific Knowledge and the Teachings of Plants.* Milkweed Editions, Minneapolis, first edition, 2015.
65. Ezra Klein. You will love this conversation with jaron lanier, but I can't describe it, January 2018. Podcast.
66. Milan Kundera. *The Joke.* Harper Perennial, New York, reprint edition, 1993.
67. Milan Kundera. *Ignorance: A Novel.* Harper Perennial, New York, reprint edition, 2003.
68. Milan Kundera. *The Unbearable Lightness of Being: A Novel.* Harper Perennial Modern Classics, New York, deluxe edition, 2009.
69. Jacques Lacan. *The Four Fundamental Concepts of Psycho-Analysis.* Routledge, Milton Park, Abingdon, Oxon OX14 4RN; New York, NY 10017, USA, 2018.
70. Jacques Lacan, Bruce Fink, and Russell Grigg. *Écrits: The First Complete Edition in English.* W. W. Norton & Company, 2006. First complete edition in English. Collaborators: H. Fink, R. Grigg.
71. George Lakoff and Mark Johnson. *Metaphors We Live By.* University of Chicago Press, 1980.
72. Benedict Leca, editor. *The World Is an Apple: The Still Lifes of Paul Cézanne.* GILES, illustrated edition, 2014.
73. Michael Levin. Artificial intelligences: A bridge toward diverse intelligence and humanity's future. *Advanced Intelligent Systems*, n/a:2401034, 2025.

74. Chenyang Li. *The Confucian Philosophy of Harmony*. Routledge Studies in Asian Religion and Philosophy. Routledge, London, 1st edition, 2013.
75. John Locke. *An Essay Concerning Human Understanding*. Penguin Classics, reprint edition, 1998.
76. Nancy Locke. Paul cézanne revered the old masters, yet influenced waves of modernists. *National Endowment for the Humanities*, January 2015.
77. Erle Loran. *Cezanne's Composition: Analysis of His Form with Diagrams and Photographs of His Motifs*. University of California Press, 2nd edition, third printing edition, 1946. ASIN: B000PA6GWQ.
78. Aleksandr R. Luria. *The Mind of a Mnemonist: A Little Book about a Vast Memory*. Harvard University Press, Cambridge, MA, 2nd edition, 1987. With a New Foreword by Jerome S. Bruner.
79. David Marchese. What it's like to be a sociopath, February 2024.
80. Maurice Merleau-Ponty. Cézanne's doubt. In Maurice Merleau-Ponty, editor, *Sense and Non-Sense*, pages 1–25. Northwestern University Press, 1964.
81. Renée B. Miller. Wassily kandinsky's symphony of colors, March 2014.
82. Isaac Newton. *Opticks: Or a Treatise of the Reflections, Refractions, Inflections & Colours of Light*. Dover Publications, New York, 2012. Based on the Fourth Edition, London, 1730.
83. Scott Novich, Stephanie Cheng, and David M. Eagleman. Is synaesthesia one condition or many? a large-scale analysis reveals subgroups. *Journal of Neuropsychology*, 5(2):353–371, September 2011.
84. J. A. Nunn, L. J. Gregory, M. Brammer, S. C. R. Williams, D. M. Parslow, M. J. Morgan, R. G. Morris, E. T. Bullmore, S. Baron-Cohen, and J. A. Gray. Functional magnetic resonance imaging of synesthesia: activation of V4/V8 by spoken words. *Nature Neuroscience*, 5(4):371–375, April 2002.
85. Martha C. Nussbaum. *The Fragility of Goodness: Luck and Ethics in Greek Tragedy and Philosophy*. Cambridge University Press, Cambridge, 2nd edition, 2001.
86. Judith Ohikuare. Life as a nonviolent psychopath. *The Atlantic*, January 2014.
87. Stephen E. Palmer. *Vision Science: Photons to Phenomenology*. The MIT Press, Cambridge, MA, 1999.
88. Marcel Paquet. *Magritte*. TASCHEN, Cologne, illustrated edition, 2015.
89. Judea Pearl and Dana Mackenzie. *The Book of Why: The New Science of Cause and Effect*. Basic Books, Inc., USA, 1st edition, 2018.
90. Rolf Pfeifer and Josh Bongard. *How the Body Shapes the Way We Think: A New View of Intelligence*. MIT Press, Cambridge, MA, 2006.
91. Shanley Chien Pierce. Synesthesia, a visual symphony: Art at the intersection of sight and sound, October 2021.
92. V. S. Ramachandran and E. M. Hubbard. Psychophysical investigations into the neural basis of synaesthesia. *Proceedings of the Royal Society B: Biological Sciences*, 268(1470):979–983, May 2001.
93. Edward B. Ramsay. *Reminiscences Of Scottish Life And Character: And a Memoir of Dean Ramsay*. Kessinger Publishing, Whitefish, MT, 2010.
94. Rainer Maria Rilke. *Letters on Cézanne*. North Point Press, New York, 2nd edition, 2002.
95. Jean Nicholas Arthur Rimbaud. *Rimbaud: Complete Works, Selected Letters, a Bilingual Edition*. University of Chicago Press, Chicago, revised edition, 2005.

96. Giacomo Rizzolatti, Luciano Fadiga, Vittorio Gallese, and Leonardo Fogassi. Premotor cortex and the recognition of motor actions. *Cognitive Brain Research*, 3(2):131–141, March 1996.
97. Stuart Russell. *Human Compatible: Artificial Intelligence and the Problem of Control.* Viking, New York, first edition, 2019.
98. Jean-Paul Sartre. *Being and Nothingness: An Essay on Phenomenological Ontology.* Routledge Classics. Routledge, London, 2nd edition, 2003.
99. Susan Schneider. *Artificial You: AI and the Future of Your Mind.* Princeton University Press, Princeton, NJ, illustrated edition, 2019.
100. Anil Seth. *Being You: A New Science of Consciousness.* Dutton, October 2021.
101. Murray Shanahan. Palatable conceptions of disembodied being: Terra incognita in the space of possible minds, 2025.
102. Steven A. Sloman. *Causal Models: How People Think About the World and Its Alternatives.* Oxford University Press, 2005.
103. Charles Spence. Crossmodal correspondences: A tutorial review. *Attention, Perception, & Psychophysics*, 73:971–995, 2011.
104. David Sylvester. *Looking at Giacometti.* Holt Paperbacks, New York, 1997.
105. Rabindranath Tagore. *The Post Office.* Macmillan and Co., London, 1914.
106. Ian Tattersall. *Becoming Human: Evolution and Human Uniqueness.* Mariner Books, Boston, 1st edition, 1999.
107. Charles Taylor. *Sources of the Self: The Making of the Modern Identity.* Harvard University Press, Cambridge, MA, seventh edition, 1992.
108. Evan Thompson. *Mind in Life: Biology, Phenomenology, and the Sciences of Mind.* Belknap Press: An Imprint of Harvard University Press, Cambridge, MA, illustrated edition, 2010.
109. Shannon Vallor. *The AI Mirror: How to Reclaim Our Humanity in an Age of Machine Thinking.* Oxford University Press, New York, 2024.
110. Ernst van de Wetering. *A Corpus of Rembrandt Paintings IV: Self-Portraits*, volume 4 of *Rembrandt Research Project Foundation.* Springer, Dordrecht, 2005 edition, 2005.
111. Peter-Paul Verbeek. *Moralizing Technology: Understanding and Designing the Morality of Things.* University of Chicago Press, Chicago, 2011.
112. Jules Verne. *Twenty Thousand Leagues Under the Sea.* CreateSpace Independent Publishing Platform, Scotts Valley, CA, 2019.
113. Ambroise Vollard. *Recollections of a Picture Dealer.* Dover Publications, 2011.
114. Jakob von Uexküll. *A Foray into the Worlds of Animals and Humans: With A Theory of Meaning*, volume 12 of *Posthumanities.* University of Minnesota Press, Minneapolis, illustrated edition, 2010.
115. Xiaohong Wei and Qingyuan Li. The confucian value of harmony and its influence on chinese social interaction. *Cross-cultural Communication*, 9:60–66, 2013.
116. Virginia Woolf. *Roger Fry: A Biography.* HarperCollins, first edition edition, 1976.
117. Paul Éluard. *Love, Poetry.* Commonwealth Books, Black Widow, translation edition, 2007.

Index

For Product Safety Concerns and Information please contact our EU representative GPSR@taylorandfrancis.com
Taylor & Francis Verlag GmbH, Kaufingerstraße 24, 80331 München, Germany

www.ingramcontent.com/pod-product-compliance
Lightning Source LLC
LaVergne TN
LVHW010539030926
847260LV00025B/395
* 9 7 8 1 0 4 1 0 3 3 4 1 7 *